Spectrum Guide to
MALDIVES

Camerapix Publishers International
NAIROBI

Spectrum Guide to Maldives

First published 1993 by
Camerapix Publishers International,
P.O. Box 45048,
Nairobi, Kenya

© 1993 Camerapix

ISBN 1 874041 30 X

This book was designed and produced by
Camerapix Publishers International,
P.O. Box 45048,
Nairobi, Kenya

The **Spectrum Guides** series provides a comprehensive and detailed description of each country it covers, together with all the essential data that tourists, business visitors, or potential investors are likely to require.

Spectrum Guides in print:
Kenya
Pakistan
African Wildlife Safaris
Seychelles
Zimbabwe
Tanzania
Namibia
Jordan
South Africa

Publisher and Chief Executive:
Mohamed Amin
Editorial Director: Brian Tetley
Picture Editor: Duncan Willetts
International Projects Director:
Debbie Gaiger
Editor: Peter Marshall
Associate Editors: Jan Hemsing,
Barbara Lawrence
Typesetting: Kimberly Davis
Photographic Research: Abdul Rehman
Editorial Assistant: Mary-Anne Muiruri
Design Consultant: Craig Dodd

Printed and bound in Hong Kong.

Editorial Board

Spectrum Guide to Maldives is another welcome addition to the popular series of high-quality and colourfully illustrated *Spectrum Guides* on exotic and exciting countries, cultures, flora and fauna.

The guide is largely the work of three lovers of these remote and fascinating Indian Ocean islands — the photographic magic of **Mohamed Amin**, *Spectrum Guides* Publisher and Chief Executive; his colleague **Duncan Willetts**, who knows the islands well; and writer **Peter Marshall**.

The person responsible for the complex liaison and logistics involved in planning such a detailed survey of Maldives is *Spectrum Guides* International Projects Director **Debbie Gaiger**.

Editorial Director **Brian Tetley**, an English-born Kenyan, worked long and hard on research and text to produce *Spectrum Guide to Maldives*, the first fully comprehensive guide book to one of the world's most remarkable nations.

Dr Peter Marshall, a former cadet in the Merchant Navy and university philosopher, has always answered the call of the sea. One of his greatest passions is sports diving. Marshall now resides in Snowdonia National Park, one of Britain's last remaining wildernesses, as a full-time writer.

Marshall, Willetts and Amin sailed the length and breadth of this great archipelago, stopping to investigate and explore the islands and marvel at the mysteries of the tropical deep.

While the camera-packing duo of Amin and Willetts was busy recording the incredible beauty of this ancient nation of more than 1,000 islands, Marshall studied intriguing remains, dug through the archives, and mixed with islanders to complete this fact-packed guide to one of the world's truly great holiday destinations.

In Maldives, the text was checked by Abdullah Rasheed, Director General of the Department of Information and Broadcasting and Ibrahim Mohamed, Assistant Director of the Ministry of Tourism. Historical facts and place names were verified by Mohamed Waheed and Mohamed Ibraheem Loutfi of the National Centre for Linguistic and Historical Research.

Design was by **Craig Dodd**, one of Europe's leading graphic designers, while Kenyan **Abdul Rehman** oversaw photographic research.

Finally, Editorial Assistant Kenyan **Mary-Anne Muiruri** coordinated the preparation of manuscripts for typesetting, which was carried out by American **Kimberly Davis**.

Above: The national flag of the Republic of Maldives is green, red and white, symbolizing victory, blessing and success.

TABLE OF CONTENTS

INTRODUCTION

THE MALDIVES EXPERIENCE 17
TRAVEL BRIEF & SOCIAL ADVISORY 19

PART ONE: HISTORY, GEOGRAPHY AND PEOPLE

HISTORY 33
THE LAND AND THE SEA 52
THE PEOPLE 57

PART TWO: PLACES AND TRAVEL

RESORT ISLANDS 70

MALÉ 76

CENTRAL ATOLLS: 96
NORTH MALÉ RESORTS 99
SOUTH MALÉ RESORTS 118
ALIFU (ARI) 130
ALIFU RESORTS 130
VAAVU (FELIDU) 136
VAAVU RESORTS 138
MEEMU (MULAKU) 139
FAAFU (NORTH NILANDHOO) 142
DHAALU (SOUTH NILANDHOO) 144
THAA (KOLHUMADULU) 147
LAAMU (HADHDHUNMATHEE) 148

NORTHERN ATOLLS: 156
LHAVIYANI (FAADHIPPOLHU) 156
LHAVIYANI RESORT 158
BAA (SOUTH MAALHOSMADULU) ATOLL 158
BAA RESORTS 160
RAA (NORTH MAALHOSMADULU) 160
NOONU (SOUTH MILADHUMMADULU) 162
SHAVIYANI (NORTH MILADHUMMADULU) 163
HAA DHAALU (SOUTH THILADHUNMATHEE) 166
HAA ALIFU (NORTH THILADHUNMATHEE) 167

SOUTHERN ATOLLS: 171
GAAFU ALIFU (NORTH HUVADHOO) 171
GAAFU DHAALU (SOUTH HUVADHOO) 173
GNAVIYANI (FUA MULAKU) 175
SEENU (ADDU) 178

PART THREE: SPECIAL FEATURES

FLORA 190
FAUNA 196
MAMMALS 196
REPTILES 197
INSECTS AND ARACHNIDS 197
BIRDS 198
MARINE LIFE 203
UNDERWATER MALDIVES 219
DIVING GUIDE TO MALDIVES 225
SPORTING MALDIVES 235
ARTS AND CRAFTS 240
ISLAM 243
DANCE AND DRAMA 246
BOAT BUILDING 248
SAILING 252
STAMPS 258
TASTES OF MALDIVES 264

PART FOUR: BUSINESS MALDIVES

THE ECONOMY 267
ECONOMIC DEVELOPMENT 270
INVESTMENT 278

PART FIVE: FACTS AT YOUR FINGERTIPS

Visa and immigration regulations 279
Health requirements 279
International flights 279
On arrival 279
Departure tax 279
Customs 279
Liquor 279
Travel permits 279
Domestic flights 279
Boat services 280
Taxi services 280
Capital 280
Business hours 280
Currency 280
Currency regulations 280
Banks 280

Payments 280
Credit cards 280
Duty-free shopping 280
Tipping 280
Security 280
Medical services 280
Time 281
Energy 281
Postal services 281
Communications 281
Media 281
Photography 281
Climate 281
Dress 281
Religion 281
Language 281
Government 281
International relations 282
English-Dhivehi 282

IN BRIEF

Physical geography 286
Mammal profile 287
Bird profile 287
Reptile profile 288
Insect, arachnid and chelopod profile 290
Seashell profile 290
Starfish profile 291
Fish checklist 293
Demographic profile 298
Atoll names 298
Gazetteer 298
Museums and historical sites 301
Festivals and holidays 303
Public holidays 304

LISTINGS

Airlines 305
Air charter companies 305
Foreign diplomatic missions 305
Maldives missions abroad 305
Maldives trade representatives 306
Maldives tourist offices abroad 306
Resort islands 306
Hotels 309
Guesthouses and lodges 310
Island resort operators 310
Travel agents and tour operators 311
Travel agents and tour operators abroad 311
Sea freight companies 312
Taxi hire 312
Helicopter hire 312
Boat hire 312
Medical services 312
Banks 313
Cinema 313
Bookshops 313
Libraries, museums and cultural centres 313
Media 313
Government offices 313
Bibliography 314
Index 316

MAPS

Maldives 16
Malé 79
Central Atolls 97
Malé Atoll 98
Alifu Atoll 131
Vaavu Atoll 136
Northern Atolls 157
Lhaviyani Atoll 158
Baa and Raa Atolls 161
Southern Atolls 172

Half-title: Indian Ocean hideaway basking in the tropical sun. Title page: Cocoa Island offers visitors sun, sand and solitude. Overleaf: Islands bursting through the surface of the Indian Ocean, first colonized by tropical vegetation and then transformed by man's fragile dwellings. Following pages: Catching the best of the warm tropical winds off Gangehi Island. Pages 12-13: Fishermen on a calm day punt their slender craft through treacherous coral reefs. Pages 14-15: Late windsurfers off Gangehi Island Resort, making landfall by the light of the moon.

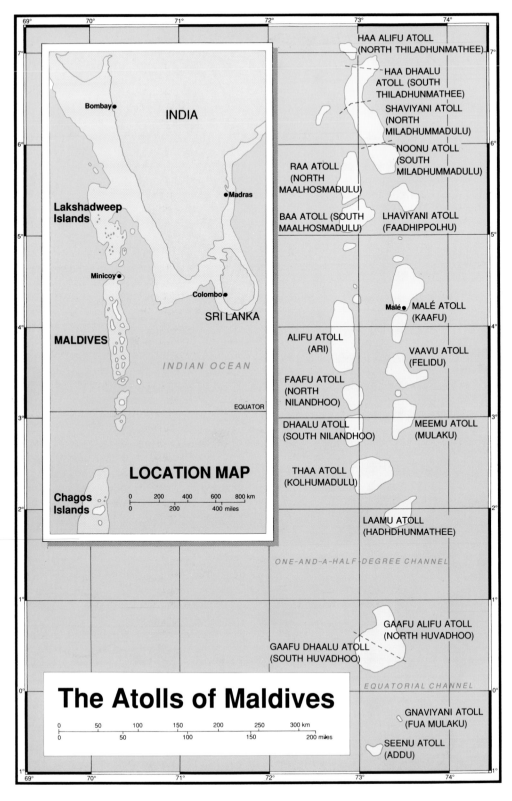

The Atolls of Maldives

HAA ALIFU ATOLL
(NORTH THILADHUNMATHEE)

HAA DHAALU
ATOLL (SOUTH
THILADHUNMATHEE)

SHAVIYANI ATOLL
(NORTH
MILADHUMMADULU)

NOONU ATOLL
(SOUTH
MILADHUMMADULU)

RAA ATOLL
(NORTH
MAALHOSMADULU)

LHAVIYANI ATOLL
(FAADHIPPOLHU)

BAA ATOLL (SOUTH
MAALHOSMADULU)

Malé • MALÉ ATOLL
(KAAFU)

ALIFU ATOLL
(ARI)

VAAVU ATOLL
(FELIDU)

FAAFU ATOLL
(NORTH
NILANDHOO)

DHAALU ATOLL
(SOUTH NILANDHOO)

MEEMU ATOLL
(MULAKU)

THAA ATOLL
(KOLHUMADULU)

LAAMU ATOLL
(HADHDHUNMATHEE)

ONE-AND-A-HALF-DEGREE CHANNEL

GAAFU ALIFU ATOLL
(NORTH HUVADHOO)

GAAFU DHAALU ATOLL
(SOUTH HUVADHOO)

EQUATORIAL CHANNEL

GNAVIYANI ATOLL
(FUA MULAKU)

SEENU ATOLL
(ADDU)

| 0 | 50 | 100 | 150 | 200 | 250 | 300 km |
| 0 | | 50 | 100 | | 150 | 200 miles |

LOCATION MAP

Bombay •

INDIA

Madras •

Lakshadweep
Islands

Minicoy •

Colombo •

SRI LANKA

MALDIVES

INDIAN OCEAN

EQUATOR

Chagos
Islands

| 0 | 200 | 400 | 600 | 800 km |
| 0 | | 200 | | 400 miles |

16

The Maldives Experience

For most vacationers, sun-baked days, moonlit nights, sandy beaches and warm, crystal-clear water form the basic ingredients for the perfect holiday. Nowhere is this more evident than in Maldives, a delightful cluster of equatorial coral islands in the deep blue Indian Ocean.

The local term for Maldives (pronounced *mawl-deevs*) is *Dhivehi Raajje*, the "Island Kingdom". The inhabitants, who call themselves *Dhivehin* (islanders) speak their own unique language, Dhivehi. Indian traders called the country *Maladiv*, Sanskrit for "garland of islands", a name that was adopted by other European languages from the Portuguese. Certainly, the country appears like a festoon of green flowers strewn across the blue velvet of the Indian Ocean. Its nearest neighbours, India and Sri Lanka, lie about 600 and 670 kilometres (372 and 415 miles) to the north and east.

The archipelago, 823 kilometres (510 miles) long, is 130 kilometres (81 miles) at its widest point. These islands are scattered over about 90,000 square kilometres (34,750 square miles). Tiny specks in a vast expanse of ocean, only 199 of some 1,190 coral islands are inhabited.

The islands form twenty-six natural atolls, each enclosed by a coral reef cut by several deep, natural channels. Each island is also surrounded by a protective coral reef and shallow lagoon. Most of these low-lying islands are no more than two metres (seven feet) above sea level and can be explored in ten minutes.

As such, there are no hills or rivers in Maldives. The most common features are tall palms, white sandy beaches, turquoise lagoons and crystal-clear waters. Some islands, especially those in the south, are covered with lush tropical vegetation. The most common plant, the coconut, is the Maldivian "tree of life". Other food crops include breadfruit, banana, mango, cassava, sweet potato and millet.

Maldives, like many other tropical island ecosystems, has few land animals. But the protective coral reefs around each island have created magnificent underwater gardens, home to millions of multicoloured fish, corals and shells.

For its people, life in this maritime environment has been difficult. Yet archaeological finds in this century suggest that the islands were inhabited at least 4,000 years ago. It is believed the first Dravidian settlers were followed by Aryan immigrants around the time of 500 BC. Today over 230,000 Maldivians clearly display a diverse mix of African, Malaysian, Indian and Arabic influence in their facial features.

There are mysterious ancient ruins scattered throughout the archipelago, as well as the beautiful remains of Buddhist and Hindu temples. In the twelfth century, Maldives converted to Islam, and today the country is 100 per cent Sunni Muslim.

Throughout its known history, Maldives has been independent except for a brief fifteen-year spell of Portuguese rule in the sixteenth century.

For centuries it drifted in the limbo of the Indian Ocean, a tropical paradise of countless tiny islands known to only a few.

For islanders, life has always been difficult. But for a few visitors the temptation to become a "lotus-eater" was irresistible. The dazzling white beaches had an allure all their own. Bounded by an infinite expanse of ocean, under the deep blue of the equatorial sky, warmed by the sun and cooled by the breezes that whispered through the palms, life seemed like a prolonged idyll. Coconuts were there for the taking and the sea teemed with fish.

But the advent of tourism in the 1970s has brought dramatic change. No longer just a scatter of dots in the Indian Ocean, Maldives now beckons the world and few can resist the entreaty.

Welcome.

Travel Brief and Social Advisory

Located at the crossways of the Indian Ocean's main shipping routes, Maldives has been known to seafarers for centuries — mainly for its fresh water, cowries, dried fish and sensual ways.

Dhivehi, a language which belongs to the Indo-Iranian group of languages, is spoken throughout Maldives. Although similar to ancient Sinhala with Tamil roots, it is unique to Maldives. The present script, which was introduced in the late sixteenth century, is written like Arabic from right to left.

Since the Second World War, however, English has become the second most commonly spoken language (and the language of learning in all secondary schools), although an increasing number speak other European languages and Arabic.

For centuries a succession of sultans ruled the country according to traditional custom, but from 1887 until 1965 the islands were a British Protectorate. The first written constitution, limiting the powers of the sultan, was proclaimed in 1932 and rewritten in 1968 when the country became a republic.

Maldives is an Islamic state, with an executive president who is also head of religious affairs. He is nominated by a parliament known as the Citizens' Majlis and confirmed by a public referendum.

The economy has long been based on fishing. Dried tuna, known as "Maldive Fish", was famous throughout the Indian Ocean. Inevitably, poor soils and limited land restrict farming and the staple food, rice, has to be imported. Traditional industry consists of boat building and handicrafts such as mat weaving, jewellery making and lacquer work.

This century shipping has become increasingly important, with Maldivians serving in foreign shipping companies as well as with Maldives National Ship Management Limited (MNSML), formerly Maldive Shipping Limited.

But when an Italian entrepreneur persuaded the Maldivian government to develop some uninhabited islands as resorts in the early 1970s, the tourist industry boomed. Today seventy resort islands welcome more than 200,000 visitors a year and tourism contributes almost a quarter of the national revenue.

Keen to expand the tourist industry, the Maldivian government makes visitors as welcome and as comfortable as possible. But it is also committed to the preservation of Maldivian customs, religion and culture.

Getting There

Malé, the capital of Maldives, is served by several scheduled air services as well as charter flights. It is about ten hours flying time from London via Dubai; four hours from Karachi; one hour from Colombo; and five hours from Singapore. There are no direct flights from the United States.

Almost all visitors arrive by air. Malé International Airport on Hulhule Island is four kilometres (2.5 miles) from Malé, about ten minutes by boat.

You'll need a valid passport and a yellow fever and cholera certificate — if you come from an infected region — to enter.

Visitors must have at least US$10 for each day of their stay, but this restriction does not apply to visitors with a tourist agency or those going there to work. You also need a confirmed hotel reservation. Visitors without reservations should consult the tourist information desk at the airport.

Opposite: Clockwise from top left: Young islander in a rapidly changing archipelago; old fisherman who has spent nearly as much time at sea as on dry land; Maldivian girl, member of a tolerant Islamic culture; young pupil of an island *makthab* school, where she learns to read and write and to recite the Qur'an.

Visas

All tourists are given a thirty-day visa on arrival, except Bangladeshis, Pakistanis, Indians and Italians, who are given a ninety-day visa. These can be extended for a nominal fee. Israeli nationals are forbidden entry.

If you want to visit any island outside the capital, you must obtain a travel permit from the Ministry of Atolls Administration on Malé — issued on request to members of organized tour groups or to individuals with a Maldivian sponsor.

Health

Many early European travellers complained about the Maldivian climate. Professor Wilhelm Geiger, who made a special study of the Dhivehi language at the turn of the century, declared the islands extremely unhealthy:

"Foreigners are usually attacked, within a short time, by severe abdominal disorders, which, if the individual does not at once leave the Islands, seems in most cases to run a swift and fatal course."

As thousands of tourists will testify, this is not so today. Malaria has now been eliminated and cholera is under control, although some islanders in the outlying atolls still suffer leprosy, filaria and occasional bouts of dengue fever. Water-borne intestinal complaints remain a problem.

None of this should bother tourists. On their special desert islands, the most common ailment is sunburn or sunstroke. Nonetheless, it is advisable to have anti-tetanus and typhus vaccinations and avoid drinking water from island wells. Either boil water or drink rainwater collected from roofs. Anti-malaria tablets are a worthwhile precaution if you plan to visit the outlying atolls in the north.

Europeans should use sun block to filter out the harmful rays of the tropical sun and sunglasses to relieve the blinding glare of the white coral sand, whitewashed buildings and sparkling seas. Cool breezes may temper the heat, but they make no less of the sun's rays. Islanders, who know best, wear hats when out fishing and seek shade during the middle of the day.

When to go

Generally warm and humid, the climate is determined by two monsoons. The rainy south-west monsoon runs from April to October, while the drier north-east monsoon prevails from December to March. Average annual rainfall is 1,967 millimetres (77 inches) and year-round temperatures vary between 30°C (86°F) and 26°C (79°F).

The best time to visit the islands is during the north-east monsoon when the skies are blue and the sun shines virtually every day. During the south-west monsoon there are frequent showers and squalls, freshwater wells fill up, and the hotels empty. Some resorts close down or slash their rates — an opportune time for bargain hunters who are not sun-lovers and prefer solitude. And though underwater diving visibility is restricted, the plankton-rich waters that well up along the western coasts of the archipelago attract manta rays and whale sharks.

Getting Around

Until the advent of tourism, the only means of travel through Maldives was by *dhoani*, local boats similar to Arab dhows that ply between the atolls and islands of the archipelago. Nowadays you can book water taxis through the individual resorts, although the *dhoani* remains the most common mode of inter-island transport.

The dependable *dhoanis* average about twelve kilometres (seven miles) an hour. There are no scheduled ferry services, but boats from Malé visit most outlying islands.

Tourist resorts, which have their own transfer boats, meet their guests at the airport.

Occasionally luxurious, privately owned schooners anchor off the resort islands and

Opposite: Malé International Airport, built on Hulhule Island.

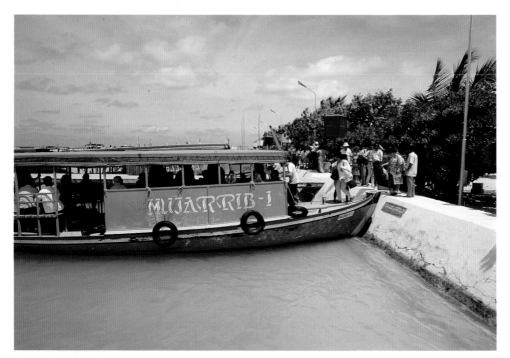

Above: Ferry boat links the capital to neighbouring islands.
Opposite: Air Maldives provides an inter-island service to a number of islands throughout Maldives.

many smaller yachts cruise between the islands, conscious of the uncharted dangers of the coral reefs.

"Cargo-*dhoanis*", ill-shaped boats with top-heavy superstructures, sail regularly from Malé to the outlying atolls. But these are slow and usually packed with local passengers and their produce. Conditions are spartan. You should be prepared to sleep on deck with others.

For those who appreciate little comfort but value independence, specially adapted "yacht-*dhoanis*" are undoubtedly the best way to travel between the islands. These traditional wooden Maldivian *dhoanis*, with diesel engines and lateen sails, have cabins equipped with basic facilities.

They may be a little cramped and short on shower water, but once you get your sea legs the benefits far outweigh the disadvantages. The food is generally more adventurous and Maldivian than in the resorts and the experienced crew of three or four, friendly and accommodating, know the best places to dive and fish.

The overwhelming advantage of the yacht-*dhoani* is the freedom it offers. With a knowledgeable skipper (who knows most of the atolls very well) you can get out of the resort satellites around Malé and make for the open sea and islands new.

By air

Malé International Airport on the island of Hulhule handles international air traffic.

Air Maldives operates domestic flights from Hulhule to Gan in Seenu Atoll, Kadhdhoo in Laamu Atoll and Hanimaadhoo in Haa Dhaalu Atoll. A fourth airport at Kaadedhdhoo in Gaafu Dhaalu was opening in 1993, and Hummingbird Helicopters are available for hire.

Independent travelling

It is difficult for independent visitors to hop from island to island, but not impossible. You can negotiate with the skippers of *dhoanis* sailing between Malé and the outlying islands to carry you along for a small fee. There is no regular timetable.

All visitors pay a daily tax during their

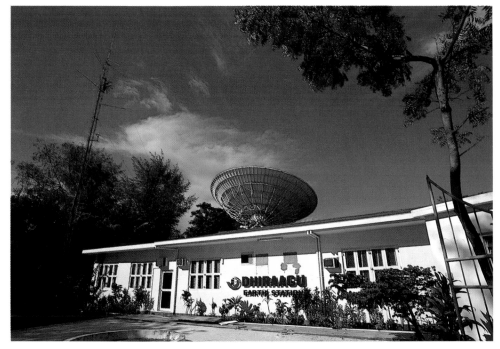

Above: Dhiraagu Earth Station, Malé, keeping the archipelago in the middle of the Indian Ocean in touch with the outside world by satellite.
Opposite: Unspoilt beaches adorn Alifu (Ari) Atoll.

stay. You need a permit to visit islands that are not resorts — only possible if you have a letter from a "sponsor" vouching for you and offering accommodation. Visitors to any inhabited island must report to the local chief.

Only Muslims with at least one parent who is Maldivian can become citizens, although Maldivian men may now marry women of Christian or Jewish faith. Gone are the days when a passing sailor married a girl for a few weeks only to divorce her as he set sail. And you can no longer land on any one of the countless deserted islands, build a shack and live happily ever after. Would-be Robinson Crusoes take note.

Where to stay

All seventy resort islands offer a wide range of facilities for every kind of visitor. Each resort is so small that it takes you no more than half an hour to stroll around the entire island. But the white coral beaches, gleaming under the Maldivian sun against a backcloth of tropical palms,

fit the image of the dreamy desert island getaway.

Visitors stay in bungalow-style rooms, fully equipped with modern conveniences. The service normally includes full board with a range of local and continental dishes as well as buffets and barbecues.

Malé has a few hotels and guesthouses, normally rented rooms in private homes. These are relatively inexpensive but do not usually serve meals.

What to do

Most activity centres on the sea. The coral reefs are excellent for diving and snorkeling and the shallow crystal-clear lagoons ideal for bathing, swimming, water-skiing, wind-surfing and other water sports.

The more leisurely practice the art of doing nothing while enjoying all the luxuries that modern society can provide. Sunbathing, lolling in hammocks under the rich vegetation, or simply strolling along the water's edge, all help visitors to unwind.

Lawn tennis, soccer, volleyball, billiards,

25

Above: Homeward bound as the sky and sea are turned to molten copper by the setting sun.

table tennis, chess and darts are among the sports on offer and excursions to fishing villages and the capital, Malé, will all make your holiday more worthwhile.

Local customs and traditions

As a devout Islamic country, alcohol, drugs, pork, dogs, firearms and pornography are forbidden. Impoverished independent travellers — backpackers — are unwelcome.

"Immodest dress" is offensive to Maldivians. Shorts and a shirt are acceptable for men, but women are expected to cover thighs and body. Standards are more relaxed on the resort islands, but returning to nature in Maldives does not mean casting off your clothes. There is a US$1,000 fine for nudity.

Traditionally, Maldivians eat with their hands. If you wish to follow suit, remember it is considered both unhygienic and ill-mannered to touch food with the left hand. Crockery is held in the left while the right hand picks up the food. If in doubt, use a spoon — as do an increasing number of wealthy Maldivians.

Although tipping is prohibited, many resorts impose a ten per cent service charge and airport porters, waiters and room cleaners appreciate an acknowledgement of their service. On Malé, Maldivians do not tip in tea-shops or restaurants.

There is no "thank you", "hello", or "good-bye" in Dhivehi. The Arabic *salaam alekum* (for "hello") and *shukriyyaa* (for "thank you") are used on rare occasions.

Bear in mind

You are in a land with its own unique traditions and customs. Respect them and you will find your holiday much more enjoyable.

Don't change your foreign currency with unauthorized dealers. There is a bank at the

Opposite: The resort island of Vilingilivaru in Alifu Atoll basks in glorious Maldivian sunshine.

Overleaf: While some visitors travel by *dhoani* to their chosen resort island, others prefer the bird's-eye view from a helicopter.

airport and all the tourist resorts deal in foreign exchange.

Keep your currency exchange receipts to change any Maldivian money you may have left into hard currency when you leave.

Alcohol is readily available on all the tourist islands, but you cannot bring it into the country or offer it to Maldivians.

National emblem

The national emblem of the Republic of Maldives consists of a coconut palm, crescent and star, two crisscrossed national flags, and the traditional title of the State.

The coconut palm, which represents the livelihood of the nation, plays an essential part in the everyday life of Maldivians.

The crescent and the star, supported by two national flags, signify the Islamic faith of the State and its authority.

The traditional title of the State, *Ad-Dawlat Ul-Mahaldeebiyya*, was first used by As-Sultan Al-Ghazee Muhammad Thakurufaanu Al-Azam, the country's most famous hero. The title *Ad-Dawlat Ul-Mahaldeebiyya* means the State of the Maldives.

National flag

The national flag consists of a white crescent on a green rectangle with a red border.

National anthem

In National Unity do we salute our Nation,
In the National language do we offer our
prayers and salute our Nation.
We bow in respect to the Emblem
of our Nation,
And salute the Flag so exalted.

We salute the colours of our Flag; Green,
Red and White
Which symbolize Victory, Blessing
and Success.

National tree

The coconut palm, the *Dhivehi Ruh.*

National flower

The *Finifenmaa*, commonly known as Pink Rose (*Rosa polyantha*).

Above: The national emblem of the Republic of Maldives consists of a coconut palm (which represents the livelihood of the nation), a crescent and star with two national flags, and the traditional title of the State.

Opposite: The Maldivian experience: sun, sea and swaying palms.

Below: The Maldivian national flower is the *Finifenmaa*, commonly known as Pink Rose (*Rosa polyantha*).

PART ONE: HISTORY, GEOGRAPHY AND PEOPLE

Above: Strange carvings on display in the National Museum, Malé, found on the sites of pre-Islamic temples. The mystery of Maldives' early history is only just beginning to be uncovered.

Opposite: Classic Maldivian beach scene — shady palms, white coral sand and deep blue waters.

History: The Legend and the Mystery

In the ebb and flow of time and tide that scour the myriad islands of Maldives, there is a story of legend and mystery waiting to be discovered.

The islands were born in the tumult of great geological change. Millions of years ago a great range of volcanoes rose from the floor of the Indian Ocean and burst through its surface. Slowly, over the years, the tumult lessened and the volcanoes sank back into the depths — leaving only coral reefs in the vast expanse of sea.

They formed a glittering necklace of gems stretching across the equator: tiny specks of coral sand and reef, covered with the lush green of coconut palms and hardy shrubs, which were completely deserted.

Yet as sailors, ever adventurous, sailed further and further in search of conquest and wealth, they drifted upon them.

In some far-off times now remembered only in distant folklore, a strange race of seagoing giants were among the first people to make their homes on these remote and distant islands.

Later, but still thousands of years ago, the Phoenicians sailed through the islands, and in the centuries that followed came Egyptian, Chinese, Greek, Roman and Sri Lankan mariners.

One legend from those misty, long-ago times before the arrival of Islam is that a single dynasty ruled this nation of scattered islands. The story goes:

"Once upon a time, when Maldives were still sparsely inhabited, a Prince of Royal birth named Koimala Kaloa, who had married the Ceylon King's daughter, made a voyage with her in two vessels from Serendib Island. Reaching the Maldives they were becalmed, and rested awhile at Rasgetheemu Island in North Malosmadulu Atoll.

"The Maldive Islanders, learning that the two chief visitors were of Ceylon Royal descent, invited them to remain; and ultimately proclaimed Koimala their King at Rasgetheemu, the original "King's Island". Subsequently Koimala and his spouse migrated thence to Malé . . . and settled there with the consent of the aborigines of Giraavaru Island, then the most important community of Male Atoll" (See "Raa Atoll: Land of Kings", Part Two).

A mixture of fact and fable, such tales as these lend to the mystery of Maldives before the arrival of Islam in the twelfth century.

The story continues with the king's order for two of his ships to return home and bring back other people of the "Lion Race", whereupon his son "reigned as a Buddhist for twelve years, and was then converted to Islam, ruling for thirteen years more before he finally departed for Mekka".

As the legend goes, the king was succeeded by his daughter, who reigned as nominal sultana until her son "married a lady of the country. From them the subsequent Rulers of the Maldives were descended".

Although official Maldivian history only begins in the twelfth century, literary works and archaeological remains provide clues to earlier pre-Islamic eras. Maldives was a stopping-off point for many great seafaring civilizations which roamed the high seas long before European maritime history began.

A Roman coin dated as early as 90 BC has been discovered in the archipelago (See "Alifu Atoll: Westward Ho!", Part Two). Since it was the Egyptians who taught the Romans how to cross the Indian Ocean, it may not be too fanciful to imagine the proud Egyptian papyrus ships with their colourful square sails navigating through the Equatorial Channel along the highway of the sun.

Perhaps the Maldivian men modelled the elegant curved bows of their boats from the Egyptians, and the women the beautifully embroidered collar pieces of their dresses.

Early travellers

These ancient seafarers made fairly accurate estimates of the number of islands in the

Above: Demon statue found on Malé.

archipelago. The first reference to Maldives is in the second-century writings of the Greek astronomer, mathematician and geographer, Ptolemy. He refers to it as "1,378 little islands" west of Taprobane (Sri Lanka).

Pappus of Alexandria, who lived at the end of the fourth century, follows Ptolemy with a mention of Taprobane and "1,370 adjacent islands". Scholasticus, the Theban who lived about the same time and visited the Malabar Coast, mentions a "thousand islands" and their treacherous nature, since they had "loadstone rocks which attract iron-bound vessels to their destruction".

Among the great Arab travellers who crossed the Indian Ocean was the Persian merchant Sulaiman, who lived in the ninth century. "In the sea known as sea of Herkend," he wrote, "there are nearly 1,900 islands," adding that "the ruler of these islands is a woman" and that their wealth consisted of cowries.

Al Mas'udi, the Arab traveller who visited Sri Lanka at the beginning of the twelfth century, claimed that between the sea of Herkend and the sea of Lar there were many separate islands: "There are 2,000 counted islands here. To be more accurate there are 1,900 islands here."

The Chinese were also among the early great navigators. Dating perhaps from the fifth century BC, the *Shu-Ching* or *Classic History* records "Weak Waters" in the area. Fah-Hian, who visited Sri Lanka about the year AD 412, mentions the small islands of Maldives.

Ma Huan, who travelled with Cheng Ho's great expedition to East Africa in 1433, states in *The Overall Survey of the Ocean's Shores* that Maldives is the "Three Thousand Weak Waters" referred to by tradition. He also identifies some of the islands and tells how foreign ships travel from afar to purchase ropes.

At the time of the Ming Dynasty (1368-1644), the Chinese were certainly familiar with the archipelago. They called the submerged mountain chain *Liu-Shan* (Liu-Mountains) and wrote about its geographical position, climate, products and customs.

In comparison with Eastern civilizations, Europeans were latecomers to the Indian

Above: Ancient Bohomala sculpture, possibly relic of early inhabitants who built great temples on the islands bordering the Equator.

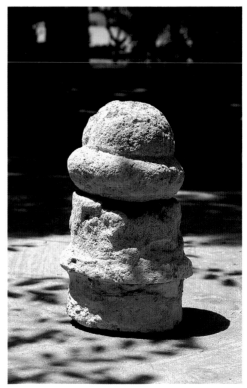

Above: Bohomala sculpture in the National Museum, Malé, probably used as a votive offering to the Hindu god Shiva.

Ocean. Vasco da Gama was the first to reach the eastern waters in 1498. Nine years later Dom Lourenço de Almeida discovered Maldives for Portugal.

When the French brothers Jean and Raoul Parmentier, aboard the *Pensée* and *Sacré*, landed on the southern island of Fua Mulaku in the Equatorial Channel, they were warmly welcomed.

In particular the headman impressed them with his geography: "The chief Priest, who was a man of much discretion and knowledge . . . showed the Captain in what quarters lay the countries of Adam [Mesopotamia, where Christians placed the Garden of Eden], Persia, Ormus, Calicut, Muluque, and Sumatra; and proved himself to be both learned and well-travelled." Such knowledge clearly reflects the extent of Maldives' trading connections at the time (See "Gnaviyani Atoll: Emeralds Across the Equator", Part Two).

These early literary references present a tantalizing glimpse into Maldives' ancient past, but only recently has a more substantial picture begun to emerge.

Recorded Maldivian history begins about the time of the islands' conversion to Islam in the year 583 of the Holy Prophet (AD 1153).

History before this date was long suppressed and most pre-Muslim artefacts destroyed. In such a conservative Islamic society, the general feeling was that it was better not to unearth what was buried.

Now a new generation of Maldivian historians, encouraged by politicians and religious leaders, has begun to explore Maldives' pre-Islamic past in search of a greater understanding of their country. While its recorded history is short, Maldives takes pride in the fact that its actual history is as old as that of its neighbours on the Indian subcontinent.

Archaeology

The first person to study pre-Islamic history in Maldives was the British civil servant H.C.P. Bell, who arrived on the wreckage of his ship in 1879. He returned twice to investigate "the pre-existence of Buddhism in the Group". The monographs of this commissioner of the Ceylon Civil Service show a great love of his subject.

During the early 1920s, Bell recorded many archaeological sites in the outlying atolls. In particular, he came across many large rounded mounds of coral stone and rubble, known locally as *hawittas*, which he thought were the remains of ancient *stupas* similar to the Buddhist *dagoba* temples in Sri Lanka.

With local help, he excavated some of the *hawittas* and found many Buddhist statues, which confirmed his view that Maldives must have been Buddhist before its conversion to Islam.

He also came across Hindu statues of Shiva and other artefacts in the southern islands which suggest that Hinduism from south India was influential there. Although Bell was little more than an amateur, he left a unique record containing much curious archaeological, historical and cultural data.

Most of the *hawittas* that Bell recorded still stand, but as local villagers use the stone for building, many are now half their size. On some islands the mounds are also called *hatteli*, meaning "seven pots", which probably refers to the spires that resemble seven superimposed kettles also found on Buddhist *dagobas* in Sri Lanka (See "Laamu Atoll: Islands of Giants", Part Two).

When asked who they think built the *hawittas*, the islanders inevitably reply "the Redin". Although no one seems to know exactly who the Redin were, some suggest that they were large people with light skin, brown hair and hooked noses. They may well have mixed with visiting sailors during the centuries.

Whoever they were, they put an enormous amount of effort, skill and wealth into the temples that they built throughout these remote islands. According to legend, they were also phenomenal sailors. One story tells how the mythical Redin would cook their food on an island in the north only to travel to another island in the south to eat it.

More light was cast on the enigma of Maldivian history in the early 1980s when President Maumoon Gayoom invited the explorer and author Thor Heyerdahl, of *Kon Tiki* fame, to investigate some archaeological sites. Heyerdahl, who visited many of the areas recorded by Bell, discovered some new sites by following local advice.

Heyerdahl found some superb craftsmanship. On the island of Fua Mulaku, near the equator, walls made from carefully cut and fitted stones reflect techniques known only to a few pre-European civilizations. The dressed stones in one sunken ceremonial bath fitted so closely that a knife blade could not slide between them.

Early settlers

Historians have argued that Maldivians are a mixture of Dravidians from south India and Sinhalese from Sri Lanka. But recent evidence suggests a more complex picture. There may be links with the Naga and Yakka people who developed the pre-Buddhist civilization in Sri Lanka, as well as Dravidians from south India (See "The People: A Mix of Many Faces", Part One).

It is also thought that Aryans from north-west India settled in Maldives two and half millennia ago, colonizing Sri Lanka at the same time. Sinhalese Buddhists undoubtedly came from Sri Lanka at a later date.

Although the principal cultural affinities of Maldivians are Sinhalese, there is a Tamil substratum. A man-beast myth in Maldives that explains the origin of the people is similar to the Sinhalese myth of the "Lion People" (See "Gaafu Dhaalu Atoll: The Kingdom of the Cats", Part Two). At the same time the Giraavaru people, who believe themselves to be the aborigines of the islands, claim descent from the Tamils. While the Dhivehi language resembles early Sinhala, most words relating to the sea and the family have a Tamil root.

Whatever the exact pattern of settlement — and historians may never know — the great variety of physical types in Maldives suggests that different groups reached these remote islands independently in prehistoric times. Later, Indonesians, Malays, Arabs and Africans all added to the racial and cultural melting pot.

The history of Maldives after the arrival of Islam in the twelfth century is clearer, but there are few records. The Koimala legend of the founding of the royal dynasty in Maldives, foreshortened by many centuries, underlies the close link with Sri Lanka and recognizes the existence of Buddhism in the archipelago before the arrival of Islam.

The official story is taken up in the *Tarikh*, a history of Maldivian sultans from AD 1153 (the date of the Islamic conversion) to 1821.

There exists, however, a copperplate book, the *Isdhoo loamaafaana*, which begins in the year AD 1105, when "the great King, Sri Maanaabarana of the house of *Theemu*, the Lord of the Lunar Dynasty became the King of this country". It lists the names of the four Buddhist kings before Islam and the length of each ruler's reign.

The Arabs

At this time the Arabs, who plied the Indian Ocean centuries before Vasco da Gama first rounded the tip of Africa, most influenced Maldivian history. Maldives, or *Dibajat* as they called it, was a strategic entrepôt on the sea routes to Malacca and China. The Arab seafarers, who landed for water, dried fish and coconuts, often stayed for long periods of time.

The Arabs also collected sacks of cowrie shells, which could be found in abundance on the shores of the islands, as ballast. In medieval times cowries were used throughout the Indian Ocean as small change. Maldivian cowries have been found as far north as the Arctic Circle in Norway and as far west as Mali.

According to legend, an Arab converted the Buddhist king Theemugey Maha Kaliminja to Islam. The story goes that when Abu al-Barakat arrived in AD 1153 he found a "colony of ignorant idolators". By exorcizing the demon god Rannamaari, who came from the sea on Malé Island every full moon to rape and kill a local

virgin offered as a sacrifice, he won the gratitude and admiration of all.

He did this by dressing as a girl and spending all night reading aloud the Qur'an. It was all too much for the sea monster, who departed forever. The Maldivian ruler was so impressed that he converted to Islam and persuaded his subjects to do the same. The old idols were broken and the temples razed.

The famous Arab traveller Ibn Battuta, who relates the story, read the hero's name from the carved inscription in the Friday Mosque in Malé as "Abu al-Barakat Yusuf al-Barbari" — from Berber land in North Africa — thereby identifying him as one of his compatriots.

Modern scholars, however, argue that it reads "Al Tabreezi" — from Tabriz in the Persian Gulf. It has also been suggested that it could refer to Beruwela in Sri Lanka. Such esoteric debate in no way diminishes the veneration accorded to the bringer of Islam, whose grave on Malé is a holy shrine.

A political interpretation suggests that Maldives adopted Islam because the ruling elite were unable to hold Buddhist Sri Lanka at arm's length without the support of their powerful Islamic neighbours in the Indian Ocean. Certainly twelfth-century Arabs were received with great hospitality and some were appointed *gazis* (chief judges of the Islamic law) as well as sultans.

King Kaliminja became Sultan Dharmas Mohamed Ibn Abdulla. During the next thirteen years of his reign he set about introducing Islamic law throughout the islands before sailing away on a pilgrimage to Mecca, never to be heard of again.

Almost sixty years elapsed before the conversion to Islam was complete. Indeed, according to the *Isdhoo loamaafaana*, the next king, who came to power in AD 1179, sent an expedition to the southern island of Dhabidhoo in Laamu Atoll to bring the Buddhists to heel:

"The Great King, Srimat Gadanaditya, an ornament to the Lunar Dynasty, resplendent as gold, firm as an *Asala* [stone] pillar, defender of the entire hundred thousand of islands, brilliant as the sun, moon and stars, virtuous in every manner, lord of love, mine of jewels, adorned with a crown set with gems, — On the fourth year of his becoming the sole monarch he, having destroyed the shrine erected previously by the infidel kings of Dabuduv, uprooted the Buddha images, and caused the infidel Kings to read the Shadat [a Muslim creed]."

Maldivian queens

Women have always played a significant part in Maldivian society and matrilineal inheritance was well-established in early times. The country may also have been ruled by matriarchy. At the turn of the tenth century both Sulaiman the Merchant and Al-Mas'udi record the fact that the Maldive islands were ruled by a queen.

And at the beginning of the twelfth century Al-Adrisi wrote:

"It has always been a custom with them that a woman arbitrate, a custom from which they do not depart. This queen is called *Dmhra*. She wears garments of woven gold, and her headwear is a crown of gold studded with various kinds of rubies and precious stones. She wears gold sandals.

"In these islands nobody wears sandals, except this queen alone, and if anyone is found wearing sandals, his feet are amputated.

"On ceremonial occasions, and the feast days of her sect, this queen rides with her slave-girls behind her, in full procession of elephants, banners and trumpets, while the king and all other ministers follow her at a distance. . . . "

In Islamic convention no woman can be a religious leader. Nevertheless, unlike other Muslim states, Maldives continued to be ruled by a succession of sultanas.

Sultana Khadeeja Rehendhi Kabaidhi Kilege, who ruled on three separate occasions between 1342 and 1380, was one of the most memorable. Many people believe she came to power after murdering her young brother, and when she was overthrown by her husband in 1363 she had him killed as well. In 1373, her position was usurped by her second husband. He suffered the same supposed fate as his predecessor. Triumphant over the dead bodies of her treacherous husbands, she ruled alone until she died in 1380.

Above: Serene Buddha head in National Museum, Malé, found in one of the many ruins in the archipelago which was once a Buddhist *dagoba*.

Ibn Battuta

It was during the reign of Khadeeja Rehendhi that Ibn Battuta came to the islands, one of many Arab traders landing in 1344 for provisions and the cowrie shells that served as currency throughout south India and Africa (See "Raa Atoll: Land of Kings", Part Two).

His writings give the earliest descriptive account of Maldives and its inhabitants. Battuta declared that the islands were the most agreeable he had ever seen and "one of the wonders of the world" — quite a statement from a man who had visited ninety-two countries.

Battuta remained on Malé for about ten months and left a detailed record about the country, its form of government, customs and religion, painting a favourable picture:

"The people of the Maldives are upright and pious, sound in belief and sincere in thought; their bodies are weak, they are unused to fighting, and their armour is prayer.

"Once when I ordered a thief's hand to be cut off, a number of those in the room fainted. The Indian pirates do not raid or molest them, as they have learned from experience that anyone who seizes anything from them speedily meets misfortune."

Since they were such bad soldiers, the sultana's army of about 1,000 men were mainly mercenaries from neighbouring islands paid in rice each month.

Battuta found the women particularly attractive and made full use of the custom that "any newcomer could marry if he so desired, then on leaving he simply repudiated his wife".

It was easy to get married in these islands, he noted, "on account of the smallness of the dowries and the pleasure of their women's society. When ships arrive, the crew marry wives, and when they are about to set sail they divorce them. It is really a sort of temporary marriage. The women never leave the country."

It was common for young girls to hire themselves out as servants to the wealthier families. There were also slave-concubines — Battuta was given two.

Although well-received at first, eventually Battuta fell out with the sultana's husband who, as the *wazir* (prime minister), feared Battuta's growing influence and resented his haughty independence. After marrying the sultana's mother-in-law — "one of the best of women" — Battuta became *gazi* and enforced a strict interpretation of Islamic Law.

He changed the practice of divorced wives remaining in the homes of their former husbands; enforced (on pain of public beating) the observance of Friday prayers; and tried, unsuccessfully, to make women cover the top of their body.

As the *gazi* he received the entire income of three islands. His marriage to three other well-connected wives soon raised the *wazir*'s fears that he was becoming too powerful. These were unfounded, however, for after about ten months Battuta decided he had had enough and sailed for Malabar.

On his way he stopped at Mulaku in Meemu Atoll, and although he was there for only seventy days he found time to marry two wives. Eventually, on 22 August 1344, Battuta left — but not without a final sense of regret. Like so many travellers since, he came across a tiny island where a weaver and his family lived alone:

"And I swear I envied that man, and wished that the island had been mine, that I might have made it my retreat until the inevitable hour should befall me."

Battuta returned only once to Maldives, to see his son, but decided it was best to leave him with his mother.

The Ali Rajas

By now trade with the Indian subcontinent was largely in the hands of the Muslim merchants along the south-west coast of India, who were called the "Sea Kings", or the Ali Rajas of Cannanore. They maintained such a stranglehold over trade that they were also known as the "Lords of the Maldive Islands".

After Sultan Kalhu Muhammad was deposed for a second time early in the sixteenth century, he appealed to the "Sea Kings" to reinstate him — which they did in return for a regular tribute. Their monopoly, however, was soon threatened.

Above: Delicately carved tombstone on Meedhoo Island.

Above: Tombstones of two local dignitaries by the *Hukuru Miskiiy* (Friday Mosque) on Malé.

The Portuguese

The Portuguese mariners and traders who followed Vasco da Gama into the Indian Ocean demanded a share of the profitable Indian Ocean trade routes. In particular, they were impressed by the Maldivian trade. After Vincent Sodré, Vasco da Gama's commander, came across some Maldivian ships in 1503, a chronicler related:

"When he was off Calicut, he sighted four sails, which he overhauled and took. They proved to be *gundras*, barques of the Maldive islands. . . . *Gundras* are built of palm timber, joined and fastened with pegs of wood without any bolts. The sails are made of mats of the dry leaves of the palm.

"These vessels were laden with cairo and *caury* . . . good stores of silks, both coloured and white, of diverse fabrics and qualities, and many brilliant tissues of gold, made by the islanders themselves, who get the silk, gold, and cotton-thread from the numerous ships that pass among the islands on their way from the coast of Bengal to the Straits of Mecca.

"There ships buy these stuffs from the islanders, supplying them in exchange with the materials whereof they are made. Thus are these islands a great emporium for all parts."

In 1517 Sultan Kalhu Muhammad signed a treaty which allowed the Portuguese to establish a trading post in Malé. When it was burnt down the following year (with the help of corsairs from Malabar), a Portuguese armada under Joao Gomes Cheiradinheiro landed 120 men in Malé to establish a fort.

The next sultan, Hassan IX, impressed by the Portuguese, travelled to Cochin, India, in 1551 to learn more about Christianity. On New Year's Day, 1552, he was baptized a Christian. Two years later

Above: Sultan Muhammad Imaad-ud-deen VI and his entourage and ceremonial umbrellas on board a visiting British ship earlier this century. Maldives was a British Protectorate from 1887 to 1965.

he married a Christian woman from Goa. Keen to convert his ministers and chiefs to Christianity, he invited them to Cochin, but others rebelled and seized two expeditions of loyal subjects which tried to reach him. It was not until 1558 that a third expedition reached Cochin.

War of independence

The Portuguese returned to take over Maldives from Sultan Ali VI, who had been in power for only two and a half months. His death during the struggle is now a national anniversary celebrated as "Martyr's Day". The islands came under the rule of the leader of the Portuguese expedition, Captain Andreas Andre, known locally as Captain Adiri Adiri. The *Tarikh* relates:

"The Maldivians then submitted to Captain Adiri Adiri, who proclaimed himself 'Sultan'. He sent Christians to take charge in all parts of the Maldives, and enforced submission. The Portuguese ruled most cruelly for several years, committing intolerable enormities.

"The sea grew red with Muslim blood, the people were sunk in despair. At this juncture God Almighty moved the heart of Khatib Muhammad, son of Khatib Hussain of Utimu . . . to fight with the Infidels and to end the crying wrongs. Praying to God for wisdom to conquer, he took council with his younger brothers."

Eventually, after eight years of guerrilla war, the three sons of the island chief of Utheemu (Utimu) led a successful rebellion, with the help of the Ali Rajas of Cannanore, although one brother was killed. On the eve of the Portuguese deadline for all inhabitants to become Christians — or face the death penalty — the rebels landed on Malé, massacring more than 300 Portuguese (See "Malé: The Island of Dreamy Light", Part Two).

Utheemu dynasty

Muhammad Thakurufaanu, the second son of the chief of Utheemu, was declared sultan in 1573, founding the Utheemu dynasty, which reigned for 127 years through seven sultans. Never again was

Above: Locally built *bangala*, with three lateen sails, which used to trade between Maldives and the Indian subcontinent. Unfortunately these sleek vessels are no longer seen.

Maldives ruled by a foreign power.

Thakurufaanu is now remembered as a national hero for his role in regaining the country's independence (See "Haa Alifu Atoll: The Land of Thakurufaanu", Part Two). Not all subsequent rulers, however, were benevolent. The Frenchman François Pyrard de Laval, a purser shipwrecked for five years when the *Corbin* ran onto a reef in 1602, left a fascinating and detailed account of the sometimes cruel Maldivian ruler of the time (See "Baa Atoll: Land of Exiles", Part Two).

During his captivity he learned Dhivehi, and his three-volume work published in 1619 remains a mine of curious information about Maldives and a valuable historic archive.

Pyrard finally escaped when a ship from Chittagong in Bengal, intent on salvaging the cannon on board the *Corbin*, arrived. Armaments at this time were more important than men.

One of the last of the Utheemu dynasty was Sultan Ibrahim Iskandar I, who ruled from 1648 to 1687 and repelled several pirate expeditions from south India, raised many fine buildings, and introduced new customs.

He came to a sticky end after falling for a beautiful slave girl, Mariam Kabaafaanu. As his concubine she bore him a son. When he was chosen as the sultan's successor, some people believe she poisoned her lover to allow her six-year-old prince to become sultan. She later seized power for herself and appointed her brother as *wazir*.

She took many lovers, encouraging the women of her court to do the same. Her death was as dramatic as her rise to power: sailing to meet the fleet which had defeated a pirate expedition from Malabar, a spark from the victory salute blew up a powder magazine, destroying the royal vessel. The sultana's body was never recovered and her son died soon after.

The Dutch and the British

During the seventeenth century the Dutch ousted the Portuguese as the principal force in the Indian Ocean. Anxious to befriend

Above: Traditional Maldivian drummers and musicians. These large drums, once common at the sultan's court, are now rarely used, but music and dance are still central to the life of the islanders.

the new superpower, in 1645 Maldives established diplomatic ties with the Dutch Governor of Sri Lanka and exchanged tribute — a practice which continued for two centuries. In return for cowrie shells the Dutch promised an annual supply of spices, areca nut and ammunition.

In 1796 the British took over from the Dutch in Sri Lanka, and trade between Malé and Colombo increased. At that time the sultan of Maldives took himself very seriously. A letter to the governor of Sri Lanka, asking him not to welcome any enemy but to take care of any shipwreck from Maldives, opens with the words:

"Hail! The glorious, renowned, most wise, nobly-born ruler, comparable to the moon and the sun, the heroic warrior Sultan Hasan Nur-ud-din Iskandar, the warrior, the great King of the earth, to the King styled the Governor in Colombo, many thousand greetings from here."

Sri Lanka became the main buyer of Maldives' major export — dried tuna fish — but by the middle of the nineteenth century the archipelago was nearly bankrupt. Bohora merchants, who were invited from India, rapidly dominated the economy. They monopolized the import and export trade, which consisted of rice, sugar, cotton, dried fish, coconuts and tortoiseshell. Eventually one firm — Carimjee Jafferjee and Company — gained complete financial control, creating so much resentment that in 1887 local businessmen set fire to the company's stores and godowns on Malé.

To end the troubles the young Sultan Muhammad Mu'in-uddin II signed a treaty with the British governor of Sri Lanka on 16 December 1887. Maldives became a British Protectorate, but the British promised to refrain from interfering in local affairs and administration.

Modern history

The turbulent political history of Maldives continued into the twentieth century when plot and counterplot prevailed. In 1932 Muhammad Shamsuddin III, who had been recognized by the British over

Above: The former sultan's musicians welcoming visiting dignitaries with trumpets and horns.

his rival, was persuaded to accept the first written constitution in Maldivian history. It not only limited his powers but also introduced the principle of elections. When he tried to repudiate it he was replaced by Sultan Hassan Nuruddin II.

At the outbreak of the Second World War the British established two airstrips, one at Gan in the south and the other at Kelai in the north. In 1942 the Maldivian constitution was again rewritten, but the sultan was forced to abdicate the following year. Sultan Abdul Majeed Didi took his place, but he was old and soon retired to Colombo.

Prime Minister Muhammad Amin Didi assumed almost complete control of the government, introducing a modernization programme that included a National Security Service and a government monopoly over the export of fish.

The sultanate was abolished in 1953 when Amin Didi was elected president of the new republic. Food shortages and his controversial ban on smoking, however, led to riots and he died on Kurumba (Vihamanaafushi) Island soon after his arrest.

The instability continued with the abolition of the republican constitution when Muhammad Farid Didi, son of the former sultan, came to power in 1954 as the country's ninety-fourth — and last — sultan. Two years later the British were given a 100-year lease of Gan air base, but it was revoked in 1957 by the new prime minister, Ibrahim Nasir.

This angered the inhabitants of the three southernmost atolls who had benefited from the base. In 1959, claiming the government in Malé treated them like serfs, they formed the cessionist state of the United Suvadive Islands.

Abdullaa Afif Didi was elected president, a People's Council was formed and a trading corporation and a bank established. Initially Nasir agreed to a better deal with the British, but in 1962 he sent gunboats to the southern atolls, forcing Didi to flee to Seychelles (See "Gaafu Dhaalu Atoll: The Kingdom of the Cats", Part Two). Other leaders were exiled on outlying islands.

Eight years later Nasir was elected

Above: Young Maldivian woman wearing traditional costume with embroidered, tight-fitting *libaas* robe over a *feyli* underskirt.

Above: Traditional *ragavaalhu* worn by Maldivians at the turn of the century for kulhijehun, a form of martial art.

president of the second republic. Maldives became fully independent on 26 July 1965, when it joined the United Nations. Following a referendum in 1968 the country adopted another republican constitution, but a 1972 amendment gave the president far greater powers in an Islamic State.

Its English name was changed from "Maldive Islands" to the "Republic of Maldives". The legal code remained based on the Islamic code of *shari'a*.

Under the new constitution, Nasir governed with an iron hand. The main market for Maldives' biggest export — dried tuna fish — collapsed in 1972 after Sri Lanka imposed foreign currency controls. When the tourist industry was launched in the same year, Nasir was accused of using government cash to set up his own hotel and travel agency. The benefits from the new industry reached few people. After a large crowd gathered to protest against rising prices in 1974, Nasir ordered the police to open fire to disperse the crowd, though no one was killed.

When Ahmed Zaki was elected prime minister for a second term, he was banished with other government officials in the hope of forestalling any attempt to remove the president. Nasir declined his nomination for a third term in office, and departed to Singapore with a great deal of the national exchequer in 1978, after Maumoon Abdul Gayoom, the first Maldivian ambassador to the United Nations, was elected the new president.

Nasir, accused of corruption and theft, was condemned *in absentia* to twenty-five years' banishment.

Political system

Highly centralized and hierarchical, the political system of Maldives is based on three tiers. At the bottom is the

Above: One of the copperplate books, called *loamaafaana*, recording the early Islamic dynasties of Maldives.

Above right: Beautifully carved Arabic inscription on a tombstone in Malé.

Right: Ornate tombstones, handsome testimony to the lost art of stone carving which was once admired throughout the Muslim world.

Above: Guard of honour salutes President Maumoon Abdul Gayoom at Malé's Islamic Centre before addressing the Citizens' Majlis.

administration of the inhabited islands, ruled by a local island chief *(katheeb)* and one or two deputies who work with an island council.

At the second level is atoll administration. For convenience, the atolls have been grouped into twenty districts, each ruled by an atoll chief *(atholhu verin)* and his deputies. The atoll chief is responsible for the economic and political arrangements on the atoll. A *gazi* (Islamic judge) deals with judicial matters by interpreting and applying the principles of *shari'a* to individual cases.

At the top is the legislative body known as the Citizens' Majlis. It consists of forty-eight members, two elected from each district and eight nominated by the president. The president is nominated by the Citizens' Majlis and confirmed by a public referendum. The president holds supreme authority: he is commander-in-chief of the armed forces and protector of Islam in the country. He can appoint cabinet ministers who are not necessarily members of parliament.

Modern society

Change is most profound in the capital and nearby islands, where the influence of the outside world is felt strongly. The days when Maldivians relied on the wily merchants of southern India or Sri Lanka to manage their economy have long gone. They now run their own businesses and there are a growing number of wealthy entrepreneurs on Malé. Government officials work in the morning, but do other jobs in the afternoon. As they become more dynamic, they also learn what it is to work under pressure.

In the 1980s the economy grew rapidly.

Opposite: Dhivehi, with Arabic phrases in red. The present script, introduced in the sixteenth century, reads like Arabic from right to left. Dhivehi belongs to the Indo-Iranian group of languages.

Above: Fishing is the mainstay of the Maldivian economy and employs about forty per cent of the country's workforce.

Fishing is still the backbone of the country, employing about forty per cent of the workforce. Maldives National Ship Management Limited handles sixty per cent of the imports and operates ten cargo and container vessels.

The tourism industry has expanded the most, however, and is now the major foreign exchange earner. Although there are new schools and health clinics in the outer atolls, Malé remains the hub of the scattered archipelago. And while no one goes without food or shelter, Maldives is one of the poorest countries in the world.

Still predominantly an Islamic seafaring nation, Maldives is rapidly entering the modern world. In the 1970s the country's ornate doors began to creak open.

As tourists continue to discover this "lost paradise" in the midst of the Indian Ocean, the ancient ways and rhythms of these unique islands are slowly being disrupted. With the dawn of the 1990s it is difficult to say what the long-term effects will be. What is certain is that the enigma that is Maldives will remain for a long time to come.

Opposite: Slow boat home under the caress of the moon.

The Land and the Sea: Fragile Islands in the Sun

The Maldivian archipelago is made up of about 1,190 small, tropical, palm-covered coral islands stretching across the equator from 7° latitude north. Together with the Lakshadweep (formerly Laccadive) Islands to the north and the Chagos Islands to the south, they form part of a vast submarine mountain range, on the crest of which coral reefs have grown.

The islands form a double line of twenty-six natural atolls 130 kilometres (81 miles) across, stretching 823 kilometres (510 miles) from north to south. Spread across more than 90,000 square kilometres (34,750 square miles), the total land area is only 298 square kilometres (115 square miles).

Every atoll (the English word "atoll" comes from the Dhivehi word *atholhu*) is enclosed by a coral reef cut by several deep, natural channels and a lagoon. Strong currents, swinging round with the monsoon winds, flow between the atolls.

The reef structure, peculiar to Maldives and consisting of a series of circular reefs in a line, is known as *faro*. Small and low-lying, the islands are rarely more than two metres (seven feet) above sea level and extremely vulnerable to surging tides and storms. Most can be walked across in ten minutes; only a few are longer than two kilometres — the longest is eight kilometres (five miles).

Although the islands are protected by coral reefs from storms and waves, inevitably some are washed away. Indeed, in 1812 and again in 1955, devastating gales destroyed many northern islands. In 1964 the island of Hagngnaameedhoo in Alifu Atoll was inundated by high waves, while the capital, Malé, was flooded by a severe storm in 1987.

If, as some scientists predict, the sea level continues to rise as a result of global warming, then Maldives, with its ancient and unique culture, may all be swept away within fifty years.

Exactly how the atolls were formed is still unresolved. In 1842, after studying atolls in the Pacific and Atlantic, Charles Darwin suggested that they were created when volcanic land rose from the sea and a coral reef grew around its edge.

As the volcano gradually sank back into the sea it left the coral reefs encircling a shallow water-filled lagoon. Islands developed when currents and tides swept coral debris into sand bars, which eventually were colonized by plants and trees.

Although Darwin added a postscript to say that there was something special about the Maldive islands, most scientists accept his theory. More recently, however, Hans Hass has suggested that during hundreds of thousands of years a platform of coral reefs built up on the submerged mountain chain in the Indian Ocean until they burst through the surface.

Porous and unstable, the coral platform sagged in the middle, leaving only a ring of the hardest and highest coral — the rims of the atolls — where debris and sand accumulated and vegetation took hold to form islands.

These tiny specks of land separated by great stretches of water have long been a great puzzle. Just as the early history of Maldives is shrouded in mystery, so no one knows exactly how many islands there are in the archipelago. The British Admiralty chart lists some 1,100 islands, and a recent government count found 1,196. But if sand bars and coral outcrops were included the figure would be close to 2,000.

Accurate definition is further confused by the fact that islands come and go. Some combine, others split in two and occasionally islets emerge from the coral reefs. A 1955 storm created three new islands in Shaviyani Atoll, while others have slowly eroded. Around 1960, for instance, the fairly large island of Feydhoo Finolhu in Malé Atoll vanished through a combination of natural erosion and inhabitants taking away sand. It was later rebuilt.

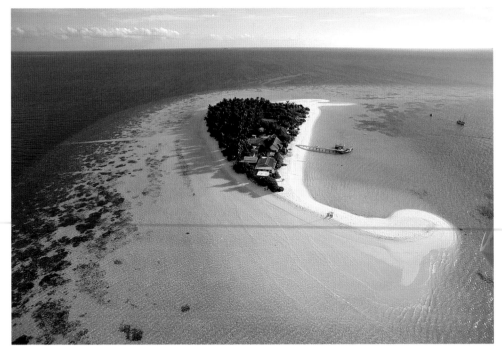

Above: Wind and wave create wondrous abstract patterns in the Maldivian archipelago.

Overleaf: Schooner anchored off Kuda Bandos Island.

To compound matters, as yet there is no agreement on what exactly constitutes an island in the archipelago: what, for instance, is the status of a large sand spit? Yet all this is part of the mystique of travelling through Maldives, where you may come across an island which has no name, is not shown on any map and has no human footprint on its shores.

Officially, 199 of the islands are populated. Many more show signs of past settlement, and some desert islands are used regularly by neighbouring islanders for collecting firewood, coconuts and even cultivation. As a rule of thumb, when the number of males who attend the local mosque falls below forty, islanders move to a more populous island.

Climate

Set in the tropics, for most of the year Maldives is hot and humid. The temperature, usually about 30°C (90°F), rarely drops below 26°C (73°F). Sea breezes take the sting from the sun except, perhaps, at midday when it reaches its zenith.

The islands, which extend latitudinally from almost one degree south of the equator to fractionally over seven degrees north, and lie scattered along and on either side of the seventy-three degree east longitudinal line, show little climatic variation.

Conveniently for sun-lovers, leisure-seekers and holiday-makers in search of an escape from the rigorous winter conditions of Europe and elsewhere, the temperatures vary little throughout each twenty-four hours, encouraging the idyllic freedom of a total outdoor life all the year round.

It is during Europe's worst time of the year, November through to March, that the equatorial-tropical climate of Maldives exerts its maximum appeal.

As an added bonus, the indoor climate in the majority of the resort hotels is gently moderated by air conditioning.

The tidal range is seldom more than a metre (three feet).

The year is divided into two main seasons according to the monsoons. The

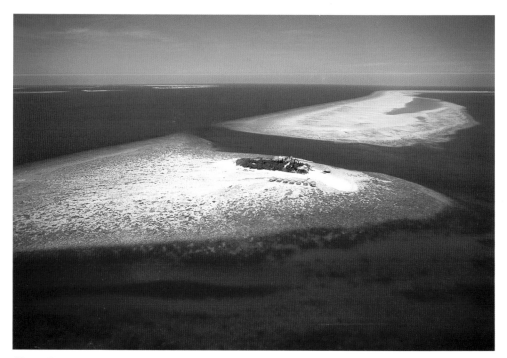

Above: Sweeps of coral on an atoll rim. Outside, the sea bed suddenly drops down more than a thousand fathoms.

north-east monsoon blows from December to March when, after some initial strong winds and squalls, the sky turns an endless blue and the sun shines from six in the morning to six at night. A wet, south-west monsoon blows from April to October.

The average annual rainfall is 1,967 millimetres (77 inches), although it is more variable in the south. The cloudbursts are so heavy that the islands are often awash. Even in the rainy season, however, the tropical sun bursts through and quickly dries the coconut leaves and coral sand.

Maldivians, who live by the subtle changes in the weather, have developed their own complex calendar based on the rising and setting of individual stars matched with the sun or the moon.

Under the *nakaiy* system the Maldivians divide the year into two distinct seasons: *hulhangu* and *iruvai*. *Hulhangu* (the south-west monsoon), which has eighteen *nakaiy*, is a season of strong winds and stormy weather. *Iruvai* (north-east monsoon), when the wind blows from the east, has nine

nakaiy. Each *nakaiy* lasts thirteen or fourteen days.

The first *nakaiy* in the *hulhangu* season, for instance, is called *assidha* (from 8 April to 21 April) when the first rains fall. The following *nakaiy* are good for clearing and planting. During the sixth *nakaiy*, *adha* (from 17 June to 30 June), seafarers steer towards the middle of storm clouds as they tend to divide and give a clear path. And towards the end of the *hulhangu* season, fishing is generally good.

The first period of the *iruvai* season is *mula* (from 10 December to 22 December), when winds blow from the north-east and the sun shines. During this period, fishing is usually good on the eastern side and in the northern atolls. And so on (See "The People: A Mix of Many Faces", Part One).

Nothing shows as clearly as this subtle and complex calendar the Maldivians' profound practical knowledge of nature and their careful adaptation to their environment.

The People: A Mix of Many Faces

The population of Maldives, which has increased rapidly in recent years, stood at about 200,000 in 1991 and is expected to reach about 300,000 by the turn of the century.

It is now the seventh most densely populated country on earth. But apart from severe overcrowding in Malé, there is no crisis of space. There are still nearly a thousand uninhabited islands for occupation.

The origins of the Maldivian people are shrouded in mystery. The first settlers may well have been Naga and Yakka people from Sri Lanka and Dravidians from southern India.

Some say they were probably followed by Aryans, who sailed their reed boats from Lothal in the Indus Valley about 4,000 years ago. Hinduism brought by Tamils and Buddhism brought by Sinhalese in turn gave way to a growing Arab influence and to Islam in the twelfth century.

Located at the crossways of the Indian Ocean shipping lanes on the main seaway around the Indian subcontinent, the islands have long been a meeting point for African, Arab, Indonesian and Malay mariners.

Throughout the centuries all contributed to the racial and cultural melting pot of Maldives. The faces of today's Maldivians reflect the influence of the various regions of the Indian Ocean.

Maldivian society

Maldivian society is distinguished by strong social divisions. Traditionally the upper class, with names like Kaloa, Fulu, Maniku and Didi, were close friends and relatives of the sultan and his family. Yet even among these families there were marked differences.

Well into this century Bell noted that "a Didi marrying a Maniku lady raises her to his own rank; but the children of a Maniku father and Didi mother are, strictly speaking, not entitled to the appellation Didi". Years ago it was unacceptable to eat with a member of an inferior class, and people of a lower class mixing with a superior only sat on a low stool.

Now these distinctions are breaking down. Indeed, the terms Maniku and Didi are sometimes used as nicknames.

Today advancement is based more on merit than birth, although education is now less important than wealth in commanding respect from others. The number of islands a person leases or the number of boats they own is also crucial to their social standing.

The boat owner takes about half the day's catch, while the skipper, *keyolhu*, earns about one-fifth. The rest is divided equally among the fishermen. The men who make the boats — *maavadi meehaa* — are respected craftsmen; on their skill depends the fishermen's lives and thus the well-being of the community. The medicine man, *hakeem*, stands on the same social rung. Skilled tradesmen like blacksmiths and jewellers also command a great deal of respect.

At the bottom of the social heap is the toddy-tapper, *raaveri*, who looks after the coconuts and taps sap for toddy and syrup.

Although long ago Maldives was ruled by sultanas and may have had a matrilineal system of inheritance, it is very much a man's world today.

Traditionally, men eat before the rest of the family and make all the major decisions, while the women stay at home and look after the family. The sharp division of labour not only reflects the exigencies of island life, but the injunctions of traditional Islam.

Yet despite the clear divisions between rich and poor, especially in Malé, there is no dire poverty. The island community and the extended family act as a safety net for its members. Even in the capital, no one sleeps in the streets or goes to bed hungry. In this sense, being small has its blessings, for every one knows each other and is willing to lend a hand. Alms-giving remains one of the fundamental tenets of Islam.

Above: At the close of day, children come out to play on the beach.

Giraavaru people

In the western quarter of the capital, Malé, live the survivors of the Giraavaru people who were translocated from the neighbouring island of Giraavaru after severe erosion of the island. They were first moved to Hulhule and subsequently to Malé when the airport was expanded.

They claim they are the original inhabitants of Maldives and throughout the centuries have kept themselves apart from the rest of society. Generally they are considered descendants of Tamils from southern India, although some argue that they may share their ancestry with the aborigines of Australia.

The women tie their hair in a bun on the right side of the head — other Maldivians tie it on the left. They also decorate the top of their *libaas* (dress) with a special style of silver embroidery. The women are extremely modest; it is said that they rarely completely undress themselves.

The Giraavaru not only have different customs, but also speak with a different accent from the people on Malé. In some ways it is closer to the dialect found on Seenu Atoll in the south. Tragically, the Giraavaru are at the abyss of extinction, down to no more than 150.

As the young marry outside their group and move into mainstream society, it is unlikely that the Giraavaru will remain a distinct community for much longer — yet another unique group unable to survive the struggle towards a modern homogenous society (See "Malé: The Island of Dreamy Light", Part Two).

Maldivian character

The people of Maldives have long been an enigma to visitors. Earlier accounts tended to express the prejudices of the observers rather than offer objective information, if such were possible.

The Arab traveller Ibn Battuta found them "upright and pious, sound in belief and sincere in thought". The French Parmentier brothers felt that they were "poor-looking creatures" although their compatriot François Pyrard declared Maldivians to be "quick and apprehensive, subtle and crafty".

Not surprisingly, the Portuguese who tried to colonize the country in the sixteenth century had a low opinion of them; according to the chronicler, Duarte Barbosa, they were "dull and malicious". While admitting they were "feeble folk", his fellow countryman Joao de Barros added that they were "very clever; and above all they are mighty magicians".

Since they offered little defence against aggressors, the Maldivians had to rely on guile to survive. They were fortunate in fostering the belief that if they were harmed, then harm would befall the perpetrator. As Battuta put it, "their armour is prayer".

The British, who became their protectors in the nineteenth century, were both attracted by their peacefulness and annoyed by their apathy. Captain Moresby, who undertook a maritime survey for the British Admiralty in 1834-1836, observed that the Maldivians "always treated us with kindness and respect, yet with shyness and suspicion, supposing our motives".

His assistants, Lieutenants I.A. Young and Wilmott Christopher of the Indian Navy, who left an interesting account of their stay, also reported that the Maldivians were "a quiet, peaceable race, hospitable and kind to strangers, though suspicious and distrustful of them".

Such attitudes, of course, were a product of island life. Nearly all commentators have remarked on the Maldivians' superstitious nature and of their fear of *jinni* (spirits) despite their faith in Islam.

In 1922 British civil servant and antiquarian H.C.P. Bell wrote that "a delightful spirit of ease and contentment seems to prevail universally", although he stressed their insularity, even in the capital. Maldives "desires nothing so greatly as to be left by the outside world as much as possible alone, to 'lotus-eat' and remain undisturbed in its sea-girt happy isolation."

Maldivians are totally adapted to their maritime environment. Like all seafarers, they carefully observe the patterns of nature around them and shape their lives accordingly. They take a keen interest in the weather, which determines when they go fishing, plant crops or sail over the horizon.

Their calendar, *nakaiy*, refers to any one of the twenty-eight seasonal divisions of the year and the clusters of stars that represent them (See "The Land and the Sea: Fragile Islands in the Sun", Part One). The origins of the calendar probably lie in the Indus Valley Civilization in Pakistan; the root of the word *nakaiy* is the Sanskrit word *nakshatra* for star or heavenly body.

The system not only determines the seasons for fishing and agriculture but also predicts the future through astrology. It thus offers a fascinating combination of common sense, scientific observation and downright superstition: during certain seasons, for example, it is considered auspicious to dig a well, to start wearing jewellery, or to lay the keel of a new boat.

Superstitions

Although all Maldivians are Muslims, they are also extremely superstitious, believing in mysterious supernatural beings called *dhevi*. The origins of this belief in spirits almost certainly antedates Islam, for many of the words used to describe them are from Sanskrit and Pali.

The scholar Hassan Ahmed Maniku suggests that a *dhevi* refers to "the idea of an invisible, but sometimes visible, being capable of moving across the high seas, land, and even through barriers. It may be helpful or harmful. It may require supplication, rebuke, or even sacrifice".

To describe the *dhevi*, Maldivians often use the Arabic word *jinni* — which in Islam are considered a third group of created beings apart from humans and angels.

They are said to be made of fire and have superhuman powers, although on Judgement Day they will be called to account with human beings. A story is told that when a student informed his Islamic professor in Egypt that he was from Maldives, the venerable scholar replied: "Ah, that is where Allah has exiled all the *jinni* of the whole world."

Lieutenants Young and Christopher observed that "the most absurd and superstitious fancies exert a powerful and pernicious influence on the people".

Certainly they believe that spirits live all around them in nature: in the sea, in the sky, in the trees and in the rain. At night, for instance, many islanders lock their doors and windows, and keep a small kerosene lamp burning to keep out evil spirits.

Hassan Maniku goes so far as to argue that primitive Maldivian society managed to produce "a religion of its own". While many of these beliefs have been condemned by the Islamic authorities throughout the centuries, they betray remarkable originality and vision and form a unique treasure trove of folklore and stories.

The islanders see no clash between their belief in Islam and in *dhevi*. Often they give long recitals from the Qur'an or other Arabic texts to ward off the evil eye and keep evil spirits at bay, but they do not rely completely on the power of the holy word.

When extraordinary events occur, many islanders turn to the local wise man immersed in *fanditha*, a special knowledge that is part science and part magic. If the rains fail, the fishing is poor or a woman is barren, the *fanditha* is consulted.

With his potions and charms he calls upon spirits to achieve his end. In an uncertain world where the unknown is feared, a belief in *fanditha* gives Maldivians a sense of control over their destiny.

There are many different spirits and stories connected with the *dhevi*. The most famous, about Rannamaari, the sea monster in the reign of Koimala who demanded the sacrifice of a virgin on Malé Island and who was thwarted by a young Arab reading the Qur'an, was recorded by Ibn Battuta (See "History: The Legend and The Mystery", Part One). During his stay in the fifteenth century, François Pyrard de Laval noted that the Maldivians believed in:

"A king of the sea, to who in like sort they make prayers and ceremonies while on a voyage; or when they go fishing, they dread above all things to offend the kings of the winds and of the sea. So, too, when they are at sea, they durst not spit nor throw anything to windward for fear lest he should be offended, and with like intent they look abaft."

Many fishermen still believe in a *dhevi* called Odivaru Ressi who lives in the sea, usually harming fishing boats, fishermen, fish bait and schools of fish, although it can also be benevolent. Sometimes it appears overhead as a long dark or red shadow, or as a sailfish, black marlin or wahoo. If it takes possession of the boat it can ruin the fishing and cause itching all over the body.

The *dhevi* who is the lord of death is called Vigani. It inhabits the seas and may be seen on water near the horizon. Some describe Vigani as a small man or in the shape of a greyish monkey with a thick covering of hair. Sometimes it is also said to have a long, elephant-like trunk which it uses to suck food from the graves of the dead. Vigani is said to be the cause of sudden death and major epidemics.

Hassan Maniku observes: "In some islands when too many people die suddenly, *fanditha* men look for signs and determine the cause to be from Vigani by looking at the sunset and the crimson clouds on the west.

"If a small compact cloud in the shape of a fish is seen glowing, then the cause of death is attributed to Vigani. He then performs *fanditha* and tries to cut the cloud into pieces.

"If he is unable to do this, it means that the entire community will be obliterated. Then the community moves to another island and settles there."

The spiritual leader of all *dhevi* is *Buddevi*, who lives in jungles, on the beach, near thick undergrowth or around abandoned houses. It can even appear where the water drips from coconut leaves after a shower of rain. It may be seen as a cat or a well-built man. It is said that whoever sees this malevolent *dhevi* falls ill.

Traditional medicine

Islanders still rely on traditional medicine men and women. At the crossroads of the Indian Ocean, healing secrets from Indians, Arabs, Persians, Malaysians, Sri Lankans and Chinese were acquired and synthesized, then used to develop local herbal remedies.

Legends abound about the feats of such special healers as Buraki Ranin, the sixteenth-century queen of Sultan Muhameed, who was said to cure sword wounds overnight with her own dressings.

Above: Although her ancestors were once queens, this island girl is likely to become a fisherman's wife.

Above: Young woman receiving a modern education in Malé.

The treatise written by Sheikh Hussain of Meedhoo in Seenu Atoll — who died in 1916 — forms the foundation of today's traditional medicine.

Known as *hakeems*, practitioners of this medicine are well-respected by the village communities. A basic tenet of their philosophy is that good health is a result of a proper balance between the hot, cold and dry "humours" in the body, so "cold food" is recommended for someone with fever, and dry fish for flu.

Some *hakeems* are schooled in *Unani* medicine, which treats the whole person, combining ancient remedies with new drugs. In recent years there has been an attempt to integrate traditional and modern medicine. Advice and training, for instance, is offered to local midwives who learned their skill from older practitioners.

Simple life

Most Maldivians lead a simple existence in harmony with nature. To many Europeans, they no doubt appear relaxed and laid back. One of the great attractions of Maldives is that it does offer a way of life adapted to the environment; a life style in which the people have few material desires.

However, it would be wrong to conclude that Maldivians lead a life of "lotus eaters" in a lost paradise. To scratch a living the islanders spend long, hard hours fishing at sea, entirely at the mercy of the elements.

Women worry about making ends meet; men worry about their catch. Most families experience enforced separation, with the men either working in the resorts or foreign shipping lines.

There is a large element of stoic resignation in the Maldivian approach to life. Perhaps because they go away and return so often, Maldivians have no word in Dhivehi for "goodbye" or "hello". At the same time, the burning interest in political intrigue and the volatile nature of their personal relations must surely reflect the need to express emotions that are necessarily repressed in close-knit, all-embracing island communities.

Homes

All land is owned by the government. Villages are laid out on a rectangular plan, and each family is granted an area known as a *goathi*, measuring fifteen metres (49 feet) by thirty metres (98 feet). Surrounded by small coral walls, within each *goathi* is a garden with several shady trees including mango, breadfruit, coconut, areca nut palm, banana and papaya. Most have several chair-like hammocks on wooden frames, *joali*, fixed in the sand or hanging from a tree, and a swinging wooden bed, *udhoali*, an ideal place to relax on a hot, sultry day.

The main house in the centre of the compound has several rooms and is used for sleeping. Food is cooked in a separate, coral shack, *bodhige*, with a thatched roof and no windows, containing two or three hollows for stoves. Most families also have a deep well for water. The "bathroom" is behind an inner coral closure called a *gifili*, where a latrine is dug in the coral sand.

The rectangular houses were originally constructed from *cadjan* (woven palm fronds), but walls are now commonly made from coral fragments held together with lime made from burning coral slowly for a long time. Coral is mined in the adjoining reefs to a depth of a metre (three feet) or so. An even stronger "cement" can be made by mixing the lime with ash, charcoal and "syrup" made from coconut sap.

Although iron is hotter, islanders prefer corrugated iron roofs to thatch because it does not have to be replaced every few years. Inside, the houses are very dark. The small windows are not placed to create a cross breeze. Flat wooden benches serve as beds at night and seats during the day, and there is invariably a swinging bed, *udhoali*, hanging from the rafters. Most families keep their valuables in a wooden trunk under a bed.

During the day, a great deal of time is spent in the shade of the verandah or under spreading breadfruit trees. Swings and hammocks attached to wooden frames are favourite lounging spots for grandparents and children. At night the doors and windows of many houses are shut tightly to keep out any passing *jinni*.

Family life

The close-knit island communities practise mutual aid to survive difficult circumstances. Extended families take care of their own members and it is usual for the mother's family to look after the children.

When they are together families say little and rarely express emotions. It is not often anyone raises their voice, even at the children. Few children speak to their remote but respected fathers.

Women usually serve the family two meals of rice and fish a day, adding to their limited housekeeping budget by mat weaving or making coir. About one-third of the houses and coconut trees are owned by women, giving them a degree of economic independence.

Since men usually work away from home either fishing, in the resorts or sailing with a shipping company, the women are responsible for the everyday running of the household. On some islands there are few men between the ages of eighteen and forty-five.

Women usually spend about three hours a day on household chores: cleaning the house and compound and preparing food. Their chores include tending fires made from scarce wood in the smoky kitchens, making the morning unleavened bread, *roshi*, and preparing rice and fish broth, *garudia*, for the main evening meal.

Preparing the golden honey from coconuts, *dhiyaa hakuru*, involves several hours of stirring, as does the concentrated fish paste, *rihaakuru*, which goes with most meals.

There are also coconuts to grate for curries and boil for oil, and the time-consuming task of making the rock-hard black fillets of tuna, *hiki mas* (See "Tastes of Maldives", Part Three).

The main opportunity for relaxation and gossip comes when the women sit on their verandahs or in their yards cleaning the evening's rice spread out on a tray.

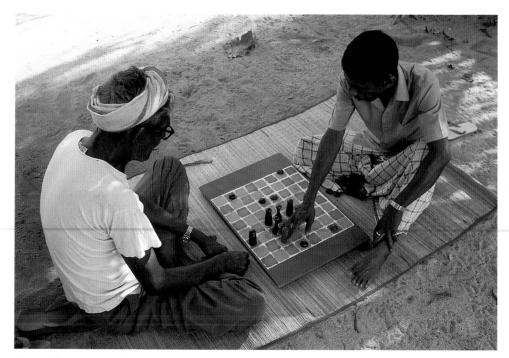
Above: Chess, a favourite game of islanders, is played with great speed and gusto.

Their greatest preoccupations are the education of the children, food and the daily catch.

In the early history of Maldives, it was common to have a sultana as ruler, and it has been suggested that the society was once a matriarchy. Now, under the Islamic law of *shari'a*, men deal with religious and judicial affairs. Women cannot be judges or priests and they say their prayers in their own mosques. According to the present constitution, the president is the religious and political leader.

Traditionally, Maldivian women never wore *purdah* and until this century they often went topless. Now, however, an increasing number of women and young girls cover their heads, legs and arms — in a tradition known locally as *burugaa*.

It's usually the job of young girls to collect water from the well in a metal pot which they carry home on their heads. Their mothers walk to the local village store, *fihaara*, which stocks basic items like rice, sugar and onions, as well as a few luxuries like condensed milk, sweets, oil and soap. All women, young and old, clean the compound and the road or path outside it, carefully picking up all the leaves and spreading the coral sand evenly. This is done with a hand broom, *iloshi fathi*, made from the thin flexible spines of coconut leaves.

To earn extra money women make coir rope, a long and drawn-out process. The husks of coconuts are first left to rot in swamps for three months or so, then beaten with heavy sticks to release the fibres.

The fibres are then washed, dried and woven together, usually across the weaver's thighs. When several strands are woven together they form an extremely strong and waterproof rope, capable of mooring a large *dhoani* to its anchor.

Formerly Maldivian coir and cables were exported widely to the Far and Middle East. It was also the Maldivian practice to sew the planks of the ships together with coir. A ship's hull held together with nails is rigid and can splinter to pieces against an Indian Ocean reef. If sewn with coir, however, it maintains a certain resilience and flexibility.

Women also make *cadjan* for screens and

Above: Immaculately turned-out pupils in a government-run school in the capital.

walls by threading dried palm leaves together with coir. They weave beautiful and intricate mats, especially in the southern atolls, showing the same skill in developing their abstract patterns as their husbands do in building their boats — simply by using their imagination and trained eye.

Marriage and divorce

Education is broadening the horizons of Maldivian women, who traditionally were expected to remain at home and look after the family. Girls usually marry very young, at about fifteen or sixteen.

The ceremony often takes place in the groom's house or in the island office. The bride does not even attend. It's enough for the husband-to-be, his father, the uncle of the bride and two witnesses to confer with with the local judge, *gazi*, to formalize the marriage.

Under Islamic law, men are allowed up to four wives — in the past it was considered a mark of esteem and piety to have as many. But today it is becoming rare for a man to have even two. Each wife is considered equal and lives in a different house. Although some marriages are still arranged, there is an increasing desire for romantic love, partly inspired by Hindi romance films and Western literature.

It's even easier to divorce than to marry — at least for men. The husband merely says "I divorce you", *thalaaq* — not three times as is usual in Islam, but once — and then reports the fact to the *gazi*.

It's more difficult for women, who must take their case to the *gazi* and prove cruelty, desertion or adultery. There are strong Muslim sanctions against adultery. The culprits are liable to be beaten. It therefore makes sense to form temporary liaisons within the marriage bond, even for a few months (and in some cases weeks). One well-placed inhabitant of Malé is reputed to have been married eighty-six times.

Ten times wed is not uncommon, but four times is the average. Eight out of ten married people divorce at least once. Married couples are usually from the same island and endogamy is preferred.

Little fuss is made over weddings. Sometimes a newly married couple arrange a small reception, *kaiveni sai*, with tea and snacks and perhaps some dancing with their friends. More elaborate affairs, however, are creeping in.

The wedding of a daughter of a wealthy family, for instance, who marries a civil servant in Malé, can be a grand affair, with local dignitaries and up to 250 guests attending a feast.

On such occasions, the trees are often decorated with tinsel and coloured paper. If there is a generator on the island, the whole compound blazes with lights.

Health

Maldivian standards of living have improved gradually in the last few decades, and life expectancy is now sixty-four years.

In the past "Maldives fever" — malaria — was notorious among travellers and seafarers. The islands were thought to have an unhealthy climate, but probably the greatest cause of illness and disease was contaminated water in village wells.

Where twenty years ago no modern doctor was available for the outlying atolls, considerable progress has been made in health care. New health centres have been set up in all the atolls and health programmes reach even the most remote villages.

Nevertheless, there are still cases of filaria and leprosy and occasional outbreaks of dengue fever. Malaria, which laid so many travellers low in the past, has been totally eradicated.

Education

Most children are still educated in privately owned schools, *makthab*, run by an Islamic teacher. From the age of three, children can be seen in a large room or under a tree learning to write with a wooden board covered in fine sand on which they trace their letters with a stick, or to recite sections from the Qur'an. They are taught to read and write Dhivehi and some Arabic, as well as to do simple arithmetic.

For centuries this was the only schooling available. But now there are new government primary schools in the outer atolls, quite a few built with help from the Japanese — schools so new that many of the headmasters are recent graduates. Standards are high. By the age of seven children are expected to speak and write in three languages with three different alphabets — Dhivehi, Arabic and English. At present the emphasis on Arabic and English is about equal.

The main secondary schools are in Malé — two private schools which teach in English and two government Arabic schools. Students go abroad to university.

But for most, the island on which they were born remains the centre of their world. There is no word in Dhivehi for "village" or "town", only for "island" (*rah*).

Above: A woman carries drinking water home from the village well. Because of the proximity of the surrounding sea, the water in wells on the islands is often brackish.

Fishing

Traditionally fishing has been the mainstay of the economy and the islanders' principal source of sustenance. Even today it still employs half the Maldivian workforce.

The fishing *dhoanis* are privately owned and usually keep a crew of eight or so, although in the north they tend to carry more. For these hardy seafaring folk, the day is long. They wake at five in the morning to catch reef fish, which are used as bait and kept alive in the bilge water of the boats.

They then search the sea for tuna shoals, travelling for up to four hours using their steady diesel engines when the wind is poor.

Finding the tuna is difficult. Usually birds circling in the sky point the fishermen in the right direction. Now the real work begins. Squeezing the live bait in their hands to stun them, the men slip the fish overboard into the water to attract the tuna.

Once the tuna begin to feed, the fishermen splash the surface of the water to make them more excited. Now it's time to cast the fixed lines strung with feathered hooks and whisk the unsuspecting tuna into the bottom of the boat. The hooks have no barbs so that the fish can be flipped off easily. The action is fast. On a good day one boat can catch more than a thousand fish, but the average catch is smaller.

The tuna are blue-fin (*raagon'di*), the larger yellowfin (*kanneli*), and skipjack (*kandu mas*).

With the hold full, the long haul home begins, muscles tired and throats dry after the day's strain and excitement under the sun. The fishermen usually reach land in the late afternoon and carry their catch ashore to gut the fish and give them to the women to dry or to cook.

Any excess is boiled, then smoked for a day, dried in the sun and exported as "Maldive Fish". The rock-hard fillets, *hiki mas*, were at one time in great demand throughout Sri Lanka.

Now government freezer ships move around the atolls, collecting the fish directly from the fishermen. It saves the long process of drying and provides ready cash.

Above: After a long, rewarding day at sea, Maldivian fishermen return home with their catch, which is immediately brought ashore for cleaning and drying.

Opposite: With the fathers away all day fishing, island life is close-knit and cooperative, with elder brothers and sisters giving a helping hand to their hard-pressed mothers.

PART TWO: PLACES AND TRAVEL

Above: The capital, Malé, is one of the 1,200 or so islands of Maldives which stretch down the Indian Ocean across the equator. No one knows the exact number of islands in the archipelago.

Opposite: Built on white coral sand, villas at Kuramathi Tourist Resort nestle under swaying coconut trees.

Resort Islands: A Touch of Paradise

With seventy resort islands to choose from, wherever your final destination in Maldives may be, one thing is certain — you will experience one of the most unusual and exotic holidays in the world. Serenity, tranquillity and natural harmony are its key elements.

A resort island is a place of no news and no shoes where the sand caresses bare feet and the head fills with a succession of poetic sights, sounds and scents: the red orb of the sun sinking into the infinite sea amid the fragrance of frangipani and hibiscus.

It is a place to admire the banyan, bamboo, coconut and mangrove trees and marvel as a heron dips its long beak into a shoal of tiny silver fish at the water's edge, where crabs scuttle away as you walk home along a moonlit beach.

Tourists are enticed by such slogans as "Robinson Crusoe with Air-Conditioning" or "Where French Chic Goes Native". For those who do not want to feel too disorientated a "Romantic Island Hideaway with a Mediterranean Atmosphere" is an alternative.

Even on the more sophisticated islands, the atmosphere is relaxed and informal. Visitors are told: "Strictly Prohibited: Hurry, Worry, Rush, Rush." Another sign reads: "Natives are Friendly".

You live in artificial luxury and natural splendour on a tiny speck of land where coconut palms tower above the tropical shrubs and flowers, surrounded by a wide strand of dazzling white coral sand that leads to the warm, turquoise waters of a sheltered lagoon. Beyond the coral reef the sea floor drops hundreds of fathoms into the deep blue of the Indian Ocean.

Getting there

The vast majority of tourists arrive by air at the international airport on Hulhule Island. Once there, each resort provides transportation to your vacation island. It is also possible to hire a *dhoani* at the airport to ferry you to nearby Malé.

When to go

The best time for divers and snorkelers to visit is between December and March. The best time for yachtsmen and windsurfers is November to March, when winds average seven to twenty-one knots.

The experience

These islands lie in the cleanest ocean in the world and in enchanted moments you may treasure all your life you learn the graceful art of doing nothing — and doing it well — simply sunbathing, daydreaming, swimming or strolling through the whispering palms beneath the pin-bright stars of the southern constellations in the balm of an indigo tropical night.

For the more active, a whole range of water sports is available: snorkeling, windsurfing, sailing, canoeing, scuba diving, water-skiing, parasailing and fishing. The water sports are run by international schools.

Because of its extreme underwater visibility, beautiful coral reefs and variety of marine life, Maldives offers some of the best diving in the world (See "Underwater Maldives", Part Three).

Idyllic

Although most visitors usually go to Maldives to get away from it all, the islands may feel crowded during the November to March high season. Nevertheless, would-be Robinson Crusoes can usually find a quiet spot on a lonely dot of land. The crescent-shaped island of Baros, for instance, is only 500 metres (1,640 feet) long and 200 metres (656 feet) wide.

Some resorts, like Rihiveli, meaning "Silver Sand", have three adjoining uninhabited islands, reached by wading through the shallows, for extra privacy (See

Opposite: Traditional Maldivian fishing boat lies at anchor after another day at sea.

"Central Atolls: Diamonds in The Sun", Part Two).

Yet even on the larger and more populous islands, it's easy to become hooked on the Maldivian life style. Many diving instructors who have lived on the same island for years feel no sense of claustrophobia or isolation. Some say the islands are what they have been looking for all their lives.

Generally, the resorts are self-contained communities, but you can arrange visits to neighbouring desert islands and even some settled islands where Maldivians make handicrafts.

The resorts combine the ideal of a tropical island paradise with creature comforts. While Maldives supplies the sand, sun and sea, virtually everything else — from light bulbs to alcohol to tropical fruit — is imported.

Resorts vary widely, from absolute luxury in post-modernist architecture to rustic villas of coral and thatch where you awake to the rustle of the breeze in the palms and the distant pounding of the surf on the reef. On some islands wooden bungalows on stilts stretch out over the water. Others have beautiful terraces above the lagoon where you can watch the reef fish in the translucent water below.

In fact, lack of fresh water may be the only real problem. The traditional supply is a well dug into the sand, but although the water that filters through is drinkable it is usually brackish.

While Maldivians like this water to wash in, foreigners usually hanker for a fresh shower to wash away the sand and salt of the day. Now, although almost all resorts have desalination plants, every effort is made to catch rainwater from roofs, on many islands all that is available for washing is brackish water.

The resorts, managed by different companies, have developed their own styles and standards. Some companies dovetail their programmes for particular tastes and nationalities.

Kurumba (Vihamanaafushi), for instance, the first tourist resort to be opened in Maldives, has a freshwater swimming pool and a sports centre fully equipped with a gym, tennis courts, sauna, jacuzzi and billiard room. Cocoa Island (Makunufushi), offering the feel of a private island for only eight or ten guests, is a hideaway for the very rich seeking relaxation and seclusion.

At the other extreme, the Club Méditerranée or the Italian Club Vacanze, offer nonstop fun with such non-Maldivian activities as aerobics, archery and squash, as well as water sports. And with a private garden for each room, the Laguna Beach (Velassaru) resort, which maintains one staff member for every guest, has been rated one of the world's top 300 hotels.

As the number of tourists increases, resorts are being built further and further away from Malé and the airport. Helengeli, for instance, lies about fifty kilometres (31 miles) from the airport, along the ancient boat route to the northern atolls. Kuramathi is sixty kilometres (37 miles) away. The most distant resort, Kunfunadhoo on Baa Atoll, takes about nine and a half hours to reach by motorized *dhoani* — and about three hours by speed boat.

Above: Convivial break in one of the capital's many tea-shops. They are usually male-only domains.

Opposite: Club Méditerranée, Farukolhufushi.

Overleaf: Ihuru Tourist Resort, with jetty stretching across the shallow lagoon, is neighbour to the equally beautiful Vabbinfaru Paradise Island.

Malé: The Isle of Dreamy Light

Although tiny, Malé, the capital of Maldives, has been the political, economic and cultural hub of this far-flung archipelago for centuries. Since the arrival of Islam in the twelfth century, it has been known as the "Island of the Sultans".

Set in the middle of the Malé Atoll, Malé covers just 1.8 square kilometres (more than half a square mile). Fifty years ago it was a sleepy village lost in the limbo of the Indian Ocean. Today Malé, the capital of a nation caught up in a race to join the rest of the world, contains the greatest wealth in the country and is the administrative and religious centre of the islands.

Earlier this century, with its clean rectangular streets of coral sand and its one-storey coral buildings behind neat palisades, visitors were struck by its peace and charm. Englishwoman Lawson Robins visited the capital in 1920 — one of the few white women to do so — and noted that there was no telegraph, no ox carts, no motor cars and no carriages. It was "a land of quietness and peace. . . . Some of the best houses have walls of whitewashed coral stones; but most are in a tiny compound surrounded by a fence of *cadjan*. Trees and shrubs flourish: we saw firs, oleanders, bamboos, palms and other plants. . . . Each street was carpeted with white coral sand, soft and clean."

When the English traveller T. W. Hockly visited Malé in 1934 he, too, recorded: "The roads are all of white coral sand and I have never seen any place kept cleaner. There were several small shops and a few houses where plantain, papaya and mango trees, and many shrubs were flourishing luxuriously.

"The poorer inhabitants have their houses walled with mats or *cadjans* made from palm leaves, about six to seven feet in height. Every little dwelling stands in its own compound. They are roofed with *cadjans* or corrugated iron sheets."

When H.C.P. Bell stayed on Malé in 1921, he remarked that "with its teeming population of over 5,200 souls, [it] is far too overcrowded already". Yet the capital now boasts 70,000 inhabitants — nearly a third of the population — and a floating population of several thousand people who come to sell their wares and buy goods.

Malé has changed irrevocably. To cope with the swelling numbers, land was reclaimed from the shallows to the south and west, and the island is now one-third larger.

Building blocks and cement bricks have replaced the *cadjan*, and the sand in the streets is now grey. Paved roads criss-cross the shopping centre and many trees have vanished, felled when President Muhammad Amin Didi ordered wider main roads.

Indeed, so large is the population and so scarce is land that the traditional single-storey coral houses are being replaced by taller, modern buildings, although few higher than five storeys and most only two. In every quarter of the island there are signs of hectic building and changing pace as new money and new people sweep away the soporific past.

Although Malé has no factories or skyscrapers, it is home to all government offices, banks, communications and the key institutions which control the nation's economic and social life.

Islanders from all over the archipelago do business in Malé's waterfront offices, the "Singapore Bazaar" and the small shops in the narrow lanes where most goods are imported. If the atolls depend on the sea for their livelihood, ultimately Malé depends on the atolls for its economic well-being.

The modern infrastructure of the nation was only laid down in the late 1970s. The first commercial jet landed in 1977 at the only operating airport on neighbouring Hulhule Island. In the same year a satellite

Opposite: Only one and a half square kilometres in size, Malé is one of the smallest capitals in the world.

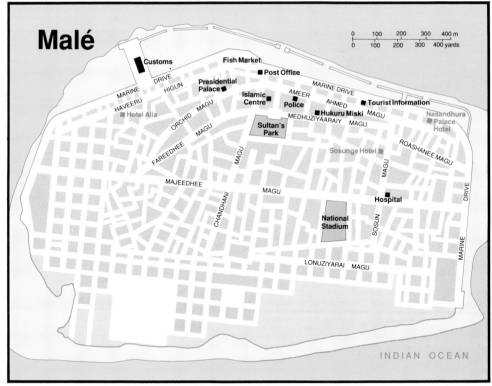

Malé

0 100 200 300 400 m
0 100 200 300 400 yards

Customs
Fish Market
Post Office
MARINE DRIVE
DRIVE
MARINE
HAVEERU
HIGUN
Presidential
Palace
Islamic
Centre
AMEER
AHMED
Tourist Information
Hotel Alia
ORCHID
MAGU
Police
MEDHUZIYAARAIY
Hukuru Miski
MAGU
Nasandhura
Palace
Hotel
Sultan's
Park
FAREEDHEE
MAGU
Sosunge Hotel
ROASHANEE MAGU
MAJEEDHEE
MAGU
MAGU
CHANDHANI
MAGU
Hospital
National
Stadium
SOSUN
MARINE
DRIVE
MAGU
LONUZIYARAI MAGU

INDIAN OCEAN

© Camerapix 1993

earth station on Malé made international telecommunications possible. The following year, colour television was introduced to Malé and, since then, each year brings newer technology.

Malé, provides everything from special medical attention to the main secondary government and private schools in the country. To progress in Maldivian society you have to start in the capital. Indeed, the political history of Maldives is largely the history of Malé's major families.

Like many developing capitals, Malé draws the young. Education in the outlying atolls is still based on traditional private schools, *makthab*, where pupils learn the rudiments of the Qur'an and Dhivehi. Most English-medium secondary schools and further education institutes are in Malé. GCE O-level graduates from such schools remain in the capital, as they have to serve the government for between two and three years. A-level graduates serve four years when called upon. Even after they have honoured this bond few wish to return to the atolls. Jobs are easier to find in Malé and life is more exciting. Malé has only one cinema due to the rising popularity of home videos, and there are nightly transmissions on local television.

Getting there

Malé is so small that there is no room for an airport. Airliners land on neighbouring Hulhule Island, which for years served as the holiday retreat for the sultans who lived in Malé. This long, thin stretch of land, providentially near the capital, serves as a natural aircraft carrier permanently anchored in the sea, with the only runway in the world that begins and ends in water. Just as your wide-body jet seems about to splash into the sea, the wheels suddenly bounce onto the asphalt.

Opposite top: Opposite the jetty on Marine Drive is the small town square.
Opposite: Fishing boats return with their catch to the fish market on Malé.
Overleaf: Malé's inner harbour, sheltering the craft which form the lifeline between the atolls.

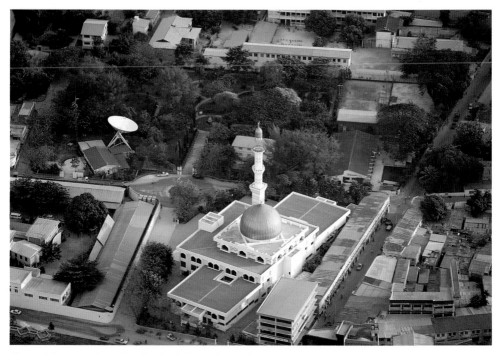

Above: Minaret and satellite dish in Malé pointing to the heavens, centre of the country's faith and international communications.

Now one form of transport is abandoned for another. Alongside the airport, *dhoanis* and launches wait at the jetty to take passengers to the capital and surrounding resort islands.

Where to stay

There are a few reasonably priced private and government-run guesthouses and small hotels in the capital.

The most expensive are the Hotel Alia and Nasandhura Palace Hotel, which have the only licensed bars in Malé. Hotel Alia, in the west of the island, has seventeen rooms as well as a palm-covered bar and air-conditioned restaurant.

Nasandhura Palace Hotel, in the east of the island, has twenty-eight air-conditioned rooms with harbour views and a restaurant. The Sosunge, once a government guesthouse, now houses the School of Hotel and Catering Services.

Hilaaleege, a government-owned guesthouse, probably warrants one star by international standards, but it has its own quiet and pleasant atmosphere with friendly service. However, it only accommodates official guests.

There is also a wide range of privately owned and registered guesthouses scattered across the island (See Listings for "Accommodation").

Getting around

The best way to discover Malé is by foot. Although it only takes about twenty minutes to walk the length of the island, many citizens ride about on bicycles. Row upon row of solid Raleigh bicycles outside government offices show how the pace of life is quickening. There are no buses, but several taxi services. All charge a standard Rf 10/- per trip anywhere in Malé without luggage, with an additional charge of Rf 5/- for luggage. All operate 24 hours and can be called by telephone. Note that you should check the fare before you hire one.

Sightseeing

The lifeblood of the nation, great liners, tankers and cargo ships which bring all the islands need for building, food and power,

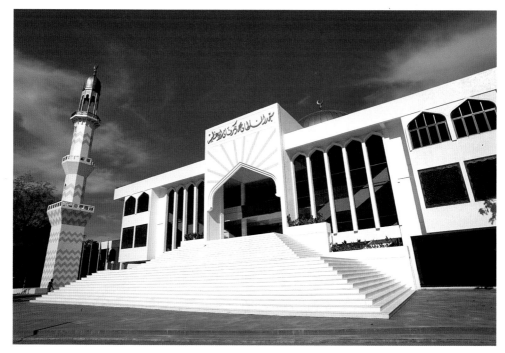

Above: Islamic Centre, Malé. Maldives is a Sunni Muslim nation adhering to a relaxed form of Islam.

ride high at their moorings in the roadstead as you cross the **channel** from the **airport** to **Malé**.

This expanse of ocean between the islands of **Funadhoo**, **Dhoonidhoo**, and **Viligili** is the **outer harbour** where *dhoanis* buzz around the silent, brooding beasts of the high seas like insects. The cargoes are ferried by towed lighters to the wharfs of the **inner harbour** north of the capital.

Enclosed by a **coral stone breakwater** with narrow entrances, it was built between 1620 and 1648. Various sections of the **waterfront** have different functions: one for the ferry boats and *dhoanis* to the outlying islands, another for fishing boats and local cargo. In front of the **Headquarters of the Security Forces** is a new wooden **official jetty**.

Malé is divided into four districts. **Henveiru** occupies the north-east side and **Maafannu** the north-west. The two smaller wards, **Galolhu** and **Machchangolhi**, lie in the centre and to the south.

Most houses have Dhivehi names, but some reflect the British influence — often quite incongruously and sometimes poet-ically: Snow Down, Sky Villa, Rose Burn, Night Flower, Blue Bell, Lightning Villa, Dreamy Light and Crab Tree. Green and blue are favourite colours and windows tend to be high and narrow which, according to legend, prevents evil spirits from entering.

Tribute to Islam

Dominating the Malé skyline from the sea is the shining gold dome and thin minaret of the new and striking **Islamic Centre**. Located between **Medhuziyaaraiy Magu** and **Ameer Ahmed Magu**, it was opened in 1984 and contains a **library** and **conference hall**. Its central feature, the **grand mosque**, holds more than 5,000 people. The main **prayer hall** has **wood carvings** and Arabic verses inscribed by Maldivian craftsmen.

Named after the national hero, Sultan Muhammad Thakurufaanu, who ousted the Portuguese in the seventeenth century, the Islamic Centre not only honours the Muslim faith but reflects the new prosperity that is enveloping the islands.

There are several other Islamic monu-

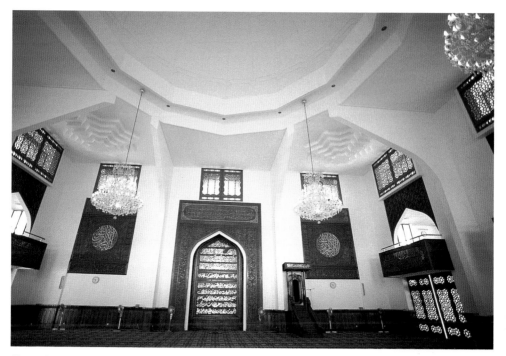

Above: Interior of the grand mosque, Malé.
Opposite: Minaret and grand mosque of the Islamic Centre, Malé.

ments on Malé. Opposite the old Friday Mosque sits the **Medhu Ziyaaraiy memorial**, which commemorates the person who converted Maldives to Islam in AD 1153 — one Al-Sheikh Abu al-Barakat Yusuf al-Barbari, also referred to as Al-Sheikh Abdul Rikaab Yusuf al-Thabreyzee (See "History: The Legend and The Mystery", Part One).

Nearby is the most beautiful mosque on Malé — the *Hukuru Miskiiy* or **Friday Mosque** — built in 1656 during the reign of Sultan Ibrahim Iskandar. The interior and exterior walls are intricately carved with Arabic verses and ornamental patterns. The compound encloses the ancient **tombstones**, all beautifully carved, of many past sultans and dignitaries.

In 1675 the same sultan, inspired by the minarets he had seen on a pilgrimage to Mecca, built the nearby **Munnaaru Minaret**, where the chief *mudhimu,* or muezzin, on the island called the faithful to prayer before the Islamic Centre was built.

The most remembered episode in Maldives' past is commemorated by the **Bihuroazu Kamanaa Miskiiy**, the **tomb** of Muhammad Thakurufaanu, who in 1573 was instrumental in regaining the country's independence from the Portuguese. That day, the first of the Islamic month of the *Rabeeu'l Awwal*, is celebrated as Maldives' National Day. Thakurufaanu, who died in 1585, is also remembered for minting the country's first coins, improving education and religious services, and expanding trade (See "Haa Alifu Atoll: The Land of Thakurufaanu", Part Two).

Sultan Ali VI is remembered in the **Ali Rasgefaanu Ziyaaraiy memorial**. Popularly known as Ali Rasgefaanu, he ruled the country only two and a half months before he was killed in the Portuguese invasion of 1558. The memorial is on the spot where the sultan fell after being hit by an enemy arrow. He was standing in the shallows, but land reclamation has brought the memorial inland.

Successive rulers used the inspiration of Sultan Ali and Muhammad Thakurufaanu as national heroes to weld the scattered people of Maldives into one nation.

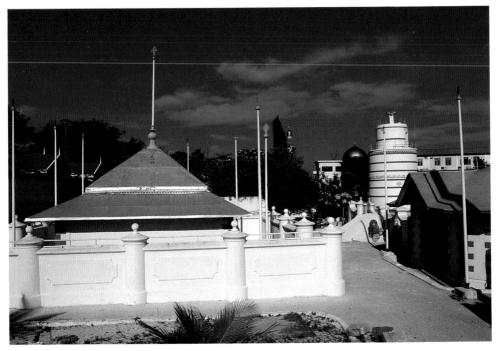

Above: The Medhu Ziyaaraiy, tomb of Abu al-Barakat Yusuf al-Barbari, who converted Maldives to Islam.
Opposite: Malé shop displays the colourful leisure-wear of the tropics.

Historic Buildings

Other buildings in Malé speak of the tempestuous political history which threatened to split the islands as different factions fought for the sultanate. Sultan Shamsuddin III built the **Presidential Palace**, known as the **Muleeaage**, for his son just before the First World War. But the sultan was deposed and his son never took office. When the country became a republic in 1953 the colonial-style building was designated the **Presidential Palace**.

However, the **Sultan's Palace** was razed to the ground — except for one three-storey wing. The **gardens** became a **public park** and now only the massive **iron gate** at the **entrance**, opposite the Islamic Centre on **Medhuziyaaraiy Magu**, speaks of its former glory. The **Sultan's Park** forms a quiet green oasis in the now bustling capital, with ponds covered by water lilies and leafy trees filled with bird song.

The wing that survived is today the **National Museum**, housing a complete collection of royal possessions. Its most interesting exhibits, however, are **archaeological finds**. Spread out against an outside wall and in a small room are the intriguing remains gathered from temples scattered throughout the atolls: Buddha heads, Bohomala sculptures, monkey statues and a broken statue piece of the Hindu water god, Makara.

The most fascinating pieces are two five-faced statues with long feline teeth, outstretched tongues and extended ear lobes discovered recently in Malé (See "History: The Legend and The Mystery", Part One).

Most objects in the museum belonged to former sultans: thrones, sedan chairs, ceremonial parasols, palanquins and a fine collection of boxes decorated with intricate lacquer work.

Shops and markets

The main **shopping area**, a cluster of stores along and around the bottom end of **Chandhani Magu** (the main north-south

Above: Fast-growing waterfront on Malé, the capital.
Opposite: Day's catch of skipjack tuna — *kandu mas* — is delivered to the fish market on Malé.
Overleaf: Malé International Airport, situated on Hulhule Island, only ten minutes by boat from the capital.

street), is nicknamed the **Singapore Bazaar** because the majority of goods are imported from Singapore.

Apart from the **tourist shops**, other shops deal in spices, dried fish, rope and other essential items. There are more tourist shops along the waterfront — **Marine Drive**.

North of the town centre along the waterfront stand the **markets**. From mid-afternoon fishing *dhoanis* begin to sail into the harbour laden with the day's catch and the crews, under the remorseless tropical sun since dawn, carry the catch — mainly bonito, swordfish and tuna — ashore.

The **fish market**, where they are laid out in the shade, is strictly men's business. Each head of the household chooses the family fish. Only a few women on Malé have ever witnessed this daily ritual, which takes place near sundown. Indeed, a few women are so housebound that they have never seen the whole of their island home.

Men also shop in the neighbouring **wood market** for firewood — coconut and

screwpine as well as *dhakadhaa*, *uni* and *dhiggaa* — brought in by *dhoani* from the surrounding islands. The only trees left on Malé are ornamental coconuts, although some new saplings have taken root on reclaimed land in the west.

Nearby a **covered market** displays the staples of Maldivian life — rice, coconuts, eggs, oil, spices, sweet potatoes, onions, chillies, watermelons, mangoes, bananas, papayas, pomegranates, limes and non-alcoholic toddy made from coconut sap. Because there is so little fertile land, vegetables are rare and expensive. Back at home the food enters the inner sanctum of the women — the kitchen — where traditionally no man sets foot.

Entertainment

Malé offers little in terms of organized entertainment. There are no nightclubs or bars. But an evening stroll around the centre of town along **Majeedhee Magu**, alive with shoppers, music and noise, helps to absorb Malé's unique atmosphere.

Above: Scarce firewood gathered from neighbouring islands on display in the main market in Malé.

And there are **restaurants**, both European and Maldivian, and **cinemas** which screen mainly Hindi romances and adventures.

The **television station** transmits a mixture of national and foreign programmes and the Voice of Maldives **radio station** is on the air throughout the day.

If the sleepy pace, beautiful faces and marvellous seascapes begin to pall, you can make an excursion to a nearby resort island or hire a *dhoani* to find out how most islanders live and travel.

Traditionally, Maldivians are shy with strangers. With their red faces, short shorts, colourful shirts and inevitable cameras, the tourists on Malé's waterfront stand out. But Maldivians are rapidly adapting. To entice tourists, Western pop music blares out of the shops and flashy trinkets are on display.

Eating establishments

In almost every street or alleyway you will find a **tea-shop** offering piping hot tea, *sai*, and delicious snacks known as "short-eats". Maldivian women never enter the tea-shops and women visitors will find themselves objects of curiosity.

A dollar or two is enough for a small feast of rice, curry and several side dishes. You take as much as you want from the dishes, which are constantly replenished, then pay at the door.

Almost any time of the day short-eats and vegetable and fish curries are available at the **Evening Glory** and **The Crest** in **Henveiru** and at the **Majeedhee Ufaa** near the **Chandhani-Majeedhee junction**. Close to the harbour are the aptly named **Dawn Café** and **Queen of the Night**.

Other restaurants cater for European tastes and pockets, such as **Quench** and the **New Port**, a good waterfront restaurant.

A new café, **Shanghai Restaurant,** has been opened on **Rahdhebai Magu**. The **Gelatino Italiano** specializes in ice cream.

The only Indian restaurant, on **Majeedhee Magu**, is called — surprise, surprise — **Indian Restaurant**, although the **Park View** on **Chandhani Magu** features some Indian cuisine, along with continental and Chinese, on its menu. Other restaurants of note include the **Dragon** on **Marine Drive** — which specializes in Thai cuisine — and **Twin Peaks** on **Orchid Magu**.

Top: Lantern-lit island store, providing a few luxuries as well as the necessities of life.

Above: Young girls at a party. Traditionally, Maldivians eat with their right hands.

Overleaf: Thriving fishing community at ocean's edge.

Central Atolls: Diamonds in the Sun

For many, the passage between the islands of the central atolls of Maldives is an unforgettable experience. On a calm, sunny day, the wake dances away behind the boat on the deep azure of the sea like so many diamonds in the sun.

Later, as the sun sinks towards the west, the sea turns sparkling silver and an atmosphere of matchless peace overwhelms the soul as the first glimmering of stars appears in the darkening sky.

Only a few frigatebirds, flying fish and an occasional school of dolphin keep the little *dhoani* company as it sails on. With no sophisticated navigation equipment, the crew constantly scans the horizon for the first hint of an island.

As you approach the islands and atolls, all around the long swell of the Indian Ocean crashes onto treacherous coral reefs.

Charting the way through such perilous hazards requires special local knowledge. Every mariner safely home breathes a sigh of relief as their vessel enters the inner lagoon, rolling gently in the slight swell as the anchor cables take the strain and the sights and sounds of land drift over the water: the cries and laughter of children playing on the beach, flitting butterflies and the surf breaking on the sand.

Frequently, however, the sky turns suddenly dark and a squall gusts across the glassy surface, whipping up white horses. Swiftly the sea becomes a menacing and foaming blue-black. Through the centuries, usually during the north-east monsoon, many ships missed their landfall in such weather and were swept thousands of kilometres off course.

Maldivians have lived with their traditional ways and customs unchanged for centuries, but in the last few decades they have been hurled into the late twentieth century. Islanders, who are only just beginning to get used to the diesel engine and electricity, can now look up and see in the sky the metal birds which land at the new airstrips on various islands in the atolls.

To the south, running between Laamu and Huvadhoo atolls, the One-and-a-Half-Degree Channel, known locally as Huvadhoo Kandu, is the broadest stretch of water in Maldives. It takes its name from its northern latitude, and divides the central atolls from the southern atolls.

Ninety-six kilometres (60 miles) wide, with a maximum depth of 1,130 fathoms, it is the widest and most dangerous of the channels which divide Maldives. During October and November currents run up to three-and-a-half knots east, and west from December to March at almost four knots as the monsoon winds change direction.

To the north, the divide between the central and the northern atolls is the Kaashidhoo Kandu. Although neither as impressive nor as strategic as the southern channel, navigating through its often turbulent waters calls for equally superlative seamanship.

The central atolls of Maldives — Malé, Alifu, Vaavu, Meemu, Faafu, Dhaalu, Thaa, and Laamu — are the most populous. The capital, Malé, lies in Malé Atoll (See "Malé: The Isle of Dreamy Light", Part Two) and is the country's main economic artery.

These atolls, especially Malé and to a smaller degree Alifu, have been at the forefront of tourist development since the 1970s. Seventy islands, some of them once inhabited, have been transformed into exclusive tourist resorts, benefiting neighbouring islanders by providing work and a ready market for their handicrafts.

Slowly, Western-style clothes and tastes blend with age-old customs and dress. But the further away you travel from Malé and Alifu atolls, the more traditional island life remains. New schools and health clinics may appear in the various island capitals, but islanders continue to build boats and go fishing.

The most noticeable change brought about by tourism is the marked absence of young men. They leave as soon as possible, either to work in the resorts or for Maldives National Ship Management Limited. Now the women — long used to looking after

FAAFU ATOLL
(NORTH
NILANDHOO)

Himithi

VATTARU CHANNEL

Dhiggaru

Magoodhoo

Nilandhoo Dharaboodhoo

MAA KADU
CHANNEL

Ribudhoo

Mulaku

Maadheli

Muli

Kolhufushi

Kudahuvadhoo

MEEMU ATOLL
(MULAKU)

DHAALU ATOLL
(SOUTH NILANDHOO)

Buruni

Fahala

Dhiyamigili

Kandoodhoo

Guraadhoo

Thimarafushi
Veymandhoo

LAAMU ATOLL
(HADHDHUNMATHEE)

THAA ATOLL
(KOLHUMADULU)

Isdhoo

Dhabidhoo

Maabaidhoo
Mundhoo

Gan (Gamu)

The Central
Atolls

| 0 | 10 | 20 | 30 | 40 km |

| 0 | 10 | 20 miles |

Maamendhoo Gaadhoo
Hithadhoo
Kadhdhoo

ONE-AND-A-HALF-DEGREE CHANNEL

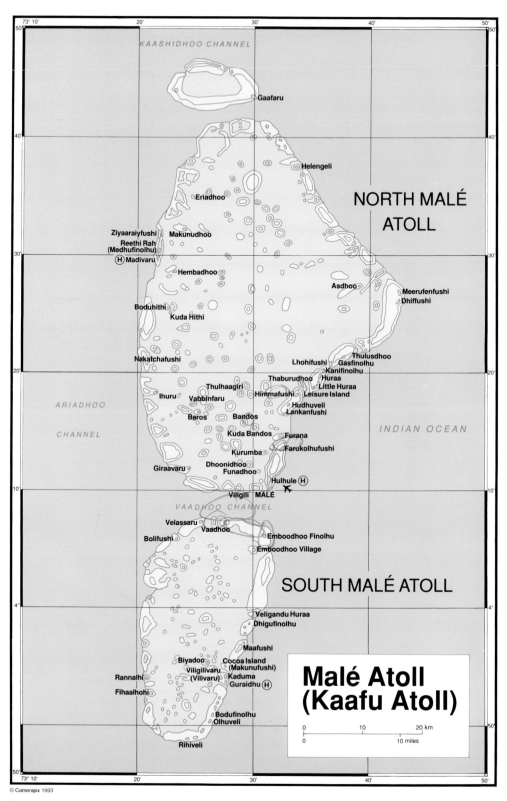

73° 10'   20'   30'   40'   50'

KAASHIDHOO CHANNEL

Gaafaru

Helengeli

Eriadhoo

NORTH MALÉ ATOLL

Ziyaaraiyfushi
Reethi Rah
(Medhufinolhu)
(H) Madivaru

Makunudhoo

Hembadhoo

Asdhoo

Meerufenfushi
Dhiffushi

Boduhithi
Kuda Hithi

Nakatchafushi

Lhohifushi
Thaburudhoo
Thulhaagiri

Thulusdhoo
Gasfinolhu
Kanifinolhu
Huraa
Little Huraa
Leisure Island
Hudhuveli
Lankanfushi

ARIADHOO

Ihuru
Vabbinfaru

Himmafushi

CHANNEL

Baros
Bandos

Kuda Bandos

Furana

INDIAN OCEAN

Kurumba

Farukolhufushi

Giraavaru

Dhoonidhoo
Funadhoo

Hulhule (H)

Viligili MALÉ

VAADHOO CHANNEL

Velassaru
Vaadhoo

Bolifushi

Emboodhoo Finolhu

Emboodhoo Village

SOUTH MALÉ ATOLL

Veligandu Huraa
Dhigufinolhu

Maafushi

Biyadoo
Viligilivaru
(Vilivaru)

Cocoa Island
(Makunufushi)
Kaduma
Guraidhu (H)

Rannalhi

Fihaalhohi

Bodufinolhu
Olhuveli

Rihiveli

Malé Atoll (Kaafu Atoll)

0   10   20 km
0   10 miles

98

Above: Club Méditerranée comes to the Indian Ocean: western design, local materials.

family and home — have even greater responsibility. But despite the absentee fathers, the close-knit communities ensure that the children are brought up in a safe and loving atmosphere (See "The People: A Mix of Many Faces", Part One).

Malé Atoll: Islands in the Stream

Malé, the economic and political centre of the country, is also the hub of Malé Atoll. There are 105 uninhabited islands, twelve inhabited, including Malé and Hulhule, and forty-three resorts in the atoll. The total population is 88,700, of whom 70,000 live on Malé.

Getting there

Resorts ferry guests from the airport to their vacation island. *Dhoanis* are also available for hire for visitors who wish to travel to nearby islands, but you will need a government permit. There are charter operators for boats and aircraft. See Listings.

When to go

Most resorts remain open year-round. Check with your travel agent or the nearest Maldives tourist office.

Where to stay

In North Malé Atoll:
Asdhoo, Bandos, Baros, Boduhithi, Eriadhoo, Farukolhufushi (Club Med), Furana, Gasfinolhu, Giraavaru, Helengeli, Hembadhoo, Hudhuveli, Ihuru, Kanifinolhu, Kanu Huraa (Tari Village), Kuda Hithi, Kurumba (Vihamanaafushi), Lankanfushi, Lhohifushi, Little Huraa, Makunudhoo, Meerufenfushi, Nakatchafushi, Reethi Rah (Medhufinolhu), Thulhaagiri, Vabbinfaru and Ziyaaraiyfushi.

In South Malé Atoll:
Biyadoo, Bodufinolhu, Bolifushi, Cocoa (Makunufushi), Dhigufinolhu, Emboodhoo Finolhu, Emboodhoo Village, Fihaalhohi, Kaduma, Laguna Beach Resort (Velassaru), Olhuveli, Palm Tree Island (Veligandu Huraa), Rannalhi, Rihiveli, Vaadhoo and Viligilivaru (Vilivaru). (See Listings for "Resort Islands").

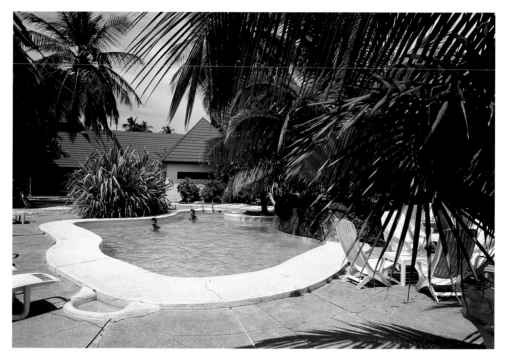

Above: All tastes satisfied on Kurumba — a man-made pool for those who want a change from the lagoon.
Opposite: Verdant tropical foliage on Boduhithi.

Sightseeing

Hulhule, home to **Maldives International Airport** in North Malé Atoll, was the site of Ibn Battuta's second visit to Maldives in 1346. For years the island was a holiday resort for the sultans who lived in Malé.

Plans to turn Hulhule into an airport began with a British survey in 1960 and work started in 1964. Today it is capable of handling the world's largest jets.

Just off the south-west edge of the island, in forty metres (131 feet) of water, lies the wreck of the freighter *Maldive Victory.* The ship, which went down in 1981, is a favourite **diving spot.**

The **Vaadhoo Kandu,** a four-kilometre-wide channel with strong currents, separates **North Malé** and **South Malé atolls.**

Since the adjoining islands have important diving spots, remember that the flood sets east and the ebb west. During the monsoons the currents race at four knots an hour — west during the north-east monsoon and east during the south-west monsoon — creating severe riptides.

Many islands in the atoll are reserved for a specific purpose, such as **Funadhoo,** which is occupied mainly by the government workers who look after the oil tanks.

When Maldives was a British Protectorate the island of **Dhoonidhoo,** just north of Malé, was the residence of the former British governor. Nowadays it is home to several prisoners who have been banished there (See "History: The Legend and The Mystery", Part One).

The neighbouring island of **Kuda Bandos,** however, has a happier atmosphere, for on Fridays, locals from the capital flock to enjoy its delightful beach and lagoon or relax in the shade of its glorious plants and trees. Throughout the rest of the week the island is open to anyone, but you cannot stay overnight.

Kaashidhoo, isolated in the northern channel, is famous for its coconut syrup; and **Maafushi** is the location of a reformatory school for orphans and delinquents opened in 1979.

About a dozen islands around Malé that were once fishing villages now enjoy

Above: The beginnings of an island. Out of the deep rises the coral reef across which waves wash debris to form land.
Opposite: Relaxing, European style, at the warm water's edge.
Overleaf: Glowing tribute to one more memorable day in Maldives.

income from visiting tourists to whom they sell souvenirs and handicrafts made elsewhere in the archipelago. **Himmafushi** and **Huraa** both fall into this category.

Other islands remain more traditional: **Thulusdhoo**, for instance, whose warehouses receive salt fish from **Raa** and **Baa atolls** to the north. In 1931 the sloop *Lord Clyde* ran aground there but was refloated.

Gaafaru, with the longest reef in Maldives, ten kilometres (six miles) long and eight kilometres (five miles) wide, has proved the undoing of dozens of ocean-going ships which took the channel between Malé Atoll and Lhaviyani Atoll.

North Malé Atoll resorts

Divers and snorkelers frequent **Helengeli**, fifty-one kilometres (32 miles) from the airport, situated on an unspoilt house reef, making diving possible without a boat. The resort caters for beginners and experienced divers alike. Underwater highlights include

a beautiful untouched coral garden. There are thirty coral stone bungalows.

Perched on the side of the Vaadhoo Channel, eleven kilometres (seven miles) west of the airport, **Giraavaru** was home to the aborigine community of the same name who were moved to Malé and various surrounding islands due to erosion of their home island.

The resort features good **beaches**, diving, and a **house reef**. Its large **lagoon** is perfect for windsurfing and water-skiing. There is a **swimming pool** and forty-eight luxury rooms, but not much shade.

Kurumba Village (Vihamanaafushi), located three kilometres (two miles) west of the northern tip of the airport and only thirty minutes by boat from the capital, was the first resort in Maldives.

Boasting a freshwater swimming pool, water-skiing, windsurfing and sailing, the island is also the **headquarters** of one of the largest dive operations in the country, a Swiss-run chain of **dive schools**. The vil-

Above: Soaking up the sun in a quiet backwater at Kuramathi Tourist Resort.
Opposite: The perfect end to another glorious Maldivian day on Thulhaagiri Island.

lage has a **conference centre**, health centre with gymnasium and jacuzzi, two flood-lit **tennis courts** and 169 rooms, seventy of which are de luxe suites.

Well inside the atoll, eight kilometres (five miles) north-west of the airport, the large island of **Bandos** shares some of Maldives' most popular dive sites with three other resorts — **Furana**, **Kurumba** and **Farukolhufushi (Club Med)** — which often become overcrowded.

Bandos, once home to Voightmann's defunct "shark circus", also offers excellent facilities for sailing, water-skiing and windsurfing with well-equipped **dive** and **water sports centres** and qualified instructors. Snorkeling around Bandos is exceptional. Non-water attractions at Bandos are tennis, squash, snooker and aerobics.

There is a **beach bar**, **coffee shop**, air-conditioned **restaurant**, disco, beauty salon, shops, 215 thatched rooms, and twenty-four VIP suites.

Its near western neighbour, **Baros**, sixteen kilometres (10 miles) from the airport and popular with British tourists, has an excellent **house reef** just ten metres (33 feet) from the **beach**. The windsurfing, water-skiing, and sailing are equally splendid. Big-game fishing at night is a regular activity, and there are excursions to other islands. The island has fifty-five excellent bungalows tucked away among the lush vegetation.

North of Baros, the lively atmosphere on **Vabbinfaru** is popular with Italians. Windsurfing, sailing and night fishing are among the daytime activities, but the crown-of-thorns starfish has caused considerable damage to the local **house reef**. Guests are accommodated in thirty-one spacious cottages.

Unique style

Quaint and comfortable **Thulhaagiri**, just a few kilometres north of Bandos, has adopted the Club Med philosophy: a unique mixture of stylishness and fantasy.

A small saltwater **swimming pool**, windsurfing and **house reef** (although again apparently damaged by the crown-of-thorns) make this locally-operated destination,

Above: International communications now connect Gangehi with the outside world.
Opposite: Cacti and bougainvillea dominate many gardens on Nakatchafushi.
Overleaf: Fishing boats at rest off Buruni Island. The raft, quite unlike any boat built in the archipelago, drifted 3,000 kilometres (1,865 miles) from Burma.

eleven kilometres (seven miles) from the airport, a delight. There are fifty-five rooms.

Ihuru Island, a small Australian-run resort north-west of Bandos, is affiliated with the Swiss tour operator Hotelplan and boasts a Swiss **dive school** with a high ratio of instructors to students. The over-dived **reefs**, which are home to at least half a dozen resident **stingrays**, are now recovering and offer excellent snorkeling.

Water-skiing, sailing dinghies, free windsurfing, interesting cuisine, an **over-the-water bar** and forty thatched bunga-lows with freshwater showers make Ihuru an idyllic island getaway.

The vast **lagoon** that surrounds the small island of **Nakatchafushi**, on the western rim of the atoll, has a long **sandspit** on its western and northern shores, the size of which varies according to the monsoon seasons. Twenty-two kilometres (14 miles) north-west of the airport, the island offers all the usual water sports, and accommo-dation in fifty-one thatched rondavels.

Once a small strip of sand with just two coconut palms, tiny **Kuda Hithi**, north of Nakatchafushi and twenty-nine kilo-metres (18 miles) from the airport, is an exclusive retreat featuring windsurfing, canoeing and *dhoani* trips.

Six luxury apartments, with their own speedboats, cater to different fantasies (the **Sheikh Room**, the **Safari Room**, etc). The nearest nightlife at Boduhithi resort is just a few minutes away by motorized *dhoani*.

Next to Kuda Hithi, **Boduhithi**, also twenty-nine kilometres (18 miles) north-west of the airport, reserved exclusively for Italian tourists, offers water-skiing, dinghy sailing and windsurfing. There are eighty-seven attractive bungalows.

Fine beach

Hembadhoo Island, one of the smaller, quieter islands located north of Boduhithi on the inside of the western rim, is known for its fine **beach** and large **lagoon**, ideal for novice windsurfers.

Above: Endless days of tropical sun on one of Kuramathi's superb beaches.
Opposite: Lone *dhoani* in the wide expanse of the Indian Ocean, keeping intact the close ties between neighbouring islands.

Full diving and water-skiing facilities are also available and twice a day a boat takes snorkelers out to the **reef**. The resort's small "**fish farm**" contains **sharks**, **rays** and **turtles**. Hembadhoo is a popular stopover (packages through Singapore Airlines) and cheaper than many other islands. One small **bar**, **dining room** and **coffee shop** — all with thatched roofs — complement the twenty-five rooms and fifteen huts.

"The Beautiful Island", **Reethi Rah** (**Medhufinolhu**), thirty-four kilometres (21 miles) north-west of the airport on the western rim of the atoll, is a haven for windsurfers with modern equipment and a high standard of instruction. If you prefer, there is a **dive school**, although the **house reef** is a fair distance — 150 metres (492 feet) — offshore. Water-skiing and sailing are also available. There are fifty rooms.

Neighbouring **Ziyaaraiyfushi**, a tiny island with seventy-nine rooms forty kilometres (25 miles) from the airport, has a great **lagoon** for windsurfing, but is usually passed over by water sports enthusiasts as it has no house reef or natural beach.

A few kilometres inside the atoll, east of Ziyaaraiyfushi, good food, **beaches** and fine **lagoon** complement the **Makunudhoo Club** on Makunudhoo Island, thirty-five kilometres (22 miles) from the airport, where divers can also explore an isolated twenty-five-kilometre-long (16-mile) **reef** littered with **many wrecks**. Above water, windsurfing, water-skiing and sailing are available. There are thirty-one rooms.

North of Makunudhoo a beautiful **beach** and good **house reef** make **Eriadhoo Island Resort**, thirty-nine kilometres (24 miles) north-west of the airport, a popular destination among German divers, windsurfers and water-skiers. Sailing, snorkeling, parasailing and "island hopping" are also popular pastimes while land sports include volleyball, table tennis, darts and badminton. There are forty-six rooms.

Along the eastern rim

Home to Club Méditerranée's property, **Farukolhufushi**, just off the northern tip of

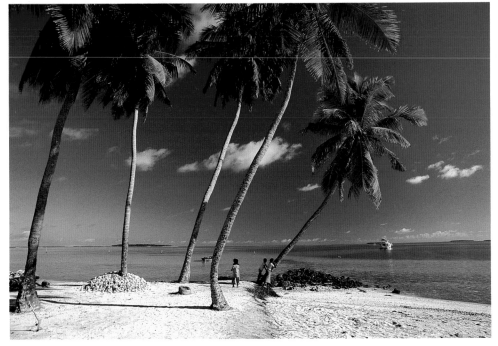

Above: Coral, sand and coconuts — the main ingredients for building island dwellings.
Opposite: Bird's-eye view of some of the countless islands which make up Maldives.
Overleaf: Walking a tightrope of glistening white sand off Cocoa Island.

the airport, is one of the finest resorts with every conceivable water sport, including an initiation dive and one "exploratory" dive a day.

Located close to Bandos, the **diving sites**, however, are often crowded during the high season. A photo lab, underwater slide show, videos and talks on underwater topics make this resort a dive haven.

For those who prefer surface activities, volleyball, aerobics, gymnastics, yoga and even silk-screen painting are on hand. The menu is limited but reasonable and the wine is free. Accommodation is in twin-bed bungalows with shower rooms and fresh water seven hours a day.

North again, still in the outer eastern reef, the **Furana resort** — which was closed for redevelopment in 1993 — runs boat dives along with introduction courses and open-water certifications.

Highlights of the diving there, three kilometres (two miles) from the airport, include **soft corals** at nearby **Kandu Oiy Giri**, **shark feeding**, diving on the **wreck** of the *Maldive Victory*, **whale sharks** off the east end of the island and **manta rays** at **Manta Point** during the monsoon. The deep **lagoon** makes an excellent yacht anchorage. Sailing, windsurfing, water-skiing, tennis and volleyball round out the day's activities.

At the time of its closure, the eighty-eight room complex had a **restaurant**, **coffee shop** and **Mr. Lee's** à la carte **Chinese restaurant**.

Another resort popular with Germans is the fifty-one room **Lankanfushi**, eight kilometres (five miles) north of the airport on the eastern rim.

Although closed for redevelopment in 1993, it was soon set to re-open as a luxury resort.

Also on the eastern rim of the atoll, fourteen kilometres (nine miles) north of the airport, is **Hudhuveli**, a sister island to Bandos, a thin **sandspit** with a large **lagoon** which caters for a young, international set. There are forty-four whitewashed thatched cottages.

Leisure and exercise

Traditionally known as Kanu Huraa Island, **Tari Village**, sixteen kilometres (10 miles) north-east of the airport, offers windsurfing and water-skiing — but no beach or lagoon. A number of sophisticated recreations, including a smart **disco** and professionally designed **tennis court**, provide land-based amusement. There are twenty-four rooms.

Little Huraa, just north of Kanu Huraa Island on the eastern rim, has few palms and a mediocre **beach**. The usual water sports are available, along with forty-three rooms.

But although only 178 metres (584 feet) wide, its neighbour, tiny **Kanifinolhu**, nineteen kilometres (12 miles) from the airport, boasts an extensive range of attractions.

The **house reef** is ten minutes sail by boat and most local **dive sites** are no more than thirty minutes away. The **dive school** is popular, along with water-skiing, sailing, windsurfing, tennis and aerobics. A **restaurant**, **bar**, twenty-four-hour **coffee shop** and **disco** all complement the attractive rooms with coral walls and thatched roofs.

Floating just a kilometre away on the same rim is **Lhohifushi**, a water wonderland with diving, sailing, windsurfing, water-skiing and eighty-four duplex-style cabins.

Gasfinolhu, an extremely small island on the eastern edge of the atoll, eighteen kilometres (11 miles) north of the airport, specializes in windsurfing. There are thirty-eight rooms.

The atoll's largest and easternmost island, **Meerufenfushi**, is also one of the most popular. Its **lagoon** is ideal for windsurfing and water-skiing and along with the **house reef** there is some excellent and uncrowded diving twenty to thirty minutes away by boat. German clientele usually predominate in the 164-room complex.

Inside the atoll, west of Meerufenfushi, **Asdu Sun Island**, a small, well-managed resort on Asdhoo Island, thirty-seven kilo-

metres (23 miles) north of the airport with spectacular **diving locations**, windsurfing and water-skiing, is a picturesque hideaway that features only thirty rooms. It boasts an Italian atmosphere.

South Malé Atoll resorts

Small and intimate, **Vaadhoo** lies on the northern rim of the atoll directly opposite **Viligili**, with **Malé** to the north-east. Eight kilometres (five miles) south-west of the airport, the island is justly famous for its diving, thanks to its fabulous location on the **Vaadhoo Channel**, which separates the two atolls and is more than 500 fathoms (3,000 feet) deep.

Perched on the edge of the channel, it is within an hour's ride of the top dive sites in Maldives. An **over-the-water bar**, modern two-storey chalets, and de luxe over-the-water bungalows, are perfect for unwinding at the end of a diving day.

With its fine **beaches**, beautiful **lagoon**, excellent **diving sites** and **windsurfing school**, tourists keep returning to Laguna Beach Resort on neighbouring **Velassaru**, twelve kilometres (seven miles) south-west of the airport. Featuring 100 rooms and suites — as well as a fully equipped gymnasium — the resort also offers catamaran sailing, snorkeling, night fishing, boat excursions and tennis.

Fourteen kilometres (nine miles) south-west of the airport, **Bolifushi**, which has thirty-two chalets and fresh water, specializes in windsurfing.

Emboodhoo Finolhu, eight kilometres (five miles) south of the airport, an Australian-run resort, has lush palms, flowers and a lovely lagoon. It caters for windsurfers and water-skiers with forty rooms, including twenty-four de luxe water bungalows.

Close by to the south-west is the large island on which **Emboodhoo Village** stands, with excellent diving on one of the best **house reefs** in the atoll. Windsurfing, water-skiing and good eating have earned it a much-favoured status among its pre-

Opposite: Visitors from colder climes on a sea safari in an Indian Ocean schooner.
Overleaf: Elegant curved bow of the Maldivian *dhoani*, silhouetted against an equatorial sunset.

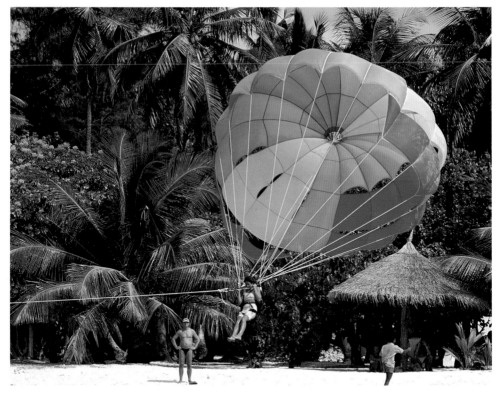

Above: Thrill a minute as a parasailer ascends.

dominantly German clientele. Parasailing, diving, snorkeling, night fishing, volley-ball, badminton and table tennis are also on offer. There are 106 rooms.

Palm Tree Island (Veligandu Huraa), one of the most recent resorts on the atoll with good diving, lies on a long **sandspit** midway down the eastern rim. This holiday spot with sixteen bungalows also features windsurfing and dinghy sailing.

Quaint and exclusive **Dhigufinolhu**'s fifty bungalows and **water sports centre**, in the north close to Veligandu Huraa, cater mainly for German clientele. The island lies well inside the atoll.

Windsurfer's delight

Thirty or more **dive sites**, with magnifi-cent precipices, overhangs and remarkable coral flora and fauna, lie no more than thirty to forty minutes off **Biyadoo**, some kilometres **south** of Dhigufinolhu.

The **reef** has five **signposted channels** which lead to a spectacular **drop-off**.

Certified divers can descend over the side of the **lagoon**, which is only twenty to thirty metres (66-98 feet) from the shore.

But the deep **house reefs** around the islands, with a maximum depth of forty metres (131 feet), are not as interesting as the **offshore sites**. The area also boasts some of the archipelago's finest snorkeling.

The efficient, well-equipped **water sports centre** looks after both diving and windsurfing, as well as special courses for catamaran sailing and parasailing.

The **hydroponic garden** grows fresh vegetables and the resort, which has ninety-six rooms in a two-storey complex, is said to serve some of the finest food in Maldives.

With a splendid **beach** and marvellous **lagoon** on the eastern rim of the atoll, **Cocoa Island** (Makunufushi), where the emphasis is on simplicity, solitude and good food, is ideal for windsurfing, water-skiing, parasailing and snorkeling.

The eight two-tiered thatched bungalows built from natural materials reflect the

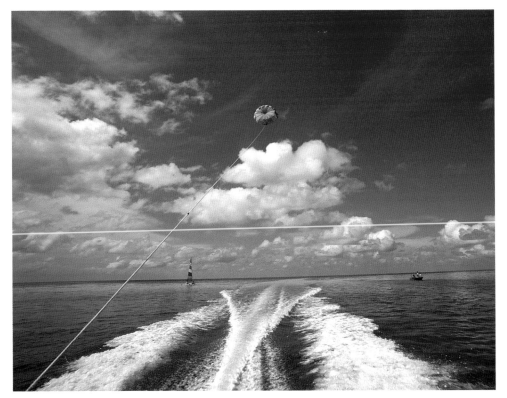

Above: Parasailing, one of the many water sports in Maldives.
Overleaf: Rihiveli lies next to two uninhabited islands which can be reached by wading through the shallows.

style of this exclusive resort well south of Veligandu.

Neighbouring **Kaduma** has a fine beach but no house reef. Windsurfing and water-skiing are popular and the resort boasts sixty-one bungalows.

The Indian-run **Viligilivaru (Vilivaru)** resort, tucked well inside the atoll west of Kaduma and south of close neighbour Biyadoo, covers five hectares (12 acres). The island boasts fine diving and snorkeling, with five **channels** through the surrounding **reef** to the **drop-off points**.

International Windsurfing Association courses are available for beginners and intermediates. Parasailing, catamaran sailing and other pursuits make the island an appealing destination. It has sixty rooms.

Fun Island Resort on **Bodufinolhu** lies far down the south-eastern rim, thirty-eight kilometres (24 miles) from the airport. With two small **deserted islands** nearby it is an ideal spot to escape the "madding crowd".

The **dive school** is run by a Dutch operator and there is also fishing, snorkeling, windsurfing and water-skiing. The 100-room complex's **over-the-water bar** and **disco** all add to the good times.

Also in the south, **Olhuveli**, on the eastern rim, thirty-five kilometres (22 miles) from the airport, is a thin strip of sand trapped in a large turquoise **lagoon** which features swimming on one side and a fast current on the other. Popular with the Swedish and the young, there are 125 rooms in this Japanese-run resort.

Rihiveli, meaning "silver sand" in Dhivehi, lies at the extreme southern end of the atoll, next to two neighbouring, uninhabited islands which can be reached by wading through the shallows.

Luxuriating in its French ambience and popular with honeymooners, it is one of Maldives' most attractive resorts, with water-skiing, windsurfing, aerobics, diving, parasailing and catamaran and sailing.

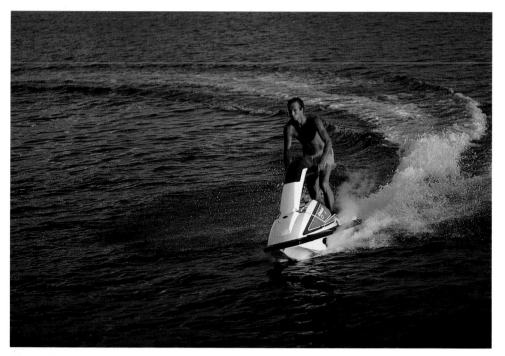

Above: Jet-ski rider, enjoying the thrill of splash and speed.

Opposite: Visiting launch gently swinging at anchor off Buruni Island, Thaa Atoll.

Below: This tiny, uninhabited oasis only minutes from Rihiveli Island is a favourite picnic spot for tourists.

The **bar**, open-air **dining area** and **disco** complement a high standard of service and food for guests in the island's forty-six spacious bungalows.

Fihaalhohi, a lush green island on the western rim of the atoll, forty-five kilometres (28 miles) from the airport, has an extensive **house reef**, water-skiing, good snorkeling and a large windsurfing school. It also undertakes diving instruction in English, French, German and Spanish. There are seventy-six rooms.

Fine **beaches**, an interesting **house reef** and a well-run **dive school** with English and German instruction distinguish **Rannalhi**, which lies just north of Fihaalhohi on the same rim, thirty-six kilometres (22 miles) from the airport.

The best **diving sites** are about one hour's sailing time. Although recently closed for redevelopment, Rannalhi was set to re-open in 1993 as a completely new resort, featuring 100 rooms, several restaurants, two bars and a discotheque.

Alifu (Ari) Atoll: Westward Ho!

Although, for the present, as in neighbouring Malé Atoll, the government has decided to restrict tourism in Alifu Atoll, there are about half a dozen island resorts popular with diving enthusiasts, with several more scheduled to open in the near future.

A chain of islands stretching eighty kilometres (50 miles) south, no wider than 30 kilometres (19 miles), forms the main part of the atoll. Sixty-one uninhabited islands, eighteen settled islands and twenty resorts, with a total population of 7,800, make up Alifu Atoll. The capital is Mahibadhoo. Almost a quarter of these seventy-nine islands are settled by fisherman and their families, whose life style has changed little throughout the centuries.

Getting there

Alifu Atoll lies sixty-four kilometres (40 miles) west of Malé, and Malé Atoll lies across the forty-kilometre-wide (25-mile) Ariadhoo Channel. Resorts ferry guests from the airport to their vacation island. *Dhoanis* are also available for hire by visitors who wish to travel to nearby islands, but you'll need a special government permit. There are charter operators for boats and aircraft. See Listings.

When to go

Most resorts remain open year-round. Check with your travel agent or the nearest Maldives tourist office.

Where to stay

Angaga, Ari Beach Resort (Diddu Finolhu), Athurugau, Avi Island Resort (Velidhoo), Bathalaa, Ellaidhoo, Fesdhoo, Gangehi, Halaveli, Kuda Rah, Kuramathi, Maayyafushi, Madoogali, Mirihi, Moofushi, Nika Hotel (Kudafolhudhoo), Ranveli Beach Resort (Vilingilivaru), Thudufushi, Twin Island (Maafushivaru) and Veligandu. (See Listings for "Resort Islands").

Sightseeing

In the north the large isolated **island** of **Thoddoo** is renowned not only for watermelons but its **women dancers**, who perform the *bandiya jehun* by tapping out a rhythm on metal pots.

Thoddoo contains the **ruins** of a **Buddhist temple** which, until recently, had a small two-metre (seven-foot) domed *stupa*. In 1958 a large and complete **Buddha** was found hidden in a chamber, along with a **relic casket** containing a **silver bowl**, a small **gold cylinder** and **two coins**.

One of the coins has been identified as a denarius of Caius Vibius Pansa, minted in Rome in 90 BC (See "History: The Legend and the Mystery", Part One), a time when the Romans sailed to Sri Lanka (and therefore through the Maldive islands).

Unfortunately, the contents of the temple have since disappeared. Only the magnificent head of the **stone Buddha** has reached the National Museum in Malé (See "Malé: The Isle of Dreamy Light", Part Two).

Alifu Atoll resorts

Ninety kilometres (56 miles) from Malé airport, in the centre of the southern half of the atoll, lies the 50-room **Angaga Island Resort**, where visitors can enjoy diving, snorkeling, water skiing, parasailing, sailing, fishing and island hopping — as well as a variety of "dry land" sports (including crab races!).

Helipad facilities make **Ari Beach Resort (Diddu Finolhu)**, ninety-seven kilometres (60 miles) from the airport, an easy hop from the capital by air. Seventy-six bungalows accommodate guests looking to unwind in the sun or burn up excess energy by taking part in the wide range of activities offered on the island, including diving, windsurfing, canoeing or playing tennis.

If the water sports offered at the **Athurugau Island Resort** do not tire guests out, they can opt to dance the night away at the resort's discotheque. Athurugau offers 42 bungalows and is sixty-eight kilometres (42 miles) from the airport.

In the centre of the northern tip of the

Previous pages: Gentle surf rolls over coral reef as the sun sinks over the Equator.

Alifu Atoll (Ari Atoll)

0   10   20   30   40 km
0   10   20 miles

Thoddoo

Veligandu

Rasdhu (H)

Kuramathi

Gangehi
Avi Island
(Velidhoo)   Ukulhas
Mathiveri
(H) Bodu Folhudhu
Nika Hotel
(Kudafolhudhoo)

INDIAN OCEAN

Madoogali

Maayyafushi   Bathalaa

Feridhu   Halaveli

Fesdhoo   Kandolodhu (H)   Ellaidhoo

Malhos

ARIADHOO

CHANNEL

Himandhu

Hagngnaameedhoo

Emboodhoo (H)

Moofushi   Omadhu

Athurugau   Kuburudhu   Mahibadhoo

Thudufushi

Mandhu

Huvahendhoo
Vilamendhoo
Angaga
Ranveli Beach Resort
(Vilingilivaru)
Rangali Finolhu   Mirihi   Twin Island
(Maafushivaru) (H)
Machafushi   Dhagethi
Kuda Rah
Vakarufalhi

Dhigurah

Fenfushi   Ari Beach Resort
(Diddu Finolhu) (H)
Nalaguraidhoo
Dhiffushi Mamigili   Diddu

131

Above: Boiling sea cucumbers. Maldivians do not eat these soft sea bed scavengers, but they find a ready market in Singapore.
Opposite: Young boy tries out a home-made kite in the gentle breezes of the Indian Ocean.
Previous pages: Serene gardens of the mosque on Nika (Kudafolhudhoo).

atoll is **Avi Island Resort** (**Velidhoo**), sixty-four kilometres (40 miles) from the airport. Twenty-eight bungalows dot the island resort, with diving, tennis, windsurfing and water skiing highlighting the activities on offer.

At the eastern fringe of the atoll, eighty-three kilometres (52 miles) south-west of the airport, tranquil **Bathalaa** specializes in underwater holidays, offering **drift diving** and **slow diving** in the **Vaadhoo Channel** where a forty-metre (131-foot) **drop-off** lies within thirty metres (98 feet) of the **beach**. Occasional strong currents challenge the most experienced divers and sailors.

Volleyball and thirty-six small rondavels with garden showers await the visitor.

Ellaidhoo, a resort on the eastern edge of the atoll, fifty-eight kilometres (36 miles) from the airport, features good diving, water-skiing, windsurfing and dinghy sailing. The fifty cool and airy coral cottages are built on low wooden platforms close to the water's edge.

Seventy-four kilometres (46 miles) from the airport, well inside the atoll, **Fesdhoo Fun Island** is extremely popular with an interesting **house reef**, excellent diving, windsurfing and white sandy **beach**. The nearby tiny, deserted island of **Gaathafushi** is reserved exclusively for Fesdhoo's guests. With sixty rooms, this small, high-quality resort features good entertainment.

Guests literally sleep above the water in twenty-five traditional-style bungalows at the elegant **Gangehi Island Resort**, which is seventy-one kilometres (44 miles) from the airport. Canoeing, diving, snorkeling and fishing are available for the sporting-minded.

Water-skiing, sailing and windsurfing all take place in **Halaveli**'s beautiful **lagoon**, fifty-four kilometres (33 miles) from the airport, with windsurfing excursions to the nearby resorts of **Bathalaa** and **Maayyafushi**, and two dives a day for qualified divers.

Additional trips to **nearby villages** and **desert islands** are also part of the package.

135

Vaavu Atoll
(Felidu Atoll)

0   10   20 km
0   10 miles

INDIAN OCEAN

Diggiri

Alimatha

Felidhoo
Keyodhoo

Rakeedhoo

Vattaru Reef

VATTARU CHANNEL

© Camerapix 1993

The dining room specializes in Italian food and there are forty thatched bungalows.

Nika Hotel (Kudafolhudhoo), a small but very smart resort in the north of the atoll, sixty-seven kilometres (42 miles) from the airport, was the brainchild of an Italian architect who wanted to create a village where an affluent few could enjoy their individual desires.

The Italian-run resort maintains two **dining rooms** serving international and Italian food, an Italian **wine cellar**, **bar**, **coffee shops**, **nightclub** and **disco**. In a garden setting, the twenty-six bungalows each contain a living room, bedroom, private verandah and bathroom.

Sports enthusiasts can enjoy the tennis courts, bowling alley, badminton and volleyball courts — or go snorkeling, windsurfing, water-skiing or canoeing. Big-game fishing excursions are also arranged.

Drift diving

A large island off the northern tip of the atoll, fifty-eight kilometres (36 miles) from the airport, **Kuramathi** takes more than an hour to explore. Famous for its **drift diving**, the island's waters are a favourite haunt of **hammerhead sharks**. *Dhoani* sailing, windsurfing, water-skiing and snorkeling are all available.

Universal Enterprises runs three centres on the island: **Kuramathi Village**, with 122 units, including thatched rondavels and single-storey terrace apartments; the fifty-room **Blue Lagoon Club**, with twenty of the units constructed in traditional style on stilts in the water; and the **Cottage Club** with its thirty bungalows and a large clubhouse hidden in the palms.

Each has its own restaurant and offers a variety of sporting activities, including tennis, archery, snorkeling, windsurfing and diving. Island-hopping excursions include trips to neighbouring **Rasdhu Island** and a traditional fishing village.

Popular **Maayyafushi Tourist Resort**, sixty-one kilometres (38 miles) from the airport, features a nightly **disco**, motel-style accommodation and beach barbecues. Water sports include windsurfing, sailing and excellent diving at the easily accessible **house reef** on the east side of the island. The sixty rooms are arranged in units of four.

On the north-western side of the atoll, 116 kilometres (72 miles) from the airport, the 50-room **Madoogali Resort** awaits visitors anxious to try out the diving, windsurfing, water skiing and a number of other water and land sports available.

Tiny and exclusive **Mirihi Marina**, with only twenty-six bungalows and suites, lets guests dive by day and disco by night — as well as offering volleyball, windsurfing, snorkeling, fishing, badminton, catamaran sailing and soccer. The resort is 105 kilometres (65 miles) from the airport.

On the western side of Alifu Atoll lies **Moofushi Island Resort**, 130 kilometres (81 miles) from the airport. Guests can choose from 60 air-conditioned bungalows and a wide variety of activities both in and out of the water.

The Italian-run **Ranveli Beach Resort** (**Vilingilivaru**) is most easily reached by a 25-minute helicopter ride from the airport into a helipad situated on a nearby island. A 20-minute *dhoani* ride brings you to the resort, which features 50 sea-view rooms, a disco, boutiques, a medical station, swimming pool and fully-equipped diving centre. Water sports offered include windsurfing, canoeing, fishing expeditions and "island hopping" trips capped off with a barbecued seafood feast on a deserted beach. It is seventy-seven kilometres (48 miles) from the airport.

Forty-four well-appointed suites await the visitor to **Thudufushi Island Resort**, seventy-six kilometres (47 miles) from the airport. A wide range of activities is highlighted by diving, parasailing, catamaran sailing and windsurfing.

Smaller **Twin Island** (**Maafushivaru**) has thirty-two air-conditioned bungalows to choose from, and offers tennis, snorkeling, fishing and diving amongst its sporting pursuits. It is located eighty kilometres (50 miles) from the airport in the centre of the southern half of the atoll.

Veligandu Island is just off the northern tip of the atoll, forty-eight kilometres (30 miles) from the airport and easily accessible via the helipad at nearby Rasdhu Island. Its sixty-three comfortable rooms are the perfect place to take a break from the volleyball, windsurfing, diving, sailing, snorkeling, fishing and water skiing offered at the resort.

As Alifu Atoll has only recently been opened to tourism, huge **black coral trees**, **manta rays**, **turtles** and plenty of unspoilt diving await the first visitors.

Vaavu (Felidu) Atoll: Land of the Rising Sun

Vaavu Atoll is shaped like a boot and lies across the Felidhoo Kandu Channel, nineteen kilometres (twelve miles) wide, from northern Malé Atoll.

The tidal streams, influenced by monsoon currents, are particularly strong during spring tides, setting east through the channel at the flood tide and west on the ebb.

Nineteen uninhabited islands, five settled islands and two resorts, with a total population of 1,500, make up Vaavu Atoll. The capital is Felidhoo.

Getting there

Vaavu lies sixty-seven kilometres (42 miles) south of Malé, close to the southernmost tip

Above: Lionfish are found in the reefs of Maldives.

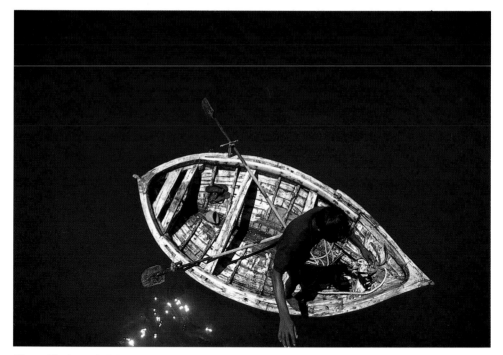

Above: Finely made little boat used as a tender to row across the coral reefs to larger fishing *dhoanis* anchored offshore.

of South Malé Atoll. Resorts ferry guests from the airport to their vacation island. *Dhoanis* are also available for hire by visitors who wish to travel to nearby islands, but you'll need a special government permit. There are charter operators for boats and aircraft. See Listings.

When to go

Most resorts remain open year-round. Check with your travel agent or the nearest Maldives tourist office.

Where to stay

Alimatha, Diggiri (See Listings for "Resort Islands").

Sightseeing

Felidhoo, the capital of **Vaavu Atoll**, has a population of only 300. The largest **village** in the atoll is on the **neighbouring island** of **Keyodhoo**, but it only has a few dozen inhabitants more. Both still rely on fishing for their livelihood.

Not far away lie **Foththeyo** and **Bodufushi**, the most easterly islands of Maldives. To the south, on the sole of the boot which makes up the shape of Vaavu, the ship *Pioneer* ran aground on the **reef** of **Higaakulhi** and was never refloated.

Also in the south, where the **Vattaru Reef** nearly bursts through the sea to form another atoll, is a fine **diving spot**. While the monsoon-driven waves are eroding the most southerly island of **Rakeedhoo**, several **new islands** are appearing among the **sandbanks** on Vattaru Reef. Mariners are advised to keep well clear.

Vaavu Atoll resorts

The Italian-run **Alimatha Aquatic Resort**, sixty-one kilometres (38 miles) south of the airport, lies close to **Vattaru Reef**, which is renowned for its exceptional diving. Water-skiing, dinghy sailing and windsurfing are available. The resort, which has seventy comfortable cabanas, specializes in Italian cuisine.

Most visitors to the atoll stop off at **Diggiri Resort**, sixty kilometres (37 miles)

Above: Lush green breadfruit tree supplies food and welcome shade.
Overleaf: Palms offer natural protection from the heat of the mid-day sun.

from the airport, is noted for its comfort and good Italian food. There are facilities for water-skiing, dinghy sailing, and windsurfing. The resort has thirty rooms.

Meemu (Mulaku) Atoll: The Backwater of Time

The awesome Vattaru Reef marks the divide between Vaavu Atoll and its closest neighbour, Meemu Atoll, a world of deserted tropical islands. Only a quarter of them are inhabited and its tiny population — which averages 100 people for each island — slumbers on in a backwater of time.

Twenty-six uninhabited and nine settled islands, with a total population of 3,600, make up Meemu Atoll. The capital is Muli.

Getting there

Meemu Atoll, 120 kilometres (74 miles) from Malé, lies just south of Vaavu Atoll. There are no resorts and the only way to see its islands is by cruising and sleeping aboard your own or a chartered craft. You need a permit to land.

When to go

The best time to visit Meemu Atoll is between December and March during the north-east monsoon.

Sightseeing

The **Vattaru Reef**, clearly visible at low tide, with fascinating **caverns**, **caves** and myriad marine life, offers opportunities for some very exciting dives.

The **north-western** side of **Meemu** is entirely deserted. Only nine of its thirty-five islands are settled. The capital, **Muli**, is the main fishing centre, and **yams** are grown on **Kolhufushi** and **Mulaku** .

One of the most interesting islands, **Dhiggaru**, has a **tea-shop**, *sai hotaa*, traditionally a male domain, run entirely by women. The island women's group uses the profits to help its development projects.

Faafu (North Nilandhoo) Atoll: Land of History

Though across the world it hardly raises an eyebrow and is so small that it is not shown on most maps, Faafu Atoll is of immense historic importance.

Strategically situated at the centre of the Maldives archipelago, it was probably a focal point for the wave of religious settlers who replaced the original inhabitants.

Certainly, as Thor Heyerdhal discovered, its wealth of ruins forms a priceless treasury of early Maldivian history (See "History: The Legend and the Mystery", Part One).

It was also once an important turtle breeding ground. Sadly, too many eggs ended up on the family table and in the tourist shops, and the species is now at risk. Only if visitors refuse to buy tortoiseshell goods will the future of these delightful and intelligent creatures be assured.

Twenty-one uninhabited and five settled islands, with a population of just over 2,600, make up Faafu Atoll. The capital is Magoodhoo.

Getting there

Faafu Atoll, 120 kilometres (74 miles) from Malé, lies south of Alifu Atoll and directly west of Meemu Atoll. There are no resorts and the only way to see the islands is by cruising and sleeping aboard your own or a chartered craft. You need a permit to land.

When to go

The best time to visit Faafu Atoll is between December and March during the north-east monsoon.

Sightseeing

In the south, **Magoodhoo**'s neighbouring **island** of **Dharaboodhoo** was a famous **turtle breeding ground**, with females laying their eggs in the sand from April to October, during the south-west *hulhangu*, monsoon. Now the species is imperilled.

Another example of the precariousness of life in Maldives is the island of **Himithi**. In 1773, all houses except one burnt down. Four years later the French ship *Duras* was wrecked on its **reef**. The island was renowned for its navigators until heavy erosion forced the people to leave in 1968.

One of the most fascinating and important archaeological sites in Maldives is on the southern island of **Nilandhoo**, which is reached on a broad swell through a shallow **coral reef**.

There Thor Heyerdahl uncovered a buried **temple**. It must have been a vast complex. The remaining **foundations**, in the middle of the **village**, measure about 115 metres (377 feet) by 170 metres (558 feet). The temple was almost certainly Hindu, for many **Bohomala sculptures** were discovered around the site (see "History: The Legend and the Mystery", Part One).

Heyerdahl and his team also excavated many small **limestone carvings** resembling towers of umbrellas, probably buried as votive offerings. Only one other had been found before in Maldives.

The original temple must have been extremely impressive. Beautifully cut facing stones were placed over a compact core of coral sand to form a pyramid, with a walled ramp on one side.

It seems that there were seven similar temples on the site and Heyerdahl also unearthed the **ruins** of a **gate**, which might have been one of seven surrounding the temple complex.

Earlier this century three mysterious **stone boxes**, roughly thirty square centimetres (nine square inches), were also found in this area. One contained a **golden cock** and a **metal plate** with indecipherable writing. Although they were sent to Malé, they have since disappeared.

The second-oldest **mosque** in Maldives, known as the *Aasaari Miskiiy*, stands on the same site. It was built by Sultan Mohamed Ibn Abdulla in AH 548 (AD 1153-66) after he completed an earlier one on Malé. The magnificent structure, with carefully fitted

Opposite: Fishing dhoani *is given a new coat of paint.*

Above: Black coral jewellery, hand-carved by the inhabitants of Ribudhoo Island, Dhaalu Atoll, known as the "Jewellers' Island". The rare black coral has to be collected by divers at a depth of thirty metres (98 feet).

stones, is decorated inside by marvellous wooden **Arabic carvings**.

It is surprisingly big for such a small community. Like many other mosques in Maldives, it was made of dressed stones taken from the earlier temple.

The exact nature of the original temple is lost, but it seems its intricately carved and dressed stones were used by Hindus to build stepped pyramids. When the country converted to Islam, it would make sense for the sultan in Malé to come to this important site and symbolically raze the temples to the ground.

The materials were probably then used to build the first mosque in the archipelago outside the capital.

Magoodhoo, north-east of Naraboodhoo, is a pious place where many women wear the *burugaa* or Muslim headscarf. Fishing is still important, although recently islanders have turned to catching and cooking **sea cucumbers** for export — so many, in fact, that the species is now in decline.

A beautiful **deserted island** opposite Magoodhoo is leased by the local *gazi* (judge), who goes there every afternoon to seek peace and quiet and cultivate the **coconut groves**.

Dhaalu (South Nilandhoo) Atoll: The Jewellers' Islands

Another atoll which has contributed to the tapestry of Maldives history is Dhaalu, famous for its beautiful mosques and ancient stone-carving crafts, which have been lost only in this century.

Opposite: The ruins of a Hindu temple on Nilandhoo Island, Faafu Atoll. Recent archaeological discoveries suggest that settlers brought Buddhism, and to a lesser extent Hinduism, to different parts of the archipelago. The islanders converted to Islam in the twelfth century.

Maldivians were justly famous in the Arab world for producing the finest of Muslim tombstones.

It is a tragedy not only that the skills have been lost, but that many ancient tombstones throughout the archipelago have been broken.

Where they have been repaired, it is often with grotesque smears of cement which obliterate their delicate and flowing filigree work.

Fifty uninhabited and eight settled islands, with a total population of 3,700, make up Dhaalu Atoll. The capital is Kudahuvadhoo.

Getting there

Dhaalu Atoll, 150 kilometres (93 miles) from Malé, lies south of Faafu Atoll and west of Meemu Atoll. There are no resorts and the only way to see the islands is by cruising and sleeping aboard your own or a chartered craft. You need a permit to land.

When to go

The best time to visit Dhaalu Atoll is between December and March during the north-east monsoon.

Sightseeing

Kudahuvadhoo's position at the southern-most end of the atoll makes it a dangerous hazard to mariners. In 1879 the 1,339-ton *Liffey* ran aground on its reef, as did the *Utheem* in 1960.

That the island has been inhabited for centuries is evidenced by an intriguing mound twenty-two metres (72 feet) in diameter and the nearby **mosque** — the oldest on the island.

Villagers came across the stone head of a **Buddha**, so large that they could hardly embrace it in their arms. But like many other priceless archaeological finds in Maldives, it too has disappeared.

During a visit to the site Heyerdahl noticed, in the rear wall of the mosque, the finest **"fingerprint" masonry** he had ever seen, more advanced, even, than that found in the famous Inca wall of Cuzco, Peru (See "History: The Legend and the Mystery", Part One).

In front of the mosque is an **outdoor gateway**, similar to the one on **Nilandhoo** in **Faafu Atoll**. A perfect six-pointed star on the **outer wall** is known locally as *Suleiman modi*, the seal on King Solomon's ring. The ancient symbol is used at the beginning and end of each text when Maldivian medicine men write their charms.

Inside the mosque's **cemetery**, two beautifully fashioned and decorated **tombstones** were carved by the master mason reputed to have done the superb stonework in the mosque wall. Each tombstone has five points on top, in contrast to Muslim stones, which only carry one point for a man and none for a woman. The inscriptions are also carved in flowing Arabic and some unknown rectilinear characters.

Uninhabited **Maadheli Island** has **ruins** whose riches have yet to be explored. Fortunately, the government in Malé has now forbidden anyone to remove stones from these ancient ruins and mounds, and no one is allowed to dig without special permission.

In the north of Dhaalu Atoll, the British Admiralty chart identifies the "**Jewellers' Islands**". The name arises from an incident hundreds of years ago in Malé when a sultan banished his chief jeweller to **Ribudhoo Island** for producing gold-plated silver and stealing the gold that had been given to him.

The exiled jeweller taught his skills to the islanders who continue to pass them down from father to son. Today Ribudhoo and its neighbouring islands are famed for their great craftsmanship in producing **gold** and **silver necklaces**, **bracelets** and **chains**.

But many islanders now fashion **jewellery** for the tourist trade from **black coral**, which only grows at a depth of thirty metres (98 feet). The "twigs" are collected by scuba divers from Malé.

Small lathes grind and shape the coral into beads, which are exported. Traditionally, Maldivian women do not wear beads. Both young and old are involved in the production process, and the island is dotted with small workshops where two or three family members work cross-legged in the shade of the coconut palms.

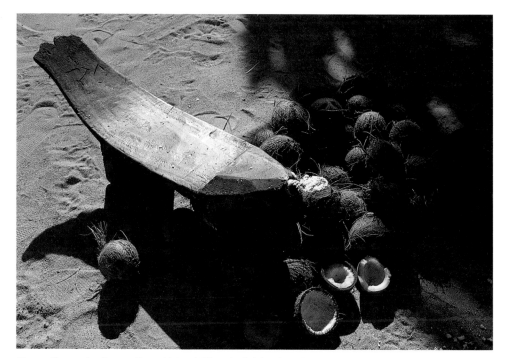

Above: Coconut splicer on Buruni Island, Thaa Atoll. Islanders sit astride the curved seat and impale the coconut on the spike.

Thaa (Kolhumadulu) Atoll: Island of Love

Hopping from one island to another, it is easy to forget that on either side of the Maldivian archipelago there are vast expanses of ocean and that the nearest landmass is thousands of kilometres away.

An occasional reminder of the enormous distances and great dangers seafarers undertook to reach the coral beaches of Maldives occurs every now and then.

Tidal streams in the Maa Kadu Channel, which extends nearly sixteen kilometres (10 miles) west and twenty-four kilometres (15 miles) east between Meemu, Dhaalu and Thaa atolls, set east on the flood and west with the ebb. Obstructed on both sides by the atolls, the strong currents are unpredictable.

The master of the 1,339-ton vessel *Liffey* discovered this in 1879 when his ship was wrecked on Kudahuvadhoo Island reef at the most southerly tip of Dhaalu Atoll.

Whales have also been washed ashore there.

Thaa Atoll is virtually a circular reef enclosing 700 square kilometres (280 square miles) of sea. There are only a few points of entry and the many submerged reefs, especially in the south and west, make navigating dangerous even for the shallow-keeled fishing *dhoanis*.

Fifty-four uninhabited and thirteen settled islands, with a total population of 7,200, make up Thaa Atoll. The capital is Veymandhoo.

Getting there

Thaa Atoll, 192 kilometres (119 miles) from Malé, lies directly south of both Dhaalu and Meemu atolls across the Maa Kadu (also known as Kudahuvadhoo Kadu) Channel. There are no resorts and the only way to see the islands is by cruising and sleeping aboard your own or a chartered craft. You need a permit to land.

When to go

The best time to visit Thaa Atoll is between

December and March during the north-east monsoon.

Sightseeing

On the eastern side of the atoll many tiny **desert islands** can be reached by wading from one to another. But Thaa also contains the largest island in the archipelago — **Fahala** — home to an abundance of lush, dense vegetation but no people.

The capital, **Veymandhoo**, has grown prosperous on the good fishing in the area. Despite its mysterious destruction by fire in 1902 — and again in 1905 — the most populous island is **Thimarafushi**.

Of historical interest is **Dhiyamigili**, birthplace of Muhammad Imaad-ud-deen, the eighteenth-century sultan who founded a dynasty that lasted more than 200 years. The **ruins** of his **residence** stand outside the **village**.

A less noble **monument** is the **grave** of Sultan Usman, who was banished to **Guraadhoo Island** in the fourteenth century after ruling for only two months.

The settled island of **Kibidhoo**, in the south-western extremity of the atoll, contains the **remains** of an excavated *hawitta*, with a circumference of about eighty metres (262 feet), which was the subject of a 1958 study. Sadly, the site has since been plundered.

The most northerly island, **Buruni**, is where the pull of **Malé** is felt most strongly. One-quarter of the men work away from home as carpenters and builders or in the tourist resorts. Those who remain go fishing, while their womenfolk weave **mats** from reeds and make **coir rope** (See "The People: A Mix of Many Faces", Part One).

The island has long been inhabited and in the **cemetery** surrounding the **Buruni Ziyaaraiy mosque** some **tombs** are almost 200 years old. An old **sundial** outside the mosque told the *mudhimu* when to call the faithful to prayer, but now a modern **Chinese clock** ticks away in the *mihrab*.

Electricity has arrived on the island and the *mudhimu*'s voice has to compete with the sound of television and radio sets. Island life is changing rapidly and irrevocably.

Despite its swift step forward into the twentieth century, Buruni will always be remembered in Maldives folklore for the story of the island girl called **Dhon Hiyala** (*dhon* means fair, and *hiyala* is a common name) whose father was elevated from the rank of low-caste toddy tapper (*raaveri*) by the sultan because of his proficient reading of the Qur'an.

In the meantime, Dhon Hiyala fell in love with a jeweller named Ali Fulhu, who gave her beautiful ornaments. But their love was not to be. The sultan's agents seized Dhon Hiyala and took her to court in Malé.

Her incensed lover followed her to the capital where they managed to escape in a boat. But when they were pursued by the sultan's soldiers, the couple jumped into the sea where they were cut into three parts by a demon.

Laamu (Hadhdhunmathee) Atoll: Islands of Giants

The wide, twenty-six-kilometre (16-mile) channel separating Thaa Atoll from Laamu Atoll, called Hadhdoo Kadu, plunges 1,118 fathoms (6,708 feet) and during spring tides has a tidal race of more than two knots.

Laamu Atoll is about forty kilometres (25 miles) long and twenty-five kilometres (16 miles) wide. It has been inhabited for thousands of years and is renowned for its ancient ruins.

Local people believe the once enormous temples were built by the legendary Redin. Collecting the fragmentary evidence together, historian Hassan Maniku writes that the name Redin refers to a group of people whom the Maldivians believe did extraordinary feats (See "History: The Legend and the Mystery", Part One).

They were able to move very fast from one island to another, using sails and oars in their boats. They are said to have come from the north and first settled on Haa Alifu Atoll but gradually spread throughout the Maldivian archipelago. They did not all die out, for some of them left when the present people arrived.

In the flux of life, of course, nothing stands still. For centuries the Maldivians

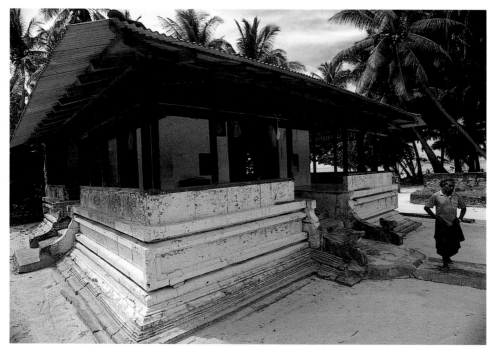

Above: The 300-year-old Friday Mosque with fine dressed stones on Isdhoo Island, Laamu Atoll.

lived with their traditional ways and customs virtually unchanged, but in the last few decades they have been hurled forward into the modern age. Now, like the mythical Redin before them, Maldivians must deal with the changes thrust upon them, adapting their life style as they advance one more step towards the coming century.

Seventy-five uninhabited and twelve settled islands, with a total population of 7,300, make up Laamu Atoll. The capital is Hithadhoo.

Getting there

Laamu Atoll, 224 kilometres (139 miles) from Malé, lies twenty-six kilometres (16 miles) south-east of Thaa Atoll. There are no resorts and the only way to see the islands is by cruising and sleeping aboard your own or a chartered craft. You need a permit to land.

When to go

The best time to visit Laamu Atoll is between December and March during the north-east monsoon.

Sightseeing

The barque *François*, with a crew of twenty-two, was wrecked in 1873 on a **reef** on **Maavah**, the atoll's westernmost island.

The capital, **Hithadhoo**, an important **fishing centre**, is located at the southern entrance to the atoll. **Freezer ships** often anchor for several weeks near the neighbouring **island** of **Maamendhoo**, collecting the daily catch from the atoll fishermen and acting as a fuel bunker for their diesel-driven *dhoanis*.

But the atoll's main interest is its **archaeological ruins**. There are no less than three denuded mounds on Hithadhoo Island as well as others on **Maabaidhoo** and **Gaadhoo**. But the most interesting ruins are on **Gan (Gamu)** and **Isdhoo islands**.

To land at **Gan** you have to wade ashore from a small boat. The black crows on the **beach** are sharp contrast to the **white coral sand** and along the water's edge **thatched sheds** shelter boats under repair or being built.

Above: Highly ornamental lacquerwork in the interior of the Friday Mosque on Isdhoo Island, Laamu Atoll.

The wide avenues that crisscross the **village** of about 2,000 people are lined with **coconut palms** and **breadfruit trees**, and the sandy paths are swept immaculately clean. **Bananas**, **watermelons**, **papayas** and **taro**, *ala*, grow there. Women pound black millet, *bimbi*, with a mortar and pestle for their babies, or rasp the pulp of coconuts for the evening curry.

Island life has remained unchanged for centuries, but now electricity has arrived and generators thump away, disturbing the island's quiet atmosphere. A new **school** built by the Japanese collects rainwater from its wide roofs.

On the south-east of the island, signs of a much earlier civilization are evident. Close to the pounding surf a mound of coral blackened by time, monsoon rains and the tropical sun, slowly crumbles away. Locals call it *Gamu Haiytheli*, meaning "the seven cooking pots of Gamu".

This neglected **monument**, standing eleven metres (36 feet) high, is about fifty metres (164 feet) in diameter. Two thousand years ago, glittering in the sun, it towered over the surrounding palms.

It's difficult to imagine the labour needed to cut and collect the coral slabs from the sea, haul them up to the mound, and fit them together like pieces in a jigsaw puzzle.

But the once proud temple is a sorry sight. Over the centuries its dressed stones have been pillaged to build village houses and the coral rubble plundered for lime. Only one or two stones lying in the surrounding bush remain, with their precise rectangular shape beautifully carved.

Archaeologist H.C.P. Bell, who visited Laamu Atoll early this century, was convinced that the mounds were the ruins of Buddhist *dagobas* or *stupas* (See "History: The Legend and the Mystery", Part One).

Opposite: Maldivian hookah smoker takes a well-earned rest. Maldivians have to work hard to survive on their far-flung islands.

On Gan, Bell excavated a mound which was then covered with high trees (now it is a denuded heap, but the large scar he dug runs down one side).

Although stripped by the islanders, Bell reported that the temple had a seven-tier pinnacle and consisted of surface dressed madrepore slabs encasing a rubble core of the same material.

Since his visit the ravages of man have been crueller than those of nature. All that now remains is a pile of rubble. To smash old pagan ruins for building material seemed more sensible than cutting new coral blocks from the reef.

Today the mound is called the same name that Bell recorded, *Hat-teli*, meaning seven cooking pots, but the pinnacle to which the term presumably refers has long since disappeared.

Shining white in the sun, way above the coconut trees, the pinnacle would have been an uncanny sight as lonely mariners from distant lands sailed through the One-and-a-Half-Degree Channel of the archipelago.

Under the summit of the mound Bell also discovered the broken face of an enormous **Buddha** and estimated its original height to be four and a half metres (15 feet).

Below the face of the giant, headless image there was also a small **seated Buddha**, but both remains have vanished.

South-west of the great mound lies a smaller *hawitta*, with a round **circular bath** close by. The island's **first mosque** was probably built on the monastery of the Buddhist monks, but it too has disappeared.

Who built the original temples still remains a mystery. The islanders say it was the legendary Redin, but Bell concluded that it was the work of Buddhists. It is quite possible that the Buddhists put a *stupa* dome on a stone-faced *hawitta* built by earlier inhabitants.

But with the arrival of Islam the new Muslims stripped the temples and used the materials to build their mosques.

An even more impressive mound stands on the island of **Isdhoo** at the northernmost tip of Laamu Atoll. From the sea, rising far above the surrounding coconut palms, it's an awe-inspiring sight. Strategically placed, the mound was a famous landmark for ancient mariners travelling across the channels between the atolls.

It too is called *Haiytheli*, meaning seven cooking pots. Two smaller **hawittas** stand nearby. There was once a metre-high **statue** of **Buddha**, but it too is gone. The discarded base lies nearby in the bushes.

There is also a **300-year-old mosque** on the island, probably built upon the foundations of an older temple, for it faces west.

Since a visit by the president in 1982 (when its position was pointed out), the congregation no longer faces the *mihrab*, but the right-hand corner of the mosque which points to Mecca.

Many ancient mosques in Maldives, built on the foundations of earlier temples and making use of older stones for new walls, face due west.

Opposite: Children of Laamu Atoll.

Overleaf: Sundown over an Indian Ocean holiday resort.

Northern Atolls: Storms and Calm, Light and Shade

Less crowded and rarely visited, the northern atolls have a charm all their own. But the weather is more unpredictable than in the other atolls. In the past, devastating storms have washed away entire islands. Hurricanes in May 1812 and January 1821 are still remembered. Another destructive storm ripped through the northern atolls in January 1955.

Often broken by deep, narrow channels, navigating the northern atolls is much easier. The free-flowing ocean currents sustain healthy coral reefs and thriving marine life. As flying fish skim through the air and schools of dolphins play alongside the boats, sailing between these atolls is pure delight.

Closer to southern India than Sri Lanka, the influence of the subcontinent is much stronger in the north. The islanders retain close links with the Lakshadweep (formerly Laccadive) Islands to the north, now a part of India, which were once largely dependent on the Ali Rajas of Cannanore.

But even though the islands are closer together and thus more interdependent, island life is much the same as in the south. Although there are fewer coconut palms, the vegetation is lush and green. Northern evenings could be played out anywhere in Maldives: children play and shout on the beach as fishermen wade ashore with the day's catch and smoke rises over the compounds where the women prepare the evening meal. Under the shade of large *cadjan* shelters carpenters repair or build boats.

The island chief, *katheeb*, welcomes visitors with great courtesy and hospitality, listening patiently to their wishes. But if these are beyond his jurisdiction he calls for help, and clearance, from the atoll office.

Despite the small compass of each island, there are always surprises. Strolling by, you might be invited to a *kaiveni sai* for a newly married couple. Music blaring out of a house and crowded courtyard may mean some recently circumcised boys are enjoying special treatment and privileged status while they recover.

There may be a local *rayyithu evvun*, where everyone turns out to help launch a new boat or to extend a jetty. It's also possible to come across a Muslim recital in Arabic, *mauloodhu*, which will continue for days as relays of readers deliver incomprehensible texts. Nonetheless, these humble fisherfolk hold the readings in great awe.

Lhaviyani (Faadhippolhu) Atoll: Ocean Wonder

Fifty-five uninhabited islands, four settled islands and one resort, with a total population of 7,000, make up Lhaviyani Atoll. The capital is Naifaru.

Getting there

Lhaviyani Atoll, 120 kilometres (74 miles) from Malé, lies eight hours sailing time across the Kaashidhoo Channel. Resorts ferry guests from the airport to their vacation island. *Dhoanis* are also available for visitors who wish to travel to nearby islands, but you'll need a special government permit. There are charter operators for boats and aircraft. See Listings.

When to go

Most resorts remain open year-round. Check with your travel agent or the nearest Maldives tourist office.

Where to stay

Kuredhdhoo (See Listings for "Resort Islands").

Sightseeing

The first ports of call on a journey north through Maldives are in **Lhaviyani Atoll**. Of the atoll's sixty small islands only four

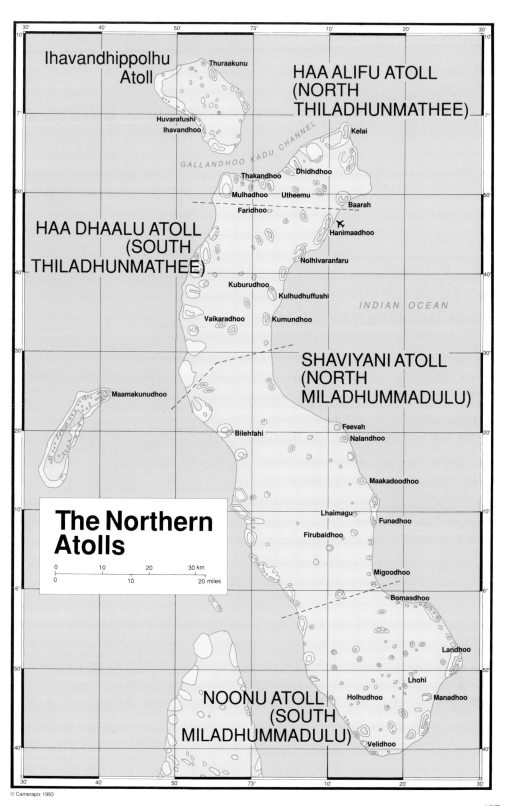

The Northern Atolls

Ihavandhippolhu Atoll

HAA ALIFU ATOLL
(NORTH THILADHUNMATHEE)

Thuraakunu

Huvarafushi
Ihavandhoo

Kelai

GALLANDHOO KADU CHANNEL

Thakandhoo
Mulhadhoo
Faridhoo

Dhidhdhoo
Utheemu
Baarah

Hanimaadhoo

HAA DHAALU ATOLL
(SOUTH THILADHUNMATHEE)

Nolhivaranfaru

Kuburudhoo

Kulhudhuffushi

INDIAN OCEAN

Vaikaradhoo

Kumundhoo

SHAVIYANI ATOLL
(NORTH MILADHUMMADULU)

Maamakunudhoo

Bilehfahi

Feevah
Nalandhoo

Maakadoodhoo

The Northern
Atolls

0   10   20   30 km
0   10   20 miles

Lhaimagu
Firubaidhoo

Funadhoo

Migoodhoo

Bomasdhoo

Landhoo

Lhohi
Manadhoo

NOONU ATOLL
(SOUTH MILADHUMMADULU)

Holhudhoo

Velidhoo

157

Lhaviyani Atoll (Faadhippolhu)

© Camerapix 1993

are occupied, but the **villages** are large. The **capital**, **Naifaru**, lies on the western rim. With more than 2,000 inhabitants and a **busy harbour**, it's known as **Kuda Malé**, the little capital.

Like nearby **Hinnavaru**, which is about the same size, the island enjoys the new prosperity brought by the expanding tourist and fishing industries.

Kuredhdhoo Island Resort is the remotest of all the Maldivian resorts and has become particularly popular with scuba divers.

Most fishermen sail thirty-metre (98-foot) diesel-driven *dhoanis*. **Container ships** collect their tuna and take it to the **canning factory** at **Felivaru**. First opened in 1977 as a joint venture with the Japanese, the factory is now owned by Maldivians.

The quality of the 15,000-18,000 tonnes of canned tuna exported each year assures it a place on supermarket shelves throughout Europe, the USA and Japan. But lack of local labour means that women from Sri Lanka keep production moving.

Lhaviyani Atoll resort

A far-flung retreat on the northern rim of the atoll, **Kuredhdhoo Island Resort**, 128 kilometres (eighty miles) from the airport, is renowned for its diving, windsurfing, and big-game fishing. There are 250 rooms.

Baa (South Maalhosmadulu) Atoll: Land of Exiles

French explorer François Pyrard was shipwrecked in Baa Atoll in 1602 when his ship *Corbin* went aground on the reef. He was held prisoner on Fulhadhoo Island for five years. While this was unfortunate, he left a fascinating account of his enforced stay for future generations.

Pyrard's movements were so closely watched that he could find no way to escape, the reason being that "few Europeans ever so much as touch there and none go to reside unless they are unfortunately cast away as I was and even in that case it is most likely they never get away".

The Frenchman only managed to escape with some companions when a fleet from Bengal suddenly arrived. At the sight of the vessels, the island king and his retinue fled, but the French castaways managed to

158

Above: Tuna canning factory on Felivaru Island, Lhaviyani Atoll. For centuries tuna has been the principal export of Maldives, although recently modern canning and freezing processes have begun to replace the traditional method of drying fish in the sun.

board the ships (See "History: The Legend and The Mystery", Part One).

Sixty-seven uninhabited islands, fourteen settled islands, and one resort, with a total population of 7,000, make up Baa Atoll. The capital is Eydhafushi.

Getting there

Baa Atoll lies 105 kilometres (65 miles) north-west of Malé, and south-west of Lhaviyani Atoll. Resorts ferry guests from the airport to their vacation island. *Dhoanis* are also available for visitors who wish to travel to nearby islands, but you'll need a special government permit. There are charter operators for boats and aircraft. See Listings.

When to go

The resort remains open year-round. Check with your travel agent or the nearest Maldives tourist office.

Where to stay

Kunfunadhoo (See Listings for "Resort Islands").

Sightseeing

Baa Atoll is separated from its northern neighbour, **Raa Atoll**, by a narrow **channel**. The **string of islands** — **Fulhadhoo**, **Fehendhoo** and **Goidhoo** — just below Baa have had more than their fair share of castaways and exiles. Indeed, Goidhoo can claim perhaps the most unusual castaways on record. In February 1963, more than 3.8 million **flying fish** landed there. Legend has it that Redin, too, were also there, and a heap of gravel and sand — one metre (three feet) high and thirteen metres (43 feet) in circumference — in the centre of the island has yet to be fully explored.

Because of their isolation, these islands are ideal for banished criminals. Since 1962, all three have been open prisons. One German tourist who stabbed his girlfriend during an argument in a Malé guesthouse in 1976 was sent to Fulhadhoo. Now a Muslim, he married a local girl and started a family — despite attempts by the German government to extradite him.

Although elsewhere in Baa Atoll many men are away at work in the resorts, in Malé, or overseas with a shipping company, everybody on the island of **Thulhaadhoo** seems involved in the production of lacquerware (*liye laajehun*) — for which Maldives is justly famous (See "Arts and Crafts", Part Three).

The **narrow alleyways** of Thulhaadhoo are crowded with craftsmen who sit cross-legged working away at different stages of their art: shaping the boxes with axes; rubbing yellow, black and red sticks of resin imported from India onto the wood as it spins round on hand lathes; or carving by hand the intricate floral patterns.

The boxes are usually made from local *funa* wood — Alexandrian laurel. The most impressive, which are used to hold the family dinner on feast days, have large circular dishes, *maaloodh foshi*, and elaborately designed lids.

The craft has brought great prosperity. Indeed the village has expanded so much that it now fills the whole island. The small **mosque** on the island was built by Sultan Mohammed Ibn Al-Haj Ali in the late seventeenth century.

The capital, **Eydhafushi**, on the other side of Baa Atoll, was once famous for woven *feyli*, a heavy white cotton sarong with brown and black strands. But since the black synthetic sarongs on sale in island shops are cheaper and easier to wash, the craft is dying out.

The arrival of electricity not only keeps the young men on the streets at night with their bikes but also enables children to do their homework.

For the first time in Maldivian history it's not axiomatic that the rising generation will take up their father's calling. Along with the unfortunate stone carvers, black-smiths and jewellers may soon also find themselves without apprentices.

Baa Atoll resorts

Opposite Eydhafushi and 100 kilometres (62 miles) from the airport, **Kunfunadhoo**, with twenty-five bungalows, maintains all the usual resort facilities. It was closed for redevelopment in 1993.

Raa (North Maalhosmadulu) Atoll: Land of Kings

According to the Maldivian chronicles, Raa Atoll is where the ruler Koimala Kaloa arrived with the king's daughter from Sri Lanka nearly two millennia ago (See "History: The Legend and the Mystery", Part One).

Subsequently, about AH 500 (AD 1100), Koimala and his wife migrated to Malé, and with the consent of the aborigines of Giraavaru Island, then the most important community in Malé Atoll, settled there (See "The People: A Mix of Many Faces", Part One).

Another celebrated visitor to Raa Atoll was Ibn Battuta, who stayed on Kinolhas in the south-east of the atoll for ten days. It was the first time he had landed on the islands. He later recalled:

"When I arrived at these islands I disembarked on one of them called Kannalùs, a fine island containing many mosques, and I put up at the house of one of the pious persons there. On this island, I met a man called Muhammad, belonging to Dhafár, who told me that if I entered the island of Mahal the Wazir would detain me there, because they had no qádi."

And, indeed, although Battuta intended to sail on to Coromandel, Ceylon, Bengal and thence China, he remained in Maldives for eighteen months, and after visiting Malé became the chief *gazi*.

The honour and hospitality accorded him in Kinolhas and neighbouring islands influenced his decision to visit the capital. The result of his stay is a detailed, colourful and fascinating period account of the country (See "History: The Legend and the Mystery", Part One).

Seventy-four uninhabited and sixteen settled islands, with a population of 9,600, make up Raa Atoll. The capital is Ugoofaaru.

Getting there

Raa Atoll, 145 kilometres (90 miles) from Malé, lies just north of Baa Atoll, from which it is separated by a two-kilometre (more than a mile) channel. There are no

RAA ATOLL (NORTH
MAALHOSMADULU)

Alifushi

Rasgetheemu

Ugoofaaru

Kadholhudhoo

Innamaadhoo

Kudafushi

Iguraidhoo

Kinolhas

INDIAN OCEAN

Viyafushi

Kunfunadhoo
Eydhafushi

Thulhaadhoo

BAA ATOLL (SOUTH
MAALHOSMADULU)

Fehendhoo
Fulhadhoo

Goidhoo

**Baa and Raa Atolls
(South and North
Maalhosmadulu)**

| 0 | 10 | 20 | 30 km |
| 0 | | 10 | 20 miles |

KAASHIDHOO CHANNEL

Above: Spectators on Eydhafushi Island, Baa Atoll, enjoy exciting inter-atoll football cup final in the late afternoon.

resorts and the only way to see the islands is by cruising and sleeping aboard your own or a chartered craft. You need a permit to land.

When to go

The best time to visit Raa Atoll is between December and March during the north-east monsoon.

Sightseeing

Raa Atoll, whose ninety islands stretch sixty kilometres (37 miles) from south to north, has played an important part in the history of Maldives.

These days Raa Atoll is famous for its **boat builders**, perhaps because the **capital Ugoofaaru** claims to have the greatest number of fishermen of all the atolls.

Most boats in Maldives are made without a plan, using primitive tools: all depends on the eye and experience of the chief carpenter. Like its cousin the Arab dhow, the basic design and construction method of the *dhoani* have changed little over the centuries.

But although modern naval architecture confirms the efficiency and seaworthiness of the ancient *dhoani* hull, change is now taking place.

The new **Alifushi Boat Yard**, where the naval architect has modified the traditional design and streamlined the hull to make more efficient use of diesel power, produces several dozen large fishing boats a year (See "Boatbuilding", Part Three).

Noonu (South Miladhummadulu) Atoll: Chain of Pearls

The northerly part of Maldives consists of a single chain of more than 200 islands stretching 140 kilometres (87 miles). For administrative purposes the islands have been divided into four groups: Noonu, Shaviyani, Haa Dhaalu and Haa Alifu.

Sixty-four uninhabited and fourteen settled islands, with a total population of

6,900, make up Noonu Atoll. The capital is Manadhoo.

Getting there

Noonu Atoll, 150 kilometres (93 miles) from Malé, lies to the east of the northern end of Raa Atoll. There are no resorts. The only way to see the islands is by cruising and sleeping aboard your own or a chartered craft. You need a permit to land.

When to go

The best time to visit Noonu Atoll is between December and March during the north-east monsoon.

Sightseeing

Noonu, the most southerly group, with its capital **Manadhoo**, may soon be brought into the tourist orbit. Certainly its beautiful islands and unsurpassed marine life make it a magnificent destination.

Until recently the **island** of **Kuredhivaru** supported a population — a coral stone slab in the island's small **mosque** is inscribed with the date AH 1121 (AD 1701) — but the people quit and moved to nearby **Bomasdhoo** earlier this century.

More **ruins** stand on the island of **Lhohi** at a place called *Haguraama Fas Gandu*, located along the south shore. Lhohi's old **mosque** was built in the mid-eighteenth century.

For millennia **Landhoo Island** has been a centre of **stone building** and **carving**. It's difficult to reach because of the rough anchorage, but hidden among its **banana plantations** and **coconut groves** are the bush-covered remains of a *hawitta*. It stands about six metres (20 feet) high.

The islanders, who call it *Maa Badhige* (**Great Cooking-pot**) and say it was built by the legendary Redin, remember when it was twice the size with a square wall around it and steps up each side. It's thought to be the remains of a Buddhist *stupa*. Recently a **statue** was found inside.

Shaviyani (North Miladhummadulu) Atoll: Land of Storm and Quake

The waters of Shaviyani Atoll, between Noonu and Haa Dhaalu atolls, are deep enough for navigation. Many centuries ago migrants from Bomasdhoo Island in Noonu Atoll sailed through these channels to settle what is now the atoll capital, Funadhoo.

Populations in Maldives usually shift because of dwindling numbers. Whenever fewer than forty men are available for Friday prayers it's customary for the community to move to a more populous island (See "The People: A Mix of Many Faces", Part One).

Thirty-nine uninhabited and fifteen settled islands, with a total population of 7,800, make up Shaviyani Atoll.

Getting there

Shaviyani Atoll, 192 kilometres (119 miles) from Malé, lies north of Noonu Atoll. There are no resorts and the only way to see the islands is by cruising and sleeping aboard your own or a chartered craft. You need a permit to land.

When to go

The best time to visit Shaviyani Atoll is between December and March during the north-east monsoon.

Sightseeing

Many islands in **Shaviyani Atoll** were affected by severe storms in May 1812, January 1821, and January 1955. Some have also experienced light earthquakes this century.

The original inhabitants of the **capital Funadhoo** (which is also known as Farukolhufunadhoo) settled there because of the fine **harbour**. The **lagoon** at its centre, which fills and empties with the tide, is called *koaru*, the nearest Dhivehi word, in a land without rivers, for "river".

Funadhoo Island has long been inhabited

Above: Trading vessels bringing basic necessities to the islanders, who import virtually everything apart from fish, coconuts and fruit.

Opposite: Taking the day's catch ashore. Fish are the staple diet of Maldivians and their main source of income.

and as the **ruins** of a **mosque** with its large **cemetery** testify, the island may have taken its name from an early resident. An old **tombstone** bears the inscription: "In memory of Ibrahim son of Funadhoo Marudhuru who died on Sunday 11, Zul-Gaidha, 1238 A.H."

Unfortunately the art of carving tomb-stones has vanished. Although a tombstone might take four or five days to complete, the family could rarely afford to pay for several days of labour. Since it involves hard work, the stone carvers simply gave up. Now only one old retired **stone carver** remains on **Landhoo** in Noonu Atoll; with him will die a unique art and an ancient tradition.

Sailing north you head for **Migoodhoo**, a beautiful **island** with an industrious population, surrounded by **beaches** of **white coral sand** two metres (seven feet) above sea level. But the centre of the island is sinking.

The water table has risen so much that the island's **freshwater lake** is expanding. During the rains, house foundations are underwater and the coral walls crack due to subsidence. Islanders constantly bring barrow loads of coral sand from the beaches for the floors of their houses and garden paths to keep their feet dry.

Maakadoodhoo, which has the largest population, is renowned for its **jaggery**-like *fathulihakuro*, a coarse brown sugar made from palm sap. In the past, the island has suffered heavily from epidemics as well as natural disasters. In 1857, 140 people died of an unknown fever and a century later it was almost destroyed during the severe storm of January 1955 (See "The Land and the Sea: Fragile Islands in the Sun", Part One).

The island of **Kaditheemu**, which supports itself from agriculture and fishing, has the oldest known written sample of **Thaana script**. It's on the door frame of the

Above: Taking firewood home to Eydhafushi Island, Baa Atoll. Because of the shortage of wood, forays are often made onto neighbouring uninhabited islands.

main **mosque**, and dates the roof from AH 1008 (AD 1588).

Nalandhoo Island, which was abandoned after the great storm of May 1812, is now formed of so many islets that on the high tide fishing boats can enter an **island lagoon**.

Evidence of the island's inhabitance is found in the shape of two *hawittas*, one on the northern coast known as **Us Fas Gandu**; the other on the north-eastern coast called **Happathi Gandu**. The Utheemu brothers hid their boat, **Kalhuohfummi**, on the island during the seventeenth-century war of independence against the Portuguese.

Another large *hawitta*, on the southern coast of the fishing **island** of **Lhaimagu**, is called *Fageeru Odi Baiy Than* by the locals.

Haa Dhaalu (South Thiladhunmathee) Atoll: Treasure Isles and Reefs

The seventy-seven islands of South and North Thiladhunmathee were split into Haa Dhaalu and Haa Alifu atolls in 1958.

Haa Dhaalu boasts one of the largest towns in Maldives, with a population of more than 5,000, a large school and a regional hospital.

Although Haa Dhaalu is contiguous to Shaviyani Atoll, the northern end of Haa Alifu forms a separate, smaller atoll.

Twenty uninhabited and seventeen settled islands, with a total population of 11,000, make up Haa Dhaalu Atoll. The capital is Nolhivaranfaru.

Getting there

Haa Dhaalu Atoll, 240 kilometres (149 miles) from Malé, lies virtually at the northernmost tip of the Maldives archipelago. There are no resorts and the only way to see the islands is by cruising and sleeping aboard your own or a chartered craft. You need a permit to land.

When to go

The best time to visit Haa Dhaalu Atoll is between December and March during the north-east monsoon.

Sightseeing

The largest **island**, **Kulhudhuffushi**, with its modern **harbour** and wide **waterfront** where children play soccer in the evening, has a teeming population. Dredgers clear the approach channel regularly.

More than half the men either work at sea on ocean-going vessels or in the tourist resorts. Those who remain are famous for their shark fishing. Large *dhoanis*, laden down with *cadjan* and coir made by the atoll women, sail frequently to Malé.

The twenty-five-kilometre (16-mile) **reef** at the south-west extremity of the atoll, where **Maamakunudhoo** is the only settled **island**, is a major hazard to shipping and the site of many **wrecks**.

The *Persia Merchant* went down along the western tip of the reef in August 1658, but the worst toll was experienced in the nineteenth century when the reef claimed the *Hayston* in 1819; the *Royal Family* on 19 August 1868; and the *George Reid* on 26 September 1872. Doubtless they were swept to their graves by the sudden storms that erupt in the area during the south-west monsoon.

Divers should note the intriguing salvage to be found in these waters and the wealth of coral and marine life, as good as any in the Indian Ocean.

Faridhoo is another interesting feature of the atoll, the highest island in the archipelago — all of three metres (10 feet) above sea level — although you could not tell. Landing to verify the fact is difficult because of perpetually rough seas.

Kumundhoo, noted for toddy tapping, has two unexplored **ruins** with **circular foundations** on its east coast. Budding archaeologists should note that they need to obtain special permission from Malé to

excavate these ancient ruins, even though locals still pinch an odd stone or two for their houses.

The amount of priceless and irreplaceable dressed megalithic stone plundered for walls and houses is painful to think about.

The inhabited **island** of **Kuburudhoo** has many coconuts for toddy tapping, but landing is difficult. There is virtually no lagoon and boats have to be hauled up the beach to avoid the pounding surf.

On the other hand, you can land on **Vaikaradhoo Island** in all seasons. The **ruins** of a *hawitta*, known locally as the *Jaadi Valhu Li Than*, stand on its western periphery. The main **mosque** dates from this century.

Haa Alifu (North Thiladhunmathee) Atoll: The Land of Thakurufaanu

The northernmost reaches of the Maldives archipelago have special significance in the hearts of Maldivians. There lies the island birthplace of the revered hero of the country, Muhammad Thakurufaanu.

The now renovated wooden palace evokes, more than any other existing building in Maldives, the life style of the rich all those centuries ago.

Haa Alifu Atoll is made up of twenty-four uninhabited and sixteen settled islands, with a total population of 10,000. The capital is Dhidhdhoo.

Getting there

Haa Alifu Atoll, 280 kilometres (174 miles) north of Malé, is the extreme northern tip of the country. There are no resorts and the only way to see the islands is by cruising and sleeping aboard your own or a chartered craft. You need a permit to land.

When to go

The best time to visit Haa Alifu Atoll is between December and March during the north-east monsoon.

Above: Fishermen returning home with the day's catch. Although engines have replaced sail, tuna are still caught by pole and line.

Sightseeing

Haa Alifu offers a good anchorage for yachts cruising through this part of the Indian Ocean. It also holds **Utheemu**, a beautiful **island** only reached by small boats which may easily be swamped by surf when the south-west monsoon is blowing, but this does nothing to discourage the many visitors to what amounts to a **national shrine**.

Utheemu is the **birthplace of Muhammad Thakurufaanu** who, with his two brothers, was a key figure in a fight to regain independence from the Portuguese. His **wooden palace** has been renovated, although the original thatched roof has been replaced by tiles.

The floor is strewn with the finest white coral sand and the small rooms contain elegant **wooden chests**, small **ornamental beds** and beautifully crafted **lacquerware**.

To enter the house you have to bow your head because the lintel is so low. This, so the story goes, is to prevent the dead from walking out before being buried. If they left the house and walked down to the beach, they could return and consume the living.

A large separate building nearby, covered with thatch, is where guests and dignitaries were received. Woven mats cover the floor and beautiful cotton hangings with colourful abstract designs adorn the walls.

Muhammad Thakurufaanu is well-remembered. His first wife, a poor girl from neighbouring **Baarah** Island, was servant to the wife of Sultan Ali (Ali was later killed by the Portuguese).

Thakurufaanu's daring exploits also endeared him to Ali's daughter. She fell in love with him at first sight and became his second wife. Yet by all accounts the two wives from such different backgrounds got on well. Such stories of royal love and Thakurufaanu's common touch made him the people's hero.

The nearby **mosque**, four-and-a-half centuries old, points west towards the setting sun, not north-west to Mecca. Thakurufaanu's father is buried in an adjoining **stone mausoleum** decorated with

white flags which flap in the sea breeze.

According to local legend, the beautiful **well** by the **mosque** was made out of a single stone which arrived on the island by divine providence. Apparently the Thakurufaanu brothers collected the stone from Seenu Atoll, but when they were caught by a storm in the One-and-a-Half-Degree Channel they threw it overboard to lighten their load.

Instead of sinking swiftly a thousand fathoms, it was miraculously washed ashore on Utheemu, at the other end of the Maldivian archipelago. Such are the stories that gather around heroes.

Another tale relates how Muhammad placed two stakes, taken from trees on Baarah, near the beach in order to make sails. The stakes took root and one tree still stands — nearly 400 years old.

Memorial Centre

The **Bodu Thakurufaanu Memorial Centre,** with **library** and **conference rooms**, was built recently and the 600 or so islanders of this remote landfall in the north are now used to important guests from Malé.

More than once the president and his ministers have made the pilgrimage to celebrate Independence Day and pay homage to the national hero.

The **tomb** of the Thakurufaanu brother captured and beheaded by the Portuguese — Ali Thakurufaanu — is found in the **cemetery** of the main **mosque** on the fishing **island** of **Thakandhoo**.

Another **monument** to a bygone era stands on **Kelai Island**, where bush has taken over the **ruins** of a former British **staging post** established in 1934. Until the end of the Second World War it functioned as the northerly counterpart to **Gan** at the other end of the archipelago. Today the island is well-known for its farming, particularly yams and *cadjan.*

In the past the island chief, *katheeb*, from Kelai played an important role in the coronation of the sultan in Malé, no doubt to ensure the loyalty of the northern atolls.

Nearby **Mulhadhoo**, a settled **island** with a large and deep **lagoon**, is distinguished by **bamboo** which grows well there.

Traditionally, although now part of the Haa Alifu administrative atoll, the most northerly true atoll is known as **Ihavandhippolhu**. It lies across the **Gallandhoo Kadu**, a five-kilometre-wide (three-mile) **channel** in which the tidal stream sets east-north-east on the flood and west-south-west with the ebb.

The atoll's traditional name derives from the **island** of **Ihavandhoo**. So good is its anchorage that in 1883 the British wanted to use it as a coal depot. But the sultan refused permission. It has long been inhabited; the construction date inscribed on the main **mosque** is AH 1112 (AD 1692).

Huvarafushi Island has a population of 2,000. At the crossroads in the centre of the **village** you can see the sea in all four directions. As far north as this, the fishing is poor and there are few coconuts for coir making. Yet it's the **commercial centre** of the atoll, with a new **school** built by the Japanese.

Renowned for music and dance, the women of Huvarafushi Youth Association regularly perform the traditional *bandiya jehun*, swinging their heads and shoulders in line as they tap out a rhythm on metal water pots.

It's a kind of harvest dance, similar to those of south India. The women also play the *bodu beru* drums, chanting away as others dance enticingly in the Arabic manner.

The northernmost island of Maldives is difficult to reach as it has no lagoon and a strong swell strikes outside the **reef**. Although this is land's end as far as Maldives is concerned, 290 kilometres (180 miles) to the north lies **Minicoy**, the southern part of the Indian state of Lakshadweep, where they still speak a Dhivehi dialect called Mahl.

In the eleventh century an Arab geographer split the archipelago into the Maldives and the Laccadives (now the Lakshadweep Islands), but the local fishermen made no such arbitrary distinctions.

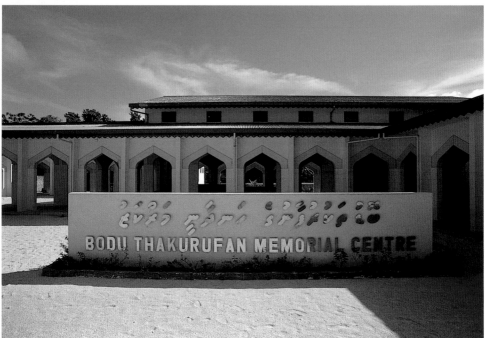

Top: Interior of the carefully preserved wooden palace of Muhammad Thakurufaanu on Utheemu Island, Haa Alifu Atoll.

Above: Memorial Centre on Utheemu Island to Muhammad Thakurufaanu, who helped regain independence from the Portuguese in the sixteenth century and is now considered a national hero.

Southern Atolls: The Path of the Sun

Isolated from Malé, the bustling resort islands, and separated from the rest of the archipelago by the broadest stretch of water in Maldives, the southern atolls reach down across the equator on the other side of the One-and-a-Half-Degree Channel.

The channel, known locally as Huvadhoo Kandu, is eighty-five kilometres (53 miles) wide and 1,130 fathoms (6,780 feet) deep.

The four atolls vary in size and character: Gaafu Alifu and Gaafu Dhaalu atolls are joined administratively to form Huvadhoo Atoll, the largest atoll in the world; Gnaviyani or Fua Mulaku Atoll, filled in the middle to make one complete island; and crescent-shaped Seenu or Addu Atoll.

These remote islands have some of the most fascinating archaeological sites in Maldives. Strategically placed on the main sea route around southern India, they also received the greatest impact from mariners who sailed the Indian Ocean through the centuries (See "History: The Legend and the Mystery", Part One).

Direct trade with Sri Lanka was more economic than with the northern atolls, Colombo being the same distance away as Malé. Until recently large sailing ships called *odis*, laden with dried fish, sailed for Sri Lanka on the south-west monsoon to return six months later on the north-east monsoon. Today it takes four or five days for a motorized cargo-*dhoani* to reach Malé.

Because of their isolation, the islanders' dialect is different. The language retains old forms of Dhivehi, reflecting the early influence of Sinhala, and people from Malé find it difficult to understand.

Small specks in the vastness of the ocean, the atolls are even isolated from one another and largely self-sufficient; the pronunciation and vocabulary change from atoll to atoll. When people visit another atoll, they usually speak the Malé dialect of Dhivehi.

Like the other atolls in the south, Huvadhoo now benefits from the recent prosperity brought by tourism. There are new government health centres and primary schools. Yet many men are forced to leave in search of work.

Gaafu Alifu (North Huvadhoo) Atoll: Islands in the Backwater

Huvadhoo Atoll, the largest in the world, seventy kilometres (43 miles) long, and fifty-five kilometres (34 miles) wide, has a lagoon which covers 2,240 square kilometres (865 miles) to a depth of eighty-six metres (282 feet). The atoll is so large that it has been divided into Gaafu Alifu in the north and Gaafu Dhaalu in the south.

Eighty-three uninhabited and ten settled islands, with a total population of 6,200, make up Gaafu Alifu Atoll. The capital is Viligili.

Getting there

Gaafu Alifu Atoll, 330 kilometres (205 miles) from Malé, lies far south of Laamu Atoll. There are no resorts and the only way to see the islands is by cruising and sleeping aboard your own or a chartered craft. You need a permit to land.

When to go

The best time to visit Gaafu Alifu Atoll is between December and March during the north-east monsoon.

Sightseeing

On the **capital** of **Gaafu Alifu**, **Viligili**, a bustling **island** of more than 1,500 inhabitants, there was once a large *hawitta* and a **road** called **Hawitta Magu**. Although the ancient mound has been washed away by the sea, the road still exists.

In these southern islands fishing remains the mainstay of the economy, but islanders on **Dhevvadhoo**, in the centre of the atoll where fishing is more difficult, are well-known for making **coir rope**.

There are several unexplored **ruins** on

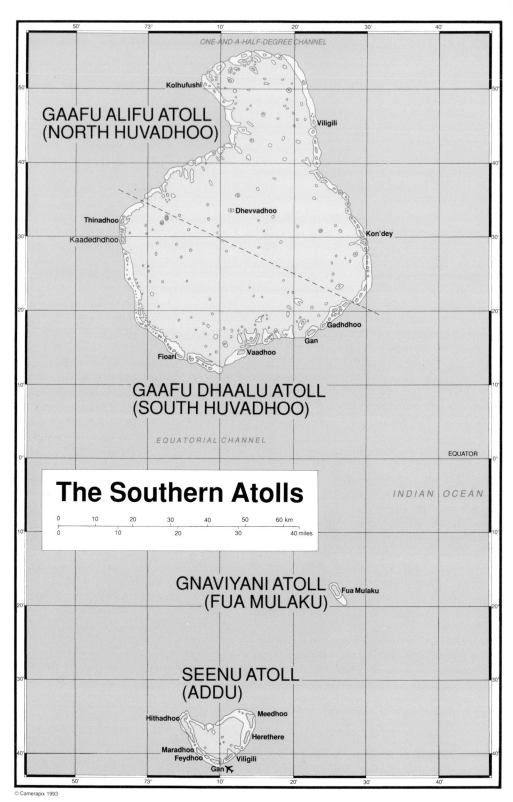

ONE-AND-A-HALF-DEGREE CHANNEL

Kolhufushi

GAAFU ALIFU ATOLL
(NORTH HUVADHOO)

Viligili

Dhevvadhoo

Thinadhoo

Kaadedhdhoo

Kon'dey

Gadhdhoo

Gan

Fioari

Vaadhoo

GAAFU DHAALU ATOLL
(SOUTH HUVADHOO)

EQUATORIAL CHANNEL

EQUATOR

The Southern Atolls

INDIAN OCEAN

| 0 | 10 | 20 | 30 | 40 | 50 | 60 km |
| 0 | | 10 | | 20 | | 30 | | 40 miles |

GNAVIYANI ATOLL
(FUA MULAKU)

Fua Mulaku

SEENU ATOLL
(ADDU)

Hithadhoo

Meedhoo

Herethere

Maradhoo

Feydhoo

Viligili

Gan

Dhevvadhoo. *Hukuru Miskiiy*, the main **mosque**, was built by Sultan Mohammed Ibn Al-Haj Ali in the seventeenth century. The **smaller mosque** was built by Sultan Ibrahim in the sixteenth century.

For fifteen years, from 1960 to 1975, **Kon'dey** was deserted, but today more than 200 people live there. There are four *hawittas* on the island, all about six metres square (65 square feet) and a metre (three feet) high. Here Thor Heyerdahl came across a **limestone sculpture**. It turned out to be the head of the **Hindu water god Makara**, a demon often decorating the entrances to Hindu temples and seen as a projecting waterspout in sacred fountains.

In 1800 the *Surat* was wrecked off the **coast** of the settled **island** of **Kolamaafushi**. The 8,460-tonne Greek ship *Nicolaos Embricos*, with a cargo of jute, gunnies, tea and cotton, went aground on the atoll's uninhabited **island** of **Maamutaa** in 1969.

Gaafu Dhaalu (South Huvadhoo) Atoll: The Kingdom of the Cats

Today, with the emphasis on welfare services and development, the southern atolls enjoy much prosperity.

One hundred and fifty uninhabited and ten settled islands, with a total population of 9,000, make up Gaafu Dhaalu Atoll. The capital is Thinadhoo. Earlier this century Thinadhoo was the capital of all the 292 islands that make up Huvadhoo Atoll.

Getting there

Gaafu Dhaalu Atoll, 360 kilometres (223 miles) from Malé, is the southern half of the world's largest atoll. An airport on **Kaadedhdhoo** was opening in 1993. There are no resorts and the only way to see the islands is by cruising and sleeping aboard your own or a chartered craft. You need a permit to land.

When to go

The best time to visit Gaafu Dhaalu Atoll is between December and March.

Sightseeing

Thinadhoo boasts its own "**5-Star**" **guest-house** — for locals only — several good **tea-shops** and two **mosques** built at the end of the seventeenth century — *Dhekunukolhu Miskiiy* and *Hukuru Miskiiy,* which was demolished and rebuilt in 1952.

An intriguing **iron knob** emerges from the sand in the **garden** of one resident. Workers abandoned an attempt to disinter it after digging down two metres. The iron pole is said to have been buried there by Captain Moresby — who was responsible for drawing up the British Admiralty chart of Maldives, which is still used today.

One of the most southerly islands is **Vaadhoo**, where you sail across a shallow foreshore in a small boat to land at a **jetty**.

The ancient **Malahandu Mosque** by the beach, which has a **bath** made with square dressed slabs, may well have been the site of an earlier temple.

The mosque is said to have been built by one Abu al-Barakat Yusuf al-Barbari (also referred to as Abdul Rikaab Yusuf al-Thabreyzee), believed to be the man who brought Islam to the island. The interior has some marvellous **wood carvings** and **painted arabesques**. The beautiful flowing **inscriptions** on the **tombstones** in the adjoining **cemetery** are carved in *Dhives Akuru*, the second-oldest script in the country.

Islanders are proud of the fact that Sultan Mohammed Ibn Al-Haj Ali, who ruled Maldives for eight years at the end of the seventeenth century, came from the island.

Thor Heyerdahl found **slabs** with unusual **ornamentation** buried next to the mosque. There are also **two mounds** on the island known as *Bodu Hawitta* and *Vidamagh Hawitta* built, it's said, by the legendary Redin.

The islands adjoining the Equatorial Channel in the southern part of Gaafu Dhaalu are scattered with many **ruins** and **artefacts** dating from long before the arrival of Islam, which suggest that earlier settlers were replaced by Hindus and Buddhists.

The most impressive ruin is that of a huge 3,000-year-old **pyramid** in the **middle** of the **jungle** on the **uninhabited island** of

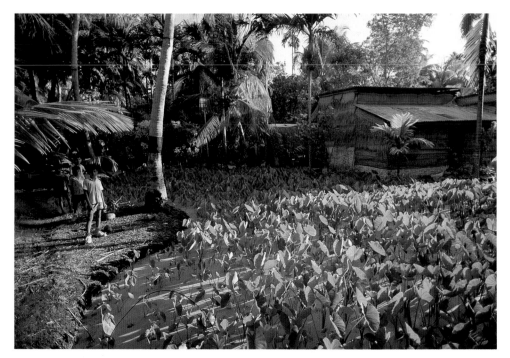

Above: Taro, growing in a swamp on Fua Mulaku, is a nutritious root vegetable which forms the staple food of the islanders.

Gan next to **Gadhdhoo**. Called *Vadamaga Hawitta*, each side of its base measures twenty-three metres (75 feet), making a ground area for the pyramid an enormous 529 square metres (5,800 square feet). Thor Heyerdahl suggested that it may have been a stepped pyramid, with ceremonial ramps on four sides like the ancient pyramids found in Mesopotamia and pre-Columbian America.

During excavations in the early 1980s he found **symbols** resembling open eyes scattered around the site and squared **blocks of stone** carved with flowers. He also found the foot of a sitting **Buddha**, a **stone bull** and **two lions**.

All the evidence suggests this extraordinary structure near the equator was once a magnificent temple. In its heyday it must have been an amazing sight, a huge pyramid of white limestone carved with marvellous skill and design, standing in a clearing in the dense green jungle and shining in the sun.

Although Gadhdhoo is only 400 metres (1,312 feet) long and 200 metres (656 feet) wide, it has a population of nearly 2,000. At the crossroads in the middle of the **village** you can see the sea at the end of each of the island's four roads. The women make beautifully intricate mats called *thundu kunaa*, from a reed called *haa* which grows on the nearby island of **Fioari**.

It seems odd that the people should choose to live on such a small island while neighbouring Gan is so much larger and empty with its abandoned Islamic **cemetery**.

People cross the narrow stretch of water from Gadhdhoo to collect coconuts and firewood, but do not stay overnight. They also bury their dead there if they have been sick or died at sea.

Local legend says the island was abandoned when Gan was invaded by huge cats which killed or chased away all the islanders. To this day the deserted island is called the "**Kingdom of the Cats**".

In reality the cats were probably Sinhalese from Sri Lanka who called themselves the "Lion People" and wore

Above: Ancient ceremonial bath adjoining Kedeyre Mosque, Fua Mulaku, with closely fitting stones dressed in a manner known only to a few pre-European civilizations.

ferocious masks with feline teeth. The legend may well refer to early Hindu settlers who were attacked by Buddhist invaders (See "History: The Legend and The Mystery", Part One).

Gnaviyani (Fua Mulaku) Atoll: Emeralds Across the Equator

One inhabited island, with a population of just over 6,000, makes up Gnaviyani Atoll. The capital is Mulah.

The forty-kilometre-wide (25-mile) Equatorial Channel separates Gnaviyani (better known as Fua Mulaku and pronounced "Foah Mulah") from Huvadhoo Atoll.

Sailing across the channel from the northern to the southern hemisphere, you pass over an unknown sea bed more than 1,300 fathoms (7,800 feet) below.

For centuries, the Equatorial Channel, where currents can run up to five knots, has been used by mariners journeying from Africa to China and the Arabian Gulf to Malaysia (See "History: The Legend and the Mystery", Part One).

They have travelled in Egyptian papyrus boats, Arab dhows, Chinese junks, windjammers, steamships and modern tankers. And all must have been impressed by this, one of the oldest shipping lanes in the world.

Alone in the middle of the Indian Ocean, just south of the equator, Fua Mulaku is one of the world's most isolated islands. Surrounded by a steep, coarse coral shingle beach, it has no sheltered mooring and boats must anchor to the lee of the prevailing monsoon.

When the north-west monsoon blows, small rowing boats collect visitors from their vessel. Only skilled island fishermen can navigate through the surf and the narrow channel to the landing spot at Rasgefaanu. Because of the dangerous currents, swimming is a grave risk.

But the island is one of the world's

great unspoilt tropical "paradises" whose tranquillity and beauty inspired one Spanish artist to convert to Islam, learn Dhivehi and change his name to Abdulla Shavi.

Married twice to local women, he now has several children. Invited back to Spain by King Carlos, he stayed only a few months before he returned to his haven in the Indian Ocean. Having won the confidence of the local people, he has collected hundreds of old stories.

Fua Mulaku is about six kilometres (four miles) long and three kilometres (two miles) wide. It is the largest island in Maldives, with a population of more than 7,000 — although most men usually work away.

Though isolated, the island is blessed with the most fertile land in Maldives. Mangoes, watermelons, papayas, limes, bananas, oranges and pineapples flourish, while taro grows so well that it has become the staple food.

The tropical vegetation is luxuriant and widespread. Areca nut trees, tall as date palms, with betel sprouting around their trunks like a liana, grow in most compounds.

Early Visitors

Among the early travellers who visited Fua Mulaku is Ibn Battuta. In 1344 he stayed on the island for seventy days while he waited for the monsoon that would carry him to the Malabar coast. In that short time he married two women (See "History: The Legend and the Mystery", Part One). Although the islanders feared Battuta's captain and crew, they presented them with cowries, coconuts, honey, betel, areca nuts and fish every day on orders from the *wazir* in Malé.

French brothers

In the sixteenth century the French brothers Jean and Raoul Parmentier rounded the Cape of Africa, in their ships *Pensée* and *Sacré*, and landed on the island on 24 September 1529. They were received by a devout man — they assumed he was the chief priest — who presented them with

lemons as offerings (See "History: The Legend and the Mystery", Part One).

"In this island," they recorded, "was a Temple or Mosque, a very ancient structure, composed of massive stone.

"The Captain desired to see the inside as well as the outside, whereupon the Chief Priest bade them to open it, and entered within. The work pleased him greatly; and chiefly a woodwork screen, with a balustrade so neatly turned that our ship's carpenter was surprised to see the fineness of the work."

Few other Europeans knew about Fua Mulaku until H.C.P. Bell landed on its shores in 1922 to explore its ruins. He loved the "bliss of solitude" and considered it the most beautiful island in the archipelago. In 1985 Thor Heyerdahl was no less affected by the peace and beauty of this lost isle in an emerald sea.

Although electricity has come to the island and the fishing *dhoanis* now have diesel engines, life has changed remarkably little since Battuta's time. Islanders are still superstitious, combining their faith in Islam with older beliefs in spirits, *dhevi* (See "The People: A Mix of Many Faces", Part One).

One story tells of a *dhevi* called Aruffanu Ferreytha, which first appeared to fishermen as a glowing flame hovering over the sea at night and came ashore as a monster vampire to suck the people's blood.

The terror finally ended when a master magician — a *fanditha* man — cast a spell and turned the monster into a big boulder on the reef. Islanders claim that if you strike it with an iron bar it bleeds.

Getting there

Gnaviyani Atoll, 430 kilometres (267 miles) from Malé, lies forty kilometres (25 miles) south of Huvadhoo Atoll across the Equatorial Channel. There are no resorts and the best way to see the island is by anchoring and sleeping aboard your own or a chartered craft. You need a permit to land. Visits to Gnaviyani Atoll may also be arranged through the Addu Development Authority on Gan Island in Seenu (Addu) Atoll.

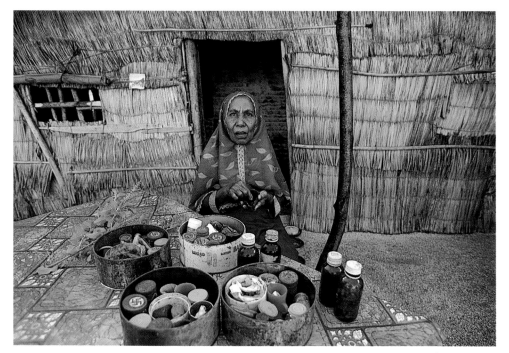

Above: *Hakeem* medicine woman in Gaafu Alifu Atoll. Although modern medicine is now reaching all the atolls, traditional medicine still plays an important role.

When to go

The best time to visit Gnaviyani Atoll is between December and March during the north-east monsoon.

Sightseeing

Once an atoll of three islands, according to local legend ships used to sail right into the middle of the lagoon. Eventually, with the entrance channel closed, the enclosed lagoon became **two freshwater lakes** — **Bandaara Kulhi** and **Dhadimage Kulhi**. Several species of **fish** thrive in their warm waters, and at night **bullfrogs** splash and bellow in the shallows. The high water table allows taro to grow in the swamps around the lakes.

Relics

Impressive **ruins** show that **Fua Mulaku** has been settled for thousands of years. Near **Huadadhoo** village, about 150 metres (492 feet) from the shore, there is a mound or *hawitta*, about twenty metres (66 feet) high and seventy-five metres (246 feet) in circumference, which was probably a bell-shaped Buddhist *stupa* on a square platform.

Towering above the coconut trees in the equatorial sun, it must have been a famous landmark. Until recently Sinhalese fishermen gave votive offerings there. Islanders call this extraordinary monument **Redinge Funi**, **"Redin's Hill"**.

Unfortunately, the original masonry has been removed for building, but a few beautifully dressed stones lie among the bush and pandanus palms growing on the mound.

Bell, who visited it in 1922, was unable to find the **stone statue** of a **Buddha** that had been reported to him. Sixty years later Heyerdahl agreed with Bell that it was probably a **Buddhist** *dagoba*, a round bell-shape carved in white plaster.

Nearby stand the **ruins** of two small *hawittas*, although most of their stones have been plundered for houses and garden boundaries. Two statues by the smaller *hawitta*, one of a naked woman and the other of a naked man holding a fish on a cord, have vanished.

Above: Young girl carries coconuts home. The nuts are central to the Maldivians' way of life, providing food and drink, building materials and coir rope.

The islanders, who called the second statue *Mahufoli Kalege*, meaning "**The Owner of the Fish**", claim that one day, just as a fisherman was giving a fish to his wife, a spirit, *jinni*, passed by and turned them to stone.

Legend says that about AH 800 the Arabs who brought Islam to Meedhoo in Seenu Atoll made their way to Fua Mulaku. In the **Dhiguvaadu Mosque**, a few hundred metres from "Redin's Hill", lies the body of Abdul Naib Kalegefan, the son of Yusuf, who was "martyred" there. The **mosque** is built from ill-fitting carved and polished limestone slabs probably taken from an earlier temple on the site.

Kedeyre Mosque, by the sea near **Dhadi Magu** village, has a beautiful and original sunken **ceremonial bath** about five metres square (54 feet square) and 1.3 metres (four feet) deep, made from blocks of different sizes.

They were cut with such precision and so carefully fitted that it is impossible to slide a knife blade between them. Excavations revealed a bench around the sides on which bathers sat as crystal-clear fresh water slowly filtered around them.

These extraordinary building skills led Heyerdahl to speculate that the people who designed it had "an exceedingly difficult technique by following an important aesthetic . . . tradition" (See "History: The Legend and the Mystery", Part One).

Seenu (Addu) Atoll: Island of Dreams

Travelling from Gnaviyani Atoll to Seenu Atoll is often difficult for the currents in the Indian Ocean change with the prevailing winds. A one-and-a-half knot current normally streams between Seenu and Gnaviyani.

The most important recent development in Seenu was the establishment of a British air base on Gan, the southernmost island of Maldives. During the Second World War, when Maldives was a British Protectorate, the Royal Navy built an airstrip on the

Above: Woven mat, known as *thundu kunaa*, made on Gadhdhoo Island, Gaafu Dhaalu Atoll, from locally gathered reeds.

island to guard the strategic sea lane to Asia and the Far East.

Later, in 1956, when the British Royal Air Force closed their base in Ceylon, they moved their operations to Gan. The islanders were simply transferred to the neighbouring island of Feydhoo. The base remained in use until 1976 when the British withdrew their forces east of Suez.

The British legacy in Seenu Atoll is very strong, and the Royal Air Force seems to have made a good impression. Suddenly appearing out of the sky with incredible machines and ideas, they must have appeared like people from another planet.

At its peak, the RAF employed some 1,200 workers. Islanders not only found work at the base, but benefited from schools and health services. Many who learned English now work in the tourist resorts of the north.

To develop Gan and strengthen ties between north and south, the Malé government set up the Addu Development Authority. So far one Hong Kong textile company has established a garment factory.

But one-third of the workers are Sri Lankan women who sign a contract for a year or two and live in the old RAF barracks. Islanders, who only work periodically for extra luxuries, prefer to stay home.

Twenty-six uninhabited islands, seven inhabited islands, and one resort, with a total population of 15,000, make up Seenu Atoll. The capital is Hithadhoo.

Getting there

Seenu Atoll, 478 kilometres (296 miles) from Malé, is the southernmost point of Maldives. Air Maldives operates regular scheduled services from Malé.

Where to stay

Gan Holiday Village is the only hotel for visitors (See Listings for "Accommodation"). You need a permit to visit the other islands.

When to go

The hotel is open year-round.

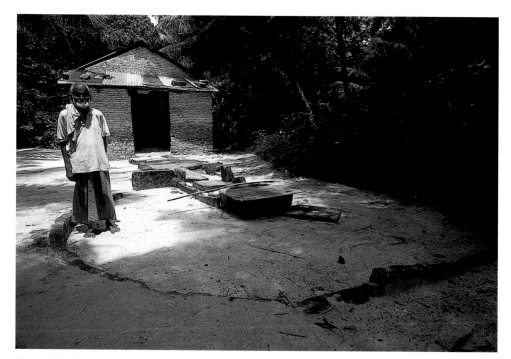

Above: Malahandu Mosque on Vaadhoo Island in Gaafu Dhaalu Atoll, said to be built by the man who brought Islam to the island in the twelfth century.

Opposite top: Beginnings of an embroidered *libaas* collar, part of the traditional costume for Maldivian women.

Opposite: The gentle art of *libaas* making in Gaafu Alifu Atoll. The embroidered collars, made with silver and golden thread, take many weeks to make.

Sightseeing

Gan Island remains a semi-deserted piece of valuable real estate. For good reason — it contains almost 3,000 metres (9,840 feet) of runway capable of handling the most advanced jets as well as hangars, permanent barracks, fuel storage tanks and a pier.

Amenities include **tennis courts**, a **soccer pitch**, an overgrown eighteen-hole **golf course** and a **swimming pool**. The **mosque**, built by the Pakistani labourers who constructed the runway, still stands.

The **gardens** and **lawns**, where the **roses**, **bougainvillea**, **frangipani** and **flamboyant trees** introduced by the British flourish, remain carefully tended. Flanked by **cannon**, the **monument** to the Indian dead of the Second World War is in good repair. Another legacy is Hammond Innes' tale, *The Strode Venturer* (1965), much of which is set in Gan.

The thirty-room **Gan Holiday Village**, in the former **sergeant's mess**, is the only official place to stay outside Malé and the resort islands. It is a good base from which

to explore the northern islands of the atoll, but there are no good beaches nearby.

To swim it's best to go by boat to the uninhabited neighbouring **island** of **Viligili** (leased by a resident of **Maradhoo**). But Gan's main interest lies more in local history than natural beauty.

The British built the causeways that join the **string of islands** along the south-west rim of the atoll — **Feydhoo**, **Maradhoo**, and **Hithadhoo**. It is possible to travel nine kilometres (six miles) by road from Hithadhoo to Gan, the only road outside Malé and the longest in the entire country. Unfortunately it has affected the natural flow of water, and silting and weed have ruined the beaches. Most people still travel from one island to the other by boat.

Another regrettable side effect of the air base was the destruction of mysterious archaeological **ruins**. In 1922 archaeologist H.C.P. Bell came across a colossal mound, about nine metres (20 feet) high with a base about eighty metres square (890 square feet), "buried in heavy scrub jungle, interspersed freely with closely growing trees". He found a casing of cut coral blocks and concluded that it must have once been a Buddhist *stupa*.

Now cleared by bulldozers, the area is completely flat. Bell recorded another **ruin**, that of an ancient **fort** in the northern extremity of neighbouring Hithadhoo, but it too has disappeared. Both would have been important **landmarks** for mariners rounding the southern tip of Asia (See "History: The Legend and The Mystery," Part One).

The capital, **Hithadhoo**, is the atoll's most northerly island. Only a pilot or some-one with local knowledge can navigate the **coral reefs** surrounding the island. The water is so shallow that visiting *dhoanis* anchor off a **long jetty** made from coral blocks. Nearby float the remains of gutted fish, waiting for the tide and breeze to carry them and their stench away.

Hithadhoo, called the "second city" of Maldives, is more like a small town. With 10,000 people, it has about two-thirds of the total population of the atoll. Its wide central road, covered in sand, is more like an air-strip where the pedestrian and bicycle rule.

Above: Soft and beautiful coral.

Opposite: Rod fishing for tuna bait on the coarse coral sand of Gnaviyani, also known as Fua Mulaku.

In the whole atoll there are only twenty taxis, although an occasional motorcycle or pick-up scatters chickens and brings mothers rushing to scoop their offspring from the sand.

The best way to see the island is by bicycle. You should also organize *dhoani* trips to uninhabited neighbouring islands and swim off the coral reefs.

Several excellent **tea-shops** on Hithadhoo satisfy the most discriminating connoisseurs of Maldivian food. Those who want a change from fish curries should try **Target Point** on **Azee Magu** for a memorable local version of Western-style cooking.

Laid out on a grid pattern, the town lanes are cut at right angles to each other. More and more houses are being roofed with corrugated iron instead of coconut thatch and building blocks have replaced the small coral stones. House compounds are surrounded by walls for privacy. Banana, coconut and betel nut palms, frangipani and hibiscus grow in most compounds, where roses are a reminder of the one-time British presence (See "The People: A Mix of Many Faces", Part One).

During the evenings young men play football in the dusty sand of the **main square** opposite the **mosque** with ceramic tiles which looks like an old colonial house. Nearby, girls play *bashi*, a game where you hit a ball over your shoulder with a tennis racket without looking. The aim is not to let the opposing team catch it. Everyone applauds with great enthusiasm.

The island's **Koravalu Mosque** was built by Sultan Mohamed Imaad-ud-deen I in the middle of the seventeenth century. The **grave** of **Sultan Hassan X**, who died in 1765 after spending more than sixty years in exile, is by **Thakurufaanu Mosque**.

New life has come to this long-established town. A modern **regional hospital**, **secondary school** and **vocational centre** reflect the government's commitment to develop its southernmost atoll. One island businessman (who has "made it" in Malé) recently opened an **Islamic centre** on Hithadhoo.

Since the local market is small, and the government freezer ships do not travel so far south, few go fishing these days. But the many half-built houses, sections added on as the money rolls in, reflect a growing prosperity.

Another British legacy is the **wreck** of the 5,583-tonne ***British Loyalty*** which ran aground on Hithadhoo's south-west reef.

On the other horn of the crescent that makes up Addu Atoll, opposite Hithadhoo, **Meedhoo**'s **long jetty**, made from coral rag, stands in its shallow foreshore.

In 1975, the population was separated into two villages — **Hulhudhoo** and Meedhoo — encouraging much good-humoured rivalry. Here, the visitor is a curiosity.

Meedhoo is a typical Maldivian village. Inevitably there is a wide central road, *magu*, which runs from one side of the island to the other, with another road crossing in the middle. Side lanes run off these main roads at right angles. The *magu* opens out at the **landing point** on the beach.

The men used to sell dried fish to Sri Lanka, but many now serve in shipping lines or the resort islands. Such a shortage of manpower, with men away for ten months of the year, clearly affects the local economy, especially the construction industry. The responsibility for the family falls upon the women, but extended families help make the separation easier.

A **recent ruin** on the north coast is that of a British Second World War **gun emplacement** built, according to a nearby stone slab, by the 8th Indian Coastal Battery.

It is the Islamic influence, however, which is most obvious. Islanders claim they converted to Islam 281 years before Malé, in AH 300 when an Arab ship which had lost its way in the Equatorial Channel landed at Meedhoo. One member of the crew, Yousuff Naib Kalheihaara Thakurufaanu, converted the islanders to Islam.

Meedhoo claims to have sent at least eight *gazis*, the chief interpreters of the law

Opposite: Islanders welcome visitors to Fua Mulaku, the largest and most remote island in Maldives.

Above: Friendly and cheerful, a young girl of Gaafu Dhaalu Atoll.

of the Qur'an, to Malé. There are **seven mosques** on the island and an extremely old **cemetery** called **Koagannu** whose **graves** are still revered. Many have beautifully **carved headstones** — rounded ones denoting a woman and those with a short stub denoting a man — inscribed with **ornamental script**. One grave, more than 400 years old, contains the remains of a famous *gazi*, **Mohamed Shamsuddeen**.

Most inscriptions are written in greyish coral stone, but the more illustrious are burnished with gold. The names are in Arabic and the rest in the ancient Dhivehi script, *Dhives Akuru*, which dates back 600 years.

The ability to carve such intricate and delicate patterns has long been lost. Only a few learned old men can still read the scripts, and many of the beautiful tombstones have been broken. Fortunately, the National Centre for Linguistic and Historical Research now conducts classes to teach *Dhives Akuru*.

Opposite: Beautifully carved tombstone on Meedhoo Island, Seenu Atoll, with early Dhivehi script known as *Dhives Akuru*. Tragically, the Maldivian art of stone carving, once famous throughout the Indian Ocean, has been lost.

PART THREE: SPECIAL FEATURES

Above: Vermilion rock cod takes flight over the reef edge.

Opposite: Skipjack tuna, the backbone of Maldives' economy.

Flora: Under the Whispering Palms

Despite the poor soil and marine environment, a surprising amount of flora grows in Maldives. Most islands are covered with a canopy of green, towering **coconut trees** and luxuriant tropical vegetation. In the south, on Gnaviyani Atoll (Fua Mulaku), the dense foliage reaches almost jungle proportions.

In such a difficult environment, the total flora adds up to only about 600 species, half of which are cultivated. The fully naturalized species number fewer than 260 and, before the islands were settled by humans, probably fewer than 100 existed. Indeed, there are more islands in Maldives than different plants.

What is striking about Maldives is that almost all the common native species of flora are identical to those of the Pacific Ocean in similar habitats some 8,000-16,000 kilometres (5,000-10,000 miles) away — while many are rare or absent in the areas between.

It is thought that the seeds and fruit floated from the Pacific to the Indian Ocean on the prevailing ocean currents and thence to the shores of the Maldive islands. Although the flora of Maldives is by no means unique, it does have five species of the genus *pandanus* which occur nowhere else.

The environment for the plant life comes entirely from broken and crushed coral thrown up on the reefs of the atolls. Wind and waves eventually create a sandbank which remains above water and enables the first salt-resistant plant pioneers to take root.

As the island grows bigger, fresh water collects in the centre, soil evolves, and the habitat becomes more diversified. Older islands develop underlying impervious layers of fine sand and hardened clay which help store fresh water. The mature soils are usually rich in phosphorous and magnesium but low in nitrogen, potash and trace elements.

As a result this means that trees with horizontal roots like the *pandanus* and coconut do well, while deep-rooted trees like **mangoes** need special attention to prevent their long roots from reaching saline water.

Coconuts seldom exceed twenty metres (66 feet). The occasional **banyan tree**, *Ficus benghalensis*, on the other hand, often grows to a towering height, providing a useful navigational landmark for passing mariners.

Ecologically, native plants have grouped themselves into five categories of vegetation, although very few are confined to only one zone. The first are the beach pioneers, of which there are about twenty species. Half of them are **sedges** and **grasses**, known locally as *hui*. The plants tend to be small and salt resistant.

Among the **non-grasses**, *Luanaea sarmentosa* (*kulhlhafilaa*), with its succulent leaves, is constant. Stabilizing grasses such as *Lepturus* or *Thuarea* are widespread along beaches, while in areas being eroded away, the small woody plant *Pemphis acidula* (*kuredhi*) is common, often with its roots revealed at the water's edge.

Going inland, the beach pioneers are followed by a littoral hedge, usually made up of shrubby plants with many branches. The most common of the ten or so widespread species are *Pemphis acidula* (*kuredhi*) and *Scaevola sericea* (*magoo*). The former provide durable dowels to hold coconut planks together in boats; the latter is widely used for firewood.

The hedge on the upper beach is not always clearly defined and often narrow. It gives way to the third zone of sublittoral thicket where small trees begin to grow. This occurs in well-drained areas not overtaken by coconuts.

The constant trees are *Cordia subcordata* (*kaani*), *Guettarda speciosa* (*uni*), *Hibiscus tilaceus* (*dhiggaa*) and *Premna obtusifolia* (*kude*). They rarely grow more than five metres (16 feet) high and are often entwined with climbers. Islanders use them for building the frames of their boats. There are about twenty other common species of

Above: Tropical loveliness of bougainvillea.

shrubs, climbers and shade-tolerant grasses in this area.

In the centre, where rainwater has reduced salinity and soil has evolved, climax forest establishes itself. Trees found in the sublittoral thicket reach maturity there, along with *Hernandia nymphaeifolia* (*kandhu*), **Terminalia catappa** (*midhili*), and on some islands the large *pandanus* or **screwpine** (*kashi keyo*). **Ground orchids** of the genus *eulophia* also occur in the luxuriant vegetation, very similar to the lowland tropical rainforest of Sri Lanka.

The final range of vegetation found on the islands are the **mangrove** and **swamp forests** which occupy water-filled depressions. In more saline areas grow mangrove forests such as *Rhizophora mucronata*, with its long prop roots which establish themselves in rough coral rubble still immersed in sea water. Other mangroves, like *Bruguiera* or *Sonneratia,* also grow in the archipelago.

In the swamp forests where the water is less saline, *Morinda citrifolia* (*ahi*) is common, and the great *Barringtonia*

asiatica (*kinbi*) tree takes root. Mangrove ferns flourish in the more open places.

Cultivated plants

The staple diet of Maldivians is locally caught **fish** and imported **rice**. Unfortunately less than five per cent of the land is fit for arable farming, and even that is poor and infertile. Nevertheless, the islanders manage to grow their main field crops of **black finger millet** (*bimbi*), **Italian millet** (*kudhi-baiy*), and occasionally **sorghum** (*dhonalha*). Although nutritious, they are considered poor man's food.

Sweet potato (*kattala*) and, especially in the south, **taro** or **yam** (*olhu ala*) are the main tubers. **Manioc** or **cassava** (*dhandialuvi*) is grown and **Indian arrowroot** (*hiththala*), which grows wild, is also sometimes cultivated.

Garden vegetables include **chillies** (*mirus*), **small onions** (*kudhi fiyaa*) and fruit such as **watermelon** (*karaa*) and **pineapple** (*alanaasi*). **Breadfruit** (*banbukeyo*) is grown on all settled islands, as is **banana** (*faiy keyo*).

Limes are the most common citrus fruit,

Above: Frangipani, its heady fragrance wafting on the sea breeze.

although oranges thrive on Fua Mulaku in the south. Another valuable plant is **betel** (*bileiy*), which grows like a vine and is often trained up **areca nut palms** (*foah*). A nutritious nut known locally as *kanamadhu* grows wild on many islands.

Medicines are taken from wild and cultivated plants; the local *fanditha* (medicine man) hands down the knowledge from generation to generation (See "The People: A Mix of Many Faces", Part One).

Perfumes are obtained from the roots of the **khus-khus** (*lansimoo*), from the flowers of the endemic *uni,* and from the introduced **frangipani**, **citronella** and **lemon grass**.

The beautiful and intricate **mats** (*kunaa*) in Maldives are made from the stems of native **sedges** (*haiburu*) coloured with dyes obtained from other plants.

One of the most useful trees is the *pandanus*. Sails were once woven from *pandanus* leaves, although today they have been replaced by imported cotton. Screens, walls, mats and roofing are still made from the leaves, as well as a soft-latticed mat about two metres (seven feet) long called a *saanthi*.

It is the **coconut**, however, that is first seen when approaching an island and which is central to the islanders' economy. It is no exaggeration to call the coconut the "tree of life" for the Maldivians. The coconut provides, of course, milk for drinking and cooking, but nothing else is wasted.

Its white pulp is used to make curries and cakes; its fibres are turned into coir; its sap (toddy) is boiled to make a type of syrup; its fronds are woven into *cadjan* for roofs, mats and walls; its trunk provides wood for boats and houses; and anything left over is used as firewood.

As Ibn Battuta pointed out centuries ago, the coconut is one of the strangest trees: "The nut resembles a man's head, for it has marks like eyes and a mouth, and the contents, when it is green, are like the brain. It has fibres like hair. . . . Among its properties are that it strengthens the body, fattens, and adds redness to the face."

Certainly anyone who has been lucky enough to taste the sweet fresh liquid of a young green coconut (*kurunbaa*) will never forget the pleasure. Nothing could be more

Above: Bright hibiscus, one of several common tropical flowers in Maldives.

refreshing after landing on a remote island at midday. However tiring the journey, you feel instantly refreshed and ready to explore. After drinking, the nut can be split open and the soft pulp scraped out.

The method of collecting the toddy or syrup from the tree has not changed for centuries. The toddy tapper, *raaveri*, cuts the stalk from which the fruit grows and ties on a small bowl for the sap, *raa*, to drip into. If done in the morning, the bowl can be emptied in the evening and another bowl may be tied further along the stalk.

The *raa* is then boiled and stirred for several hours until it is reduced to a delicious sweet liquid known as *diyaa hakuru*. If liberal amounts of sugar are added during the process, the toffee-like syrup is called *fathuli hakuru*. The finished product was once exported to India, Yemen and China, but what is not consumed locally nowadays ends up in the Malé market.

Coconut oil is made by peeling the ripe nuts, *kaashi*, and sun-drying the contents. It is then cooked and the oil extracted. The oil is used on the hair, for cooking, as a dip for bread and for lighting.

Above: One of about 600 species of flora in the Maldivian archipelago.

Overleaf: An exuberance of bougainvillea on Nakatchafushi — brilliant in colour but without scent.

Fauna: Land of the Flying Fox

Like all oceanic islands, Maldives has limited wildlife. It is possible, however, that new species await discovery, as little research has been conducted.

Most Maldivian fauna came from the Indian subcontinent via the Lakshadweep Islands or drifting on the north-easterly monsoons. Colonization may have also been borne along from Africa on the south-west monsoon, particularly to the southern atolls.

But down through the millennia interesting divergences have evolved between Maldivian species and those on the mainland. The origins of the islands' fauna is as obscure as that of the people.

Mammals

Local mammalian fauna consists of two species from the **bat family**. The most conspicuous is the **flying fox**, *Pteropus giganteus ariel*, which is found in the highest treetops of the larger islands. It could be a form unique to Maldives. Although it does much damage to the islanders' fruit trees, there is little attempt to destroy their colonies. The other bat recorded is the ***Pteropus hypomelanus maris***, but this small bat has been sighted only once in Seenu Atoll.

Other mammals present in Maldives were introduced from ships: the **black rat**, which does much damage to crops; the **house mouse**, a common pest; and the **Indian house shrew** with its high-pitched call.

Mammals of Maldivian waters are the **whales**, **dolphins** and **dugongs**, the latter indigenous only to the Indian Ocean, Red Sea and Western Pacific.

Approaching Malé in a tiny twenty-five-ton cargo vessel from Colombo, that compulsive sea-traveller Gavin Young, in his book *Slow Boats to China* (1981), described arriving after a hideous night storm at sea, heartened by the "reassuring sight" of dolphins leaping along beside the battered boat.

Above: Playful bottle-nose dolphin, so-called because its head and upper jaw line resemble the shape of early wine bottles.

Reptiles

The **reptiles** on Maldives reflect close links with Sri Lanka, since both share common species. Two nocturnal **house geckos** with large eyes are part of the *Hemidactylus* species, *frenatus* and *brookii* (known as *hoanu* in Dhivehi).

On some islands the **garden lizard** *Calotes versicolor* (*bondu*) is widespread, the males with reddish heads and yellow tails, and the females a duller brownish-grey. Rarer is the **rapid skink**, *Riopa albopunctata* (*garahita*).

At least two types of **snake** exist, both harmless to humans. One is a species of *Tylphus braminus* (*nannugathi*). The other is the **wolf snake**, *Lycodon aulicus capucinus*, which lives in dense vegetation and feeds on **lizards**.

Island reptiles also include a large **toad**, *Bufo melanostictu* (*boh*), and one **frog**, the short-headed *Rana breviceps*.

Older even as a species than the dinosaurs, five species of marine turtle are found in the seas around the islands and atolls of Maldives. In order of size they are the **leatherback**, the **loggerhead**, the **green**, the **hawksbill** and the **olive Ridley**.

The giant **leatherback turtle** (*Dermochelys coriacea*) is the largest living chelonian. Adults measure up to two metres (six to seven feet) across the front flippers and weigh up to 450 kilos (1,000 pounds). The greatest reliably recorded weight is 865 kilos (1,980 pounds). Leatherbacks are said to swim at more than seventy kilometres (43 miles) an hour.

The **loggerhead** (*Caretta caretta*) can weigh up to 408 kilos (900 pounds), is a flesh-eater feeding on sea creatures and molluscs, and may be up to 110 centimetres (just under four feet) in length.

The **green turtle** (*Chelonia mydas*) is entirely vegetarian, living mainly on seaweed and sea plants, and is 100 centimetres or just under four feet long. The young, hatching out from eggs laid on the land, by instinct first have to dig their way upwards out of the sand in which they are buried, and then find their way downward to the sea.

Hawksbill turtles, *Eretmochelys imbricata* are common and, fully grown, reach eighty five centimetres (just over two feet) in length. The females come ashore to lay their eggs in the sand during the months of June through November. During the last ten years there has been a significant drop in the number of these Maldives residents.

The smallest of the five is the sixty centimetre (two-foot) **olive Ridley**.

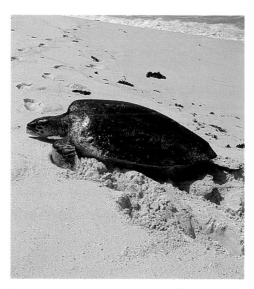

Above: Rare sight as female hawksbill turtles come ashore to lay their eggs in the sand from June through November.

Insects and Arachnids

There has been virtually no research into the insect and arachnid world of Maldives, but a small **scorpion**, with a powerful sting, and a large **centipede**, which uses its adapted front claws to give an aggressive and unpleasant bite, are well known. The large **rhinoceros beetle** causes considerable damage in coconut plantations.

Among the flyers, sixty-seven species of colourful **butterfly** have been identified so far. Very common are **paper wasps**.

Birds

There is a wide variety of **land birds** in Maldives, although as might be expected, **seabirds** are more numerous. At present, about twenty of 113 identified species can be counted as resident.

Of the resident land birds undoubtedly the most common is the **Indian house crow**, *Corvus splendens* (*kaalhu*), which arrived with the first settlers. They were released from the boats when land was considered nigh.

If the crows circled and returned to the ship, then the seafarers were mistaken; if they set off in a straight line, then land was in that direction.

Unfortunately, the crows have now become serious pests in the northern atolls, taking hard-earned fish catches drying in the sun and eating precious fruits and vegetables.

Wherever the crow lives, so does the **koel bird**, *Eudynamys scolopacea*. A member of the cuckoo family, it lays its eggs in crows' nests. The male (*kaalhu koveli*) is shimmering black with a bright green bill, while the female (*dindin koveli*) is spotted, with plumage ranging from brown to black. Its wide repertoire of extraordinary sounds fills the early morning air.

The only member of the **parrot family** living in Maldives is the **rose-ringed parakeet**, *Psittacula krameri*, an introduced bright green bird with a red bill which is now found around Malé and the surrounding islands. The **house sparrow**, which was introduced a decade ago, did not flourish and can only be found in the capital.

The **white-breasted water hen**, *Amaurornis phoenicurus maldivus* (*kambili*), which is a common bird around Alifu Atoll, is usually found in dense vegetation. With its white breast and loud call, this unique bird of Maldives has been classified as a separate race. Another water bird is the **water cock**, *Gallicrex cinerea* (*hulhi kukulhu*), which looks like a large **moorhen**.

The **kestrel**, *Falco tinnunculus* (*surumuthi*), was once considered a visitor but is now seen in Alifu Atoll year-round.

A variety of **migrant birds** pass through the archipelago at different times of the year,

Above: In Maldives, the rare and beautiful fairy tern is found only in Seenu Atoll.

including such birds of prey as **harriers**, **falcons** and even **buzzards**; many being blown off course by the monsoon winds. A large number of **wading birds** visit the islands in the winter, including at least seven species of **plover**, along with **turnstone**, **snipe**, **whimbrel**, **godwit**, **curlew** and **sandpiper**.

Herons are a common sight wading along the outer reefs or seashore. There are thirteen different types, the most common being the large **grey**, *Ardea cinerea rectirostris* (*maakanaa*). Three smaller, rarely seen herons are considered unique to Maldives: the central and paler *Butorides striatus didii* (*raabondhi*) the southern and darker *Butorides striatus albidulus*, and the **pond heron**, *Ardeola rayii phillipsi*.

Top: Grey heron, the most common of Maldives' heron types.
Above: Crab plover, an Indian Ocean speciality.
Overleaf: Taking to the glorious tropical skies of Maldives.

Above: A large grey heron, one of thirteen different types to be found in Maldives, takes off to visit another island. They can often be seen fishing for small fry at the water's edge.

Among the true **seabirds** are more than fifteen types of breeding residents, mostly **seagulls** (*Gaadhooni*) and **terns** (*Kirudhooni*). The rarest and most beautiful is the **white** or **fairy tern**, *Gygis alba* (*kandhu walludooni*), found only in Seenu Atoll in the south.

The story goes that it was introduced by a Muslim saint, and that thanks to the tern there are no crows in the southern atolls. There may well be an element of truth in the legend, since terns mob any darker bird, regardless of its size, that trespasses in their territory.

On the other hand, the tern could have followed the **frigatebird** (*Kurangi* in Dhivehi) from Seychelles. It has settled in small numbers on Huvadhoo Atoll. There are two types of these large black birds with long forked tails that fly so well: the **greater frigatebird**, *Fregata minor*, and the **lesser frigatebird**, *Fregata ariel* (*hoara*).

Unlike the frigatebirds, the **common noddy**, *Anous stolidus pileatus*, and the **lesser noddy**, *Anous tenuirostris* (*naaranga*), are seen throughout the archipelago. Since they gather around shoals of tuna, the Maldivian fishermen keep an eye open for them.

The **white-tailed tropicbird**, *Phaethon lepturus* (*dhandifulhu dooni*), with its long streaming tail feathers, is one of the most distinctive birds that flock to breed on the islands. The **red-billed** and **red-tailed tropicbirds** are also visitors, as is the small **Audubon**'s **shearwater**, *Procellaria iherminieri bailloni* (*hoagulhaa*).

Unfortunately islanders not only make pets of seabirds, but also eat their eggs and flesh. While this forms a much needed addition to their poor diet, it may well threaten the bird numbers. Rarer species, if they are to survive, will need protection in the future.

Marine Life: Maldives Beneath the Sea

Part of a great submerged mountain range that stretches across the Indian Ocean, Maldives is more underwater than above. The islands are the tips of the gigantic coral reefs that have burst through the surface of the sea, but which are in constant danger of sinking back down into the depths.

But whatever happens to the people who for thousands of years have scratched a living from these specks of sand, life in the ocean deep will continue as it has done for aeons.

It seems likely the mountain peaks once formed large volcanic islands high above the water. For millions of years coral grew around them as fringing reefs until the islands began to sink — a combination of erosion, the settling of the sea floor and a rising sea level.

What remained was a ring of coral near the surface — the rim of today's atolls. Islands were created when plants colonized sand bars built up by coral debris (See "The Land and the Sea: Fragile Islands in the Sun", Part One).

Although the shape may vary, each island follows a basic pattern. The centre, thick with green vegetation, gives way to the white coral sand of the beach. This runs into the shallow lagoon where the white sandy bottom turns the water a bright turquoise.

In turn, this gives way to a shallow platform of coral reef — the reef flat — that may dry out at low tides. At the reef edge, the land drops sharply more than a thousand fathoms (6,000 feet) into the vast depths.

Descending the outer reef there is often a sloping terrace to about ten metres (33 feet), a steep escarpment to fifty metres (164 feet), then a sloping fore-reef to ninety metres (295 feet) before the vertical drop to the ocean floor.

Corals

Corals were long thought to be plants because of their similarity to flowers, but in fact they are simple animals in polyp form.

They belong to the same phylum as **anemones** and **jellyfish** and vary in size from under a millimetre to several centimetres. Usually they are shaped like a cylinder with a central mouth which has a ring of poisonous tentacles that sweeps passing microscopic animals into their bodies.

In a remarkable example of symbiosis, many corals also feed on organic compounds leaked by the algae that live within their tissues. Although some colours come from the corals themselves, most of the spectacular reds, greens, yellows and browns that turn the reef into a kaleidoscope of colour are produced by the algae.

There are 200 or so species of coral in Maldives, all influenced by the intensity of the sunlight and the strength of the underwater swell: they tend to be small and delicate in the sandy lagoons, large and robust on the reef edge.

Corals can be both hard and soft. The beautiful soft ones lack an external skeleton. They are fleshy or water-filled, being strengthened by numerous "spicules" in their walls. Although biologically they may be more primitive than their harder cousins, they far surpass them in the brilliance of their colours.

But the hard, stony corals which build the reefs can only live in a narrow zone of warm, clear, sunlit water. During the day the corals are closed. All that can be seen are the hard skeletons and algae. Only at night, when they feed, do they open up and extend their tentacles.

There is great competition between the two different varieties for space on the reef. The hard corals emit toxic chemicals while the soft corals sting with tentacles. Often only a thin line marks the battle zone between the opponents.

From one tiny polyp, mighty things grow. Since it can reproduce asexually as well as sexually, one polyp can begin the construction of a reef. But countless must follow, building on the limestone skeletons of their ancestors over millions of years.

Deposits of calcium-producing algae and encrusting sponges complete the job by cementing the whole to create one of the most productive and beautiful environments on the planet.

Depending on sunlight and wave energy, these tiny creatures create structures of such size, strength, shape and beauty that no human architect can equal them. Fans, leaves, columns, arches and caves are only a fraction of the shapes they form. The very scale and grandeur of a coral reef defies the imagination — it's the nearest thing in the underwater world to the sublime.

Although they build massive structures, only the top part of the coral in sunlit water lives. Growth rates are exceptionally slow, between one and ten centimetres a year. Extremely delicate, corals easily suffer stress because of lack of sunlight, lowered salinity, warmer temperature and, above all, pollution. When this happens the polyps expel the symbiotic algae from their tissues and the coral becomes bleached.

If a swimmer breaks a piece of coral by walking or holding on to the reef, he can also kill part of the colony. Even touching the living coral removes a slimy mucous that protects it from infection and falling sediment. The white, featureless desert of dead coral near some of Maldives' most popular diving sites is tragic. The reef can regenerate, of course, and even protect itself, but only to a limited extent.

Dangers of the reef

Fire coral, a hydroid that secretes a stony skeleton, can give a nasty sting. Many **anemones** and **jellyfish** do not encourage close contact. **Sea urchins** have sharp spines that can even pierce a wet suit. But the most dangerous invertebrate is a member of the *Conus* species, a shell which can instantly poison a fish with its proboscis.

Symbiosis

In this wonderful underwater world, marine life has achieved a remarkable equilibrium. While all species live off each other, there are many different types of symbiotic relationships. Some, like the little bugs or isopods that live on fish, are parasitical. Others are more commensal, as in the case of the **pilot fish**, for example, which saves energy by riding the shark's bow wave and picking up its scraps.

An interesting example of symbiosis and mutual benefit is seen in the **clownfish**, which lives among the tentacles of the giant **anemone**. While poisonous to other fish, the tentacles act like protective arms for the clownfish.

In return the fish "feeds" its host scraps of food and attacks any marauding creatures. In Dhivehi clownfish are called *saiboani mas*, or soap fish, referring to the slimy covering which probably protects them from being stung by the tentacles of the anemones.

Cleaning is another mutually beneficial habit developed by certain fishes and shrimps. A prime example is the bright blue-striped cleaner **wrasse** which lives by picking parasites, dead skin and scales from other fish.

Two or three will often position themselves on coral outcrops along the upper reef slope waiting for customers to come to their "cleaning stations". **Groupers**, **eels** and **barracuda** — which could easily snap them up — allow the tiny fish to forage in their open mouths. Divers may even find one trying to nibble their ear.

The most important example of symbiosis in the reef, however, is that between the **algae** and the **hard corals**. The algae live in a protected environment and use the waste products of the polyp while producing oxygen and nutrient compounds for the coral. Coral can exist without algae, but without it they could never build huge atolls and great barrier reefs.

Reef fish

The reef fish of Maldives are divided into herbivores and carnivores. Although seaweed grows fast on the reefs in the warm

Opposite: Butterflyfish exploring a coral grotto. Since fish orientate themselves to the nearest rocks by a ventral line along their underside, they often swim upside down when close to an overhang.

Above: Grey reef sharks, a common sight in Maldives, but not dangerous because of the abundance of marine life.

waters of the Indian Ocean, it is immediately cropped back by the herbivorous fish.

The most common and fascinating are the **parrotfish**, so called because of their beaks, bright colours and "flapping" manner of swimming.

While scraping off thin layers of algae and other organic matter, they take in large amounts of coral rock which is then ground down by powerful sets of teeth.

After digesting the organic material they excrete puffs of coral sand — the main building block of the islands — an average of fourteen kilos a year per fish. Another feature which they share with many other fish is the ability to change sex as they grow older.

Another conspicuous herbivore is the **surgeonfish** with its scalpel-like blades on the sides of its tail. Although they may seem destructive, the herbivores do a useful job by breaking down plant material for other creatures. They also prevent the reef from becoming overgrown with plants that would cut out the sunlight and check the growth of the corals.

Most reef fish, however, are carnivorous, or at least omnivorous. The **butterflyfish** are specialized carnivores which feed on small animals, including coral polyps, along the reef edge and slope with their perfectly adapted snouts and teeth. On the other hand the smaller and more solitary **angelfish** feed mainly on **sponges**.

Broadly speaking, the carnivores of the Maldivian reefs may be divided into plankton eaters and ambush or roving predators.

Plankton consists of minute plants and animals that float in open water. During the day these are not visible to the naked eye, but at night they can sometimes be seen shining phosphorescent in the wake of a boat or a dolphin.

Some of the most common fish living off plankton are the **fusilier** and the **bannerfish**, which form large schools during the day in the open water. At night they take refuge in holes in the reef, when such nocturnal species as the **batfish, large-eyed soldierfish** and **squirrelfish** come out to eat.

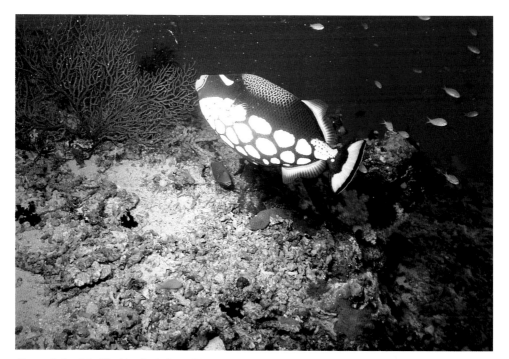

Above: Colourful white-blotched triggerfish, which scrapes algae and coral from the reef and excretes puffs of coral sand.

Plankton in the sea around Maldives increases during the south-west monsoon when the wind blows the local waters eastwards and an upwelling of nutrient-rich water occurs, causing the ocean to take on a greyish haze. The result is a bloom of plankton eaten by schools of small fish.

This is the best time to see the large filter feeders like the **manta rays**, which browse near the eastern reefs. Ancient mariners called them "Devil Rays" because of their "horns" that scoop plankton into their wide mouths.

Welling up like spectres from the mighty deep, these black shadows glide and hover over the reef to be groomed by innumerable cleaner fish. Mantas measure up to four metres (13 feet) across, dwarfing the frail diver. They appear gentle and caring, lifting a wing over a diver's head as they go by in an apparent gesture of sympathy.

Another visitor from the deep is the **whale shark**, the largest fish in the world. It too is a gentle giant, filter feeding on plankton and small animals.

The ambush or "lie-in-wait" predators are among the most extraordinary and dangerous fish of all. They float motionless until a shrimp or fish passes by and then grab it with blurring speed.

Varieties include the **hawkfish, lionfish, lizardfish, scorpionfish**, and **stonefish** — whose names all reflect their appearance. To avoid being eaten themselves, while quietly waiting to eat, some sedentary fellows like the **stonefish** and **scorpionfish** camouflage themselves so well that it is easy to mistake them for bits of coral. They have also developed a row of poisonous spines along their backs which causes severe pain when touched.

Another form of protection is seen in the case of the poisonous **puffer**, which inflates itself with large quantities of water when threatened. This is also done by the **porcupinefish** which has, as its name suggests, the additional defence of a spine-covered body.

One of the most graceful carnivores is the **spotted eagle ray**, which glides effortlessly through the water, soaring along with a few slow flaps of its wings. It feeds along

Above: Hawksbill turtle, once common in Maldives but now endangered because of their capture for food and jewellery.

---

the reef slope and in the atoll lagoons on crustaceans and molluscs.

Two or three **reef sting rays** can often be found lying on the sandy bottom of a cave in the coral slope; they are best left alone, since they may lash out with the venomous spine at the base of the tail.

Moray eels are usually considered very dangerous, and can reach up to a metre and a half (five feet). As they open their mouths to breathe in and out, the eels reveal sharp, inward-pointing teeth.

Yet in Maldives they often seem quite tame. Diving instructors get to know their daytime hideaways in the reef and stroke their soft slimy necks; they sway their heads in sensual pleasure and slowly their bodies emerge. Nevertheless, their apparent calm can be deceptive. At night they come out to look for prey. Their sense of smell is well-developed and they scavenge as well as take fish.

Maldivian fishermen hate to catch a moray eel on their hooks; with their powerful body and strong teeth they can fight a long time at the bottom of a boat.

Barracuda also have a bad reputation. Certainly they have very nasty teeth and are often curious. But they seldom attack in clear water unless, perhaps, a swimmer wears bright jewellery or flashes the white soles of their feet — which might be mistaken for tasty morsels.

Among the roving predator fish, the **bluefin jack** is a fierce customer. They usually hunt in small groups along the reef slope, but sometimes dash into the lagoon after a shoal of small fish (which have been known to beach themselves in their frenzy to escape).

By schooling, fish find safety in numbers. Many eyes are better than two in spotting would-be predators. Schooling also reduces the amount of energy needed for swimming.

Speed is related to size, so schools usually include fish of a similar age in order to move together. When a larger predatory fish attacks, they bunch up and move in the same direction with great precision, swirling around to create confusion.

To be successful, the predator has to single out a particular fish and attack it. Some predators hunt in groups for greater efficiency when stalking a school.

Fish orientate themselves by a sensory lateral line that runs the length of their body. This enables them to move with great dexterity and speed in the middle of a school without bumping into each other. They also have a ventral line along their underside that enables them to orientate themselves to the nearest rocks; they will often swim upside down with ease under the ceiling of a cave or overhang.

Sharks

The most spectacular predator in Maldives, and the one that many come to see, is the **shark**. As a scavenger and a hunter, it has an extremely strong sense of smell and can pick up the scent of blood many kilometres downstream. Its hearing is also acute, but it cannot see well — a result of living in the dim light many metres deep.

To witness a shark attack is an awesome sight. It's a creature of great power and grace, but unlike the dolphin, seems to have little desire to play or communicate. It's such a fierce and voracious predator that it becomes frenetic at the smell and taste of blood. When injured, sharks have been known to snap at their own entrails.

Nearly all human beings have a primordial fear of being dragged under water by some terrifying creature from the deep — a fear used to good effect by Jules Verne in *20,000 Leagues Under the Sea*, but with mischievous results in films like *Jaws*.

The idea of a shark darting up to grab the legs of an unsuspecting swimmer has become associated with all manner of deep psychological fears about predators and drowning.

Yet sharks have been unjustly maligned. Only the **great whites**, which have sea mammals as a large part of their diet, are a potential danger. The sharks in Maldives are especially friendly.

After the initial shock, you soon get used to them. They are rarely aggressive since their normal food supply is so abundant.

But the local ones are best left alone, like all sharks, as they may become hostile if

Above: Delicate coral fan, one of the 200 or more species in Maldives.

people splash about or corner them. If a shark looks as if it is going to attack, with nose lowered, pectoral fins sharply down, and swimming fast, the best thing to do is back off slowly and calmly — to flee only triggers their hunting instinct.

Divers advise hitting an attacking shark on the nose with something hard, getting them to bite on a plastic fin rather than a tasty arm and, as a last resort, gouging out their eyes with a thumb (although to have the *sang-froid* to do this while being torn apart seems unlikely).

In Maldives the most common sharks are the **white-tip reef shark** and the smaller **nurse shark**. They will only attack if provoked. The **grey reef shark** grow little more than two metres (seven feet), but come in shoals of a dozen or more. These are the sharks that intrepid divemasters in Maldives have fed mouth-to-mouth. The beautiful **silver-tip** makes a rarer and more

Above: Blue surgeonfish, nocturnal feeders of the reef.

memorable appearance, although the **whale shark** is fairly common on the easterly coral reefs during the south-west monsoon.

Turtles

Maldives was once famous for its turtles, especially the **hawksbill**. These ante-diluvian omnivores eat almost anything, including coral and can easily swim fifty kilometres (30 miles) an hour; the **giant leatherback** reaches up to seventy-four kilometres (46 miles) an hour.

Unfortunately the local taste for turtle omelettes and flesh, coupled with the tourist demand for tortoiseshell jewellery, has led to a serious drop in numbers, despite the fact that turtles lay vast numbers of eggs in excavated pits on the beach.

Between the months of June and November one female may return three or four times to lay up to a thousand eggs in different nests.

Dolphins and whales

Dolphins are abundant in Maldives and large schools are often seen leaping out of the water between the atolls or sporting along the edge of the reef.

The most common is the dark grey **bottlenose dolphin**, identifiable by its long and broad beak. Feeding on fish and crustaceans, these mammals offer no danger to divers. But where dolphins interact with people in other seas, in Maldives they tend to disappear when approached. They have not yet been tamed. Perhaps it is better that way.

For centuries Maldives has been re-nowned for the **ambergris** that comes from the intestinal tract of the **sperm whale**. Sometimes found floating in the sea, this white, grey or black substance, used to manufacture perfumes and cosmetics, is a great discovery for islanders and fetches a very high price. Carcasses of dead whales also wash up on the reefs from time to time.

Shells

The reefs are teeming with countless other creatures, including 5,000 different species of shell, which tend to be active at night and rest during the day. While **cowries** and **nautilus shells** are abundant, **conch, pearl**

Above: A fast-moving school of jacks, often found at the entrances through the coral reefs.

and **trident shells** are becoming rare, though still available in tourist shops.

Although not as dangerous as the **cone** shells, the most impressive shell is undoubtedly the **giant triton**, which lives off **starfish** and other **crustacea**. It grows to almost half a metre (1.5 feet), and its shell is still used on some islands to call villagers to meetings.

Cowries, *Cyprea moneta*, are the most famous, of course, used for centuries as money by the countries adjoining the Indian Ocean. The special lustre on their colourful and neat shapes comes from minute chalk algae exuded by their mantles.

At one time they were cultivated on large bushes of palm leaves tied together and cast into the sea. The molluscs were then pulled off and placed in pits on land where the flesh disappeared, leaving only the white shell.

Some cowries have been found in burial sites from 1500 BC in the Indus Valley harbour city of Lothal. By AD 600 they had reached Norway. In the early eleventh century the Arab traveller Al-Biruni records that the Maldivian archipelago was called the "Cowrie Islands". Three centuries later Ibn Battuta came across cowries in West Africa (See "History: The Legend and the Mystery", Part One).

Maldivians exchanged them with the people of Bengal, who used them as money for rice, as well as with sailors from Yemen, who used them as ballast in their ships.

Ma Huan, a Chinese Muslim who travelled with Cheng Ho's celebrated expedition to East Africa in 1433, noted that Maldivian cowries were sold in Thailand as well as Bengal.

The Portuguese Joao de Barros also noted in 1563 how important Maldives cowries were in the maritime commerce of the day:

"With these shells for ballast many ships are laden for Bengal and Siam, where they are used for money, just as we use small copper money for buying things of little value.

"And even to this kingdom of Portugal, in some years as much as two or three thousand quintals [100-150 tonnes] are brought by way of ballast; they are then

exported to Guinea, and the kingdoms of Benin and Congo, where they are used for money, the Gentiles of the interior in those parts making their treasure of it."

During the eighteenth century the cowries began to lose their value around the Indian Ocean as a medium of exchange. Yet at the turn of this century, cowries were still a common currency among the islands of Maldives. Each man on the island of Isdhoo, for example, had to pay an 18,000 cowrie tax for himself and his wife to the sultan.

Crabs

Anyone landing at a jetty of coral rubble, or walking along the foreshore at night, will immediately become aware of the enormous number of crabs which live between sand and foam as well as in the sea.

Hermit crabs abound, making use of the colourful shells for their portable homes. The **ghost crab** is common on the beaches of every island, undermining the sand with its burrows.

Keep a wary eye out for the small **porcelain crab** and its one enormous pincer. Fortunately the massive and aggressive **land crab** is largely confined to the mangrove swamps of the far north.

Visitors who fear crabs should remember, however, that if it were not for them the beautiful **crab plovers** would not be so numerous along the white coral beaches.

Ecology

While the Indian Ocean is the least polluted sea in the world, and Maldives has no major industrial pollution, there are growing threats to some of the marine life and coral reefs.

The greatest immediate problem comes from coral mining. Until this century islanders used *cadjan* for their homes, but it is now a status symbol to have a solid house and surrounding walls made from coral fragments.

Throughout the archipelago many half-built coral houses await completion by the owner who is away earning more money to buy more coral. The resort islands have copied this coral style for most buildings.

Building coral is taken from the top two metres (seven feet) of the reefs surrounding the islands, thereby killing off the coral-building polyps. A weakened coral reef makes the islands increasingly vulnerable to storms and tidal surges. In 1986 cracks were observed in the reef around Malé, the one most under stress.

Aware of the danger, the government is now encouraging the use of cement bricks, but that demands expensive imported cement and local sand, which is by no means limitless. As the population increases and tourism expands, the situation is likely to worsen.

Other human activities have also upset the natural equilibrium. The building of jetties and harbours on small islands prevents the natural circular movement of sand around the islands according to the monsoons, resulting in erosion on some sides and unwelcome deposits on others.

The leaching of waste water on inhabited islands has also encouraged the growth of weeds along the shores.

The ecological problems facing the islands are not all man-made. A coral reef is an extremely delicate and carefully balanced ecosystem. In Maldives the reefs suffer from heavy rainfall (which dilutes the salinity of the sea), strong wave action, and exposure to the sun at exceptionally low tides. In some areas these factors have led to extensive coral bleaching.

The greatest hope is that the Maldivian people, who have begun to plant trees to consolidate the sand of their islands, will recognize that their life depends on the health of the coral reefs that protect them.

While tourists have undoubtedly contributed to the degradation of the local environment in the past, they are increasingly eager to preserve and protect the unique marine wilderness of Maldives. After all, it's what they come to see and enjoy. As more people begin to appreciate the underwater world, then hopefully the

Opposite: Oriental sweetlips glide over the coral reef.

Above: A poisonous lionfish making a rare foray into open water from its home around the coral reef.

chances of preserving the beautiful and unique environment of Maldives will improve.

Crown-of-thorns

In recent times the reefs have also had to contend with an infestation of **crown-of-thorns starfish**, but it is not yet the major threat that it is in Australia's Great Barrier Reef. The crown-of-thorns starfish, a large spiny creature, feeds on reef-building corals and can reach plague proportions.

The first outbreaks in Maldives were reported in Alifu Atoll in the mid 1970s. More recently there has been an alarming outbreak north-west of North Malé Atoll where reef-building coral on several reefs has been killed.

Some scientists suggest that the sudden appearance of the crown-of-thorns results from human interference with the eco-system, coral mining and removing the giant triton shell predator. Others postulate that sudden changes in the environment precipitate the infestation.

There is little agreement on the possible long-term effects. Indeed, others again argue that it's part of a natural cycle, only observed since the advent of diving and may well have a long-term benefit by removing fast-growing coral, thereby maintaining the diversity of the coral communities. Until that is proven, the northern part of Malé Atoll appears seriously threatened.

Threatened species

Human activity is beginning to affect other species of marine life. When the country first opened its doors to tourists many divers plundered the reefs for shells, but this has now been banned. So have spear fishing and the removal of any marine life from the waters around the resort islands.

It's still possible, however, to buy tortoiseshell jewellery, which has led to a serious decline in turtle numbers, and

Opposite: A lone butterflyfish, shadowed by a school of other fish, surveys the bewitching underwater world of Maldives, one of the richest marine ecosystems in the world.

Above: Spawn of the exotic spanish dancer in Maldives' underwater gardens.

jewellery made from black coral, which has resulted in the virtual disappearance of this rare coral from the islands around Malé.

As far as fishing is concerned, only sea cucumbers and lobsters seem to be in decline because of excessive catches. It is, of course, tuna — the skipjack and yellowfin variety — which the Maldivians eat and export. Despite increased catches brought about by mechanized boats and freezer ships, tuna stocks seem to be holding up, mainly because Maldivian fishermen still use the traditional pole and line method to catch them.

Both species of tuna, however, are migratory, travelling across the Indian Ocean from Seychelles to Sri Lanka. Although Maldives has a 333-kilometre (200-mile) exclusive zone around its islands, it cannot control the fishermen from Japan, Korea and Taiwan who have been long-lining in the region for tuna since the 1950s.

More recently, French and Spanish purse seine trawlers operating from Seychelles have been sweeping up schools of tuna. As stocks decline in the Atlantic, there can be no doubt about the increasing pressure on the Indian Ocean species during the next few years.

Global warming

The greatest long-term threat to Maldives comes from global warming. It is now well-known that at the present rate industrial gas emissions will warm up the globe in what is known as the "greenhouse effect". In turn, this will lead to a melting of the ice caps and a consequent rise in sea level.

Scientists predict that water levels could rise as much as twenty-four to thirty-eight centimetres (9-15 inches) within the next forty years — a catastrophic increase for this island nation. In addition, most islands are cup-shaped with a low centre, and some, like Malé, are actually sinking. Even

Opposite: A pair of red lionfish size each other up. These colourful predators are highly poisonous.

217

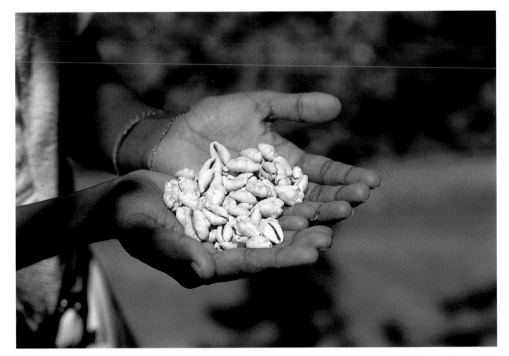

Above: Cowrie shells which grow in abundance around the islands. They were once widely used as small units of money. Maldivian cowries have been found as far afield as West Africa and northern Scandinavia.

an increase of a few centimetres would make the islands more vulnerable to surging tides and sudden storms.

Not everybody agrees with this scenario. Optimists point out that fast-growing, "catch-up" coral reefs can expand ten centimetres (four inches) a year and should be able to keep pace with the expected rise in sea level.

Unfortunately, most of the protective reefs around the islands grow slowly — the slowest a mere one centimetre every ten years. Moreover, fast corals grow where the current is weakest and the threat the least.

Even if enough coral grows to keep pace with the rise in the ocean, just as worrying are the climatic changes associated with global warming. The aberrant weather pattern known as *El Niño*, previously thought to be confined to the southern Pacific, now seems to affect the Indian Ocean, resulting in more storms.

It is all very well to say, "Don't worry. Nature knows best and will somehow take care of itself." There can be no doubt that a coral reef has a remarkable capacity to heal itself; any diver who has seen coral growing over a bottle can confirm this. The reef is a living organism and the whole is far greater than the sum of its parts. But with the present level of human interference, there is little room for nature to work its healing ways.

One day in the not-too-distant future, storm-driven waves on an exceptionally high tide may well sweep across the islands and wash them all away. If this were to happen, it would be the direct result of industrialized man's rapacious exploitation of the earth's resources. Unless they change their way of life at home, the tourists who flock to Maldives today to enjoy a touch of unspoiled "tropical paradise" will be directly responsible for its demise.

The poet John Donne once wrote: "No man is an island, entire of itself". In our fragile and polluted world, no island, however small, remains self-contained. If the islands of Maldives were to disappear, we would all be the less.

Underwater Maldives: Raptures of the Deep

Maldives is one of the great diving centres in the world with all the perfect ingredients: desert islands, warm and clear waters, thriving coral reefs and an unlimited variety of marine life. Its turquoise lagoons and magnificent coral drop-offs make it an ideal place to begin to appreciate the beauties of this quiet and slow-moving "inner universe".

The most striking impression is the sheer number and variety of fish, all with beautiful patterns and marvellous colours. There are well over a thousand species of fish, more than half of which are seen regularly on the reefs.

At first the swirling confusion of fish is overwhelming, but with careful observation you can begin to identify the different species: the groupers, fusiliers, sweetlips, butterflyfish, angelfish, surgeonfish, parrotfish, and puffers. Then there are the unforgettable encounters with sharks, manta rays and moray eels.

It takes longer to appreciate the different species of coral, but is equally worth the effort. Maldives is one of the world's richest coral areas, comparable only with the Philippines and Australia's Great Barrier Reef.

There are more than 200 different species of hard coral alone, but it is the shapes that they form which make them so amazing: caverns, fans, shafts, canyons and boulders. In the clear, sunlit water they form a kaleidoscope of colour enhanced by myriad fish moving in and out of the nooks and crannies of the reef.

So beautiful is this underwater world that at first it's difficult to know where to look. Many divers are inclined to drift or flip from patch to patch on the reef, looking for ever more breathtaking shapes and colours. If you want to unravel the reef's secrets, however, you should remain in one place. Travelling fast over the reef is like flying over the Amazon forest instead of walking through it.

Physical conditions

The year-round temperature in the waters of Maldives is a constant 20°–30°C (68°–86°F), with the lagoons often reaching 32°C (90°F). The calmest seas and bluest skies are from November to May, when the winds are north-westerly and the currents outside the atolls run west to east at an average of twenty-four metres (80 feet) a minute.

The roughest seas are experienced during June, and sometimes in October or early November, when strong winds blow from the north-east and currents run east to west at thirty metres (100 feet) a minute.

The best underwater visibility occurs towards the end of the north-west monsoon, from March to April, when forty metres (130 feet) is normal. On some occasions it is possible to see seventy metres (230 feet) down the coral edge. But in April, when plankton begins to bloom, the visibility is reduced to about twenty metres (66 feet). Nonetheless, this is possibly the most interesting time on the eastern side of the atolls, for the plankton-rich waters attract manta rays and whale sharks.

Local visibility is also affected by the rise and fall of the tide: incoming tides bring clear water, while the falling tide is filled with plankton and sediments.

To appreciate the full beauty of the corals and fish, bear in mind the effects of water on sunlight. Because of the refraction of light through water, objects seem closer and larger than they really are. Colours also change. As the diver descends deeper, more light is filtered out by water, absorbing different colours at different rates.

Within the first five metres (16 feet) all reds disappear and red coral appears black. Orange appears black within ten metres (32 feet), yellow will be completely absorbed by twenty metres (66 feet) and green by twenty-five metres (82 feet). The last colour to go is blue. It therefore makes sense to take a torch on any dive to bring out the true colours of the marine environment.

Above: Vermilion rock cod, lonely dweller of the reef.

Snorkeling

To appreciate this underwater world you don't have to be a professional diver. All you need is a silicone mask to keep out the saltwater and improve your vision.

Maldives is an ideal place to learn snorkeling, mask on face, fins on feet and air tube in mouth. By these simple devices you can enter the magical world beneath the surface. It's like being in a brightly lit aquarium full of the most exotic tropical fish.

First-time snorkelers can discover the sheer delight of floating in warm water, where every move is effortless. To wallow in a shallow lagoon with the sun on your back and the white coral sand below is one of the most euphoric experiences.

To swim for the first time through a channel in the coral reef is breathtaking. The coral edge suddenly drops away to the unknown deep, like suddenly going over an abyss in a dream. But instead of hurtling forever downward you drift and glide like an aircraft. Resist the

impulse to return to the lagoon, it's perfectly safe, despite the lurking shadows of big fish and sharks deep down by the coral face.

Scuba diving

With such amazing coral reefs and wide variety of marine life, it's not surprising that Maldives has become top of the list of the world's great diving destinations. Most resort islands run well-equipped diving centres with excellent instructors who know their patch in Maldives like the backs of their hands.

The schools offer "resort courses": three lessons that show what it's like to dive in tepid, crystal-clear waters off iridescent reefs surrounded by schools of fish.

To obtain a professional qualification like the PADI Open Water Course, which enables the holder to obtain air tanks and dive anywhere in the world, takes about twelve dives, along with a written and practical examination. Any able-bodied person should pass it without too much effort.

The minimum skills necessary to undertake a diving course are:

- Swim 200 metres (656 feet) without swimming aids.
- Swim at least twelve metres (40 feet) underwater.
- Tread water for at least five minutes.
- Float with a minimum amount of movement for at least five minutes.
- Dive to a depth of three metres (10 feet), recover a two-kilo (4.2-pound) object, and return to the surface.

Wilderness diving

Because Maldives is so popular as a diving centre, there is no "wilderness diving" near the resort islands. As many as 1,000 people — ten per cent of the tourist population — dive each day and many sites, which are shared by several resorts, become overcrowded.

At Banana Reef near Bandos, for example, up to sixty divers a day go down. This means the thud of boats can sometimes be heard overhead and on some parts of the reef divers suddenly appear like a shoal of sharks.

If a few sting rays are discovered lying in the sand of a little cave, over-eager spectators jostle each other with cameras, disturbing the fish and damaging the coral. It is particularly upsetting for the quiet diver who does not want to impress his friends with his feats but simply wishes to enjoy the privilege of underwater life.

The best way to experience a wilderness dive is to hire a yacht-*dhoani* and head off with an experienced skipper, *keyolhu*, to the outer atolls. There, off real desert islands, you will find coral reefs that have remained undisturbed for centuries (See "Diving Guide to Maldives," Part Two).

Night diving

Diving in Maldivian waters at night with lights is unsurpassed. When the sun sets, corals open up and extend their flower-like tentacles, spiders and shrimps leave their tubular sponges to search for food and moray eels, along with the other nocturnal predators, prowl the deep, dark depths.

But visibility, excellent by day, is reduced to the narrow tunnel of light from your torch — and bumping into a shark hunting by moonlight may be unnerving.

Shark feeding

One of the great attractions of Maldives for divers used to be the shark feeds, first made famous by a German photographer named Herwath Voightmann on Bandos Island. The fashion caught on and soon five locations became popular — the house reef on Bandos, Lion's Head in the Vaadhoo Channel, Banana Split near Furana, Rasfaree near Nakatchafushi and Fish Hole in Alifu Atoll.

Voightmann dressed up as an underwater superman and fed sharks mouth-to-mouth. A more notorious human "shark" who turned up in the archipelago was Richard Harley, a lawyer who staged a diving accident in the Bahamas after being convicted of taking over US$300,000 in bribes. Interpol at last caught up with him — yes, you guessed it, feeding sharks!

The knack is to feed large fish, so when the food is in the shark's mouth, there's no room for heads or hands. But tuna sends sharks into a feeding frenzy and it's preferable to use different fish.

It is still possible to see a shark feed, but the event is becoming rarer for several reasons. Firstly, there is the danger. Secondly, there is the damage done to the sharks themselves: touching a shark can harm its protective body covering, making it prone to infection.

And finally, feeding changes a shark's natural behaviour, not only making it a lazy feeder but training it to associate divers with food.

With the growing ecological awareness among divers in recent years, shark feeding is now discouraged. It is better to observe the underwater world in Maldives as it is, without human interference, particularly

Overleaf: A school of orange butterfly perch, living off the myriad hard and soft corals which make Maldives such a rich underwater habitat.

Above: Shoal of chocolate surgeonfish surging over a coral outcrop.

as it is one of the last underwater "wildernesses". In keeping with this spirit, the Maldivian government officially discourages the so-called "shark circuses", and Herwath Voightmann has moved on.

Diving philosophy

The best way to appreciate the underwater world of Maldives is to go slowly, conserving energy and looking around carefully. Nothing compares with a slow drift along a reef edge, the gentle current carrying the buoyant diver along, an honorary fish among fish, a harmless observer of the environment. There is so much unearthly beauty that afterwards many divers find it difficult to remember the exact details of all they have seen. They just recall a sense of deep contentment and peace.

Humans, of course, are land animals. But if evolutionists are right, all life began in water, so it is no surprise that many feel at home once they have learned basic underwater survival.

Many establish relationships with the fish. Dolphins are famous for offering life-changing experiences, but even moray eels, with their doleful eyes, impart a certain knowledge and mutual empathy. Dolphins tend to keep to themselves in Maldives, but some diving instructors are emphatic that they have communicated with turtles.

Restrictions and dangers

Maldives maintains a maximum diving depth of forty metres (131 feet), but some resorts have introduced their own limit of thirty metres (98 feet). To go deeper, especially in clear, warm water, is a constant temptation. It is fatally easy to succumb to an excess of nitrogen in the blood, which induces the "raptures of the deep".

The overwhelming sense of wellbeing and power leads the most experienced diver to lose all caution and care. In such a happy-go-lucky state, divers have been known to offer the regulator of their air supply to a passing fish. The feeling of elation is soon followed by confusion. Each year, experienced divers and even instructors the world over disappear, drawn ever deeper by the lure of the ocean.

Diving Guide to Maldives

It is possible, of course, to dive off any reef and discover the stunning world that waits underwater. During the last two decades certain sites have become famous; the main ones, inevitably, are close to the resort islands around Malé. These include:

Banana Split, close to **Furana** in **North Malé Atoll**, a popular spot with beginners. The twenty-metre-high (66-foot) cone-like **reef** reaches to within three metres (10 feet) below the surface.

Barracuda Giri is a **seamount** that rises from the floor of the **North Malé Atoll** lagoon. Its great variety makes it one of the best dives within the **fringing reef**. The seamount is divided by a canyon and a **huge pinnacle** adorned with **soft corals** at the **northern edge** of the site. Not only barracuda can be seen there, but also white-tip reef sharks, jacks and tuna. Closer to the coral, lionfish, clownfish and triggerfish abound.

Blue Lagoon is situated near a **thin spur** of **reef** that extends from the **island** of **Girifushi** towards the **inside** of **North Malé Atoll**. On either side there are shallow areas with slight currents and **hard corals**. The sun reflecting on the white coral sand creates the effect of a "blue lagoon". The sand gently slopes down an island of coral eighteen metres (59 feet) deep. Multitudes of reef fish graze among the hard corals which form a series of rolling **valleys** and **plateaux**.

Coral Garden is near the **same spur of reef** as Blue Lagoon. There are two main areas of interest. A large **mound** of **star coral** at one end is home to many friendly eels, groupers, rock cod and sting ray. Further towards Girifushi, the reef creates a **protective bowl** with a fantastic growth of delicate **hard corals**, some looking like fairytale castles, others like giant mushrooms.

Emboodhoo Wall in **South Malé Atoll** stretches from **Vaadhoo** to **Emboodhoo resort islands**. It has at least **five** major **diving sites** that include sheer **drop-offs** and **magnificent caverns**. These include the **Canyon** with its radiant yellow sponges on the walls and nurse sharks lying on the bottom in the current.

A series of spectacular **caverns** with soft corals to the **south** is called the **Devil's Lair**.

Further along is the **Cathedral**, a huge **cavern** eighty metres (262 feet) long and fifteen metres (49 feet) high with several **alcoves**.

Running **south**, the fringing **reef** forms a series of colourful **vertical walls** divided by stretches of sloping reef that are called the **Palisades**.

The section of **reef** stretching **south** to the **mouth** of the **Emboodhoo Channel** is called **Fusilier Reef** after the schools of fusiliers that congregate there to feed on the plankton brought in by currents along the channel. In turn they are prey for skipjack and yellowfin tuna which often arrive in large numbers.

Emboodhoo Express is the name of the **channel** entering **South Malé Atoll** towards **Emboodhoo Island**. During the winter monsoon the fast-moving current carries divers at a rapid clip over two kilometres (1.25 miles) of unforgettable **reef** among eagle rays, tuna, Napoleon wrasses and schools of fusiliers. When the current is weak, the **soft corals** near the mouth of the channel can be explored.

The Entrance lies between **Furana** and **Farukolhufushi** in **North Malé Atoll** on an **undulating sea bed** with several **gullies** and gradual **drop-offs**. Many clownfish can be seen against a profusion of yellow and pink anemones.

Hanna's Reef lies about a kilometre **west** of **Kandu Oiy Giri**. It begins in just three metres (10 feet) of water at the top of a **sandy slope** that descends gently to a large mound with splendid **soft corals**, twenty-seven metres (89 feet) below the surface. There are many **small caves** in the **western**

Above: A bewitching encounter on Maldives' coral reefs between a scuba diver and a parrotfish.

reef wall which is washed by the mild current.

Kandu Giri is the **outer reef** near **Kandu Oiy Giri**, featuring flourishing **soft corals** and shoals of sweetlips, red bass, coral trout and grouper.

Lion's Head is the most famous of the shark-feeding sites. It is named after a **coral outcrop** shaped like a lion's head that stares out into the **Vaadhoo Channel** and is part of the **North Malé Atoll outer reef**.

The sharks are grey reef, a common species around Maldives. They are only one and a half to two metres (5-7 feet) long, but at any time as many as fifteen can emerge from a depth of about eighty metres (262 feet).

The dead coral on the rough slope about twelve metres (39 feet) deep, where spectators sat and watched shark feeding, shows the resulting degradation of the environment.

Maagari, located **north-west** of **Furana** in **North Malé Atoll**, is a series of **caves** with wonderful **fan-shaped corals**.

Maldive Victory is the name of the 100-metre-long (328-foot) **freighter** that went down on Friday the Thirteenth, 1981, to the sandy bottom of Malé's **outer harbour** after hitting the **south-west edge** of **Hulhule Island**. Strong currents sweep across the hydroid-infested **wreck** which lies upright forty metres (131 feet) deep. A skilled diver can explore the **cabin** areas and **holds**. The wreck is buoyed.

Manta Point is on the **outer reef** wall beyond **Lankanfushi**, where the reef crests at fifteen metres (49 feet), then slopes down to an edge which plunges more than a thousand fathoms. As its name suggests, the site is renowned for manta rays.

They gather there at "cleaner stations", where tiny fish which inhabit the large mounds of **star coral** come out to remove parasites from their skins and gills. If small

Opposite: Spectacular pink coral transforms the reef into an aquatic garden.

groups of divers keep low and about ten metres (33 feet) away, these giant spectres from the deep do not seem to mind.

Whale sharks, the largest fish in the world, can also be seen at this point. Like the manta rays, they only come to feed between July and October (and sometimes November) when there are rich upwellings of plankton. As a result the water is also a hazy grey, adding a ghostly aspect to the slow movements of these gigantic and mysterious creatures of the deep.

The Opera House near **Bandos** in **North Malé Atoll** is an **amphitheatre** of **overhangs** and **shallow caves** where sharks and turtles are occasional visitors among the profuse reef fish.

Paradise Rock is a **mound** with **two large coral pinnacles** between **Furana** and **Lankanfushi** in **North Malé Atoll**, rising out of a flat area of the atoll's lagoon.

The marvellous **soft corals** are concentrated on the pinnacles themselves and on the underside of the **ledges** that run along most of the **mound** at about twenty metres (66 feet) deep. The rock attracts many large creatures, including Napoleon wrasses, turtles, sharks and manta rays.

Rainbow Reef is a **mound** situated in **the cut** between **Himmafushi** and **Girifushi** in **North Malé Atoll**, just **inside** the **outer reef**.

Around the edges of reef, from twelve to thirty metres (39-98 feet) deep, the crystal-clear water supports a magnificent population of **soft corals** that are visited by eagle rays and Napoleon wrasses as well as shoals of blue-barred and horse-eye jacks.

Shallow Point, situated near **Baros** in **North Malé Atoll**, is a **reef** where barracuda congregate.

Vaadhoo, the **resort island**, forms part of a small section of the **northern fringing reef** of **South Malé Atoll**. The reef drops away on all sides of the island, especially in the **north** where it falls 250 metres (820 feet) into the **Vaadhoo Channel**.

There are several excellent **diving spots** in the vicinity. The **Vaadhoo Caves** are a long series of **caves**, **caverns** and **ledges** that stretch along the island's **northern wall**. **Blue** and **yellow soft corals** flourish in the caves, while eagle rays, turtles and large tuna are regular visitors to the wall.

Around the corner from the caves, the **fringing reef** develops into the **Vaadhoo Coral Garden**, where a **steep cliff** gives way to a gently sloping reef with many **soft corals**.

Across the **mouth** of the **inlet** on the **eastern side** of Vaadhoo lies **Paradise Pass**, where schools of horse-eye jacks and spotted eagle rays can be seen soaring in strong currents of clear water. Divers glide on the incoming tide to reach **Vaadhoo's House Reef**.

In a typical dive, expect to see a couple of moray eels (happy to be stroked), lionfish and scorpion fish (to be avoided) lying motionless on the coral, blue-barred jacks, groupers and an assortment of surgeonfish, butterflyfish and angelfish.

In deep water triggerfish flap along, while parrotfish can be seen excreting clouds of coral sand and occasionally a large, dignified Napoleon wrasse appears out of the blue.

Vattaru Reef, to the **south** of **Vaavu Atoll**, has some of the best diving spots in Maldives. The **caves** and **caverns** around Vattaru Reef are unsurpassed, and since they are away from the most popular diving sites in **Malé Atoll**, they contain some of the least disturbed underwater habitats in the archipelago.

Previous pages: Photographers jostle as sleek grey reef sharks power up from the deep.

Opposite: Feather stars can best be seen on night dives when, illuminated by the diver's light, they are caught in the act of feeding on plankton and other minute organic matter.

Overleaf: Between sky and sea, savouring the main elements of Maldives.

Sporting Maldives

These myriad islands, scattered over thousands of kilometres of the Indian Ocean close to the equator, are perfect for water sport enthusiasts, amateur and professional alike. Maldives offers one location after another in which to enjoy the whole gamut of water sports: swimming, water-skiing, windsurfing, surfing, sailing (from dinghies through catamarans to ocean-going yachts and schooners), scuba diving and snorkeling.

The coral reefs on which the islands stand offer safe shallow waters, teeming with fish. The crystal-clear sea ensures visibility of up to forty metres (130 feet).

Yet where the coral reefs plunge vertically as much as 1,800 metres (6,000 feet) to the ocean bed there lies a whole new world of tropical deep-sea fish.

In the shallow waters of the atolls, more than 2,500 species of coral, including 100 endemic to the islands, thrive. Several hundred species of fish, including all the most colourful Indian Ocean species, also flourish in this benign environment.

The border between the shallow lagoons and the deep water is one of the most interesting areas for underwater enthusiasts. Wherever you happen to be staying, most water sports can be arranged from the beach of your own resort. Virtually all provide the necessary equipment for such sports as surfing, water-skiing, wind-surfing, snorkeling and diving.

Snorkeling

Snorkeling is an ideal way to explore the shallow reef areas and most resorts have excellent snorkeling areas within easy swimming distance. Almost anyone who swims can snorkel but while some take to it straight away, others often need a helping hand.

Most diving centres offer short, inexpensive snorkeling courses. If you are appre-

hensive about throwing yourself into an Indian Ocean teeming with fish, it is well worth taking one.

Snorkeling is easy, relatively cheap, and allows you to spend hours watching the world of the coral reefs. If you follow a few tips you will find it even more enjoyable. First of all, you should buy, borrow or rent a mask that fits snugly. Test this by putting it to your face without using the strap and breathe in through the nose. If it fits properly it will not fall off, even when you lean forward. If it is loose, keep trying until you find that it does fit properly. Next, choose some fins which feel comfortable on your feet, and a snorkel which fits easily into your mouth.

Ask any of the water sports staff, or dive centre instructors for a basic introduction on the proper way to use the equipment.

After this initial introduction you must now find out which are the best places in your locality to go snorkeling, how to reach them and what are the potential problems — such as waves, currents or difficult entries and exits.

Always take adequate precautions against the sun: the deceptive cool of the ocean will increase chances of sunburn. T-shirts help but remember the sensitive skin on the back of your knees and neck. Waterproof sunscreen cream or the full protection of Lycra body suits provides the best protection.

Lycra suits also protect you from minor scrapes against the coral and you can always use them afterwards for aerobics at home.

Finally, whenever possible, swim — rather than walk — around the reef edge. Walking over shallow coral not only results in cuts and scrapes but, more importantly, damages the corals, often severely.

Scuba diving

While snorkeling allows you to watch most of the shallow water fish in detail and see many different coral formations, you are restricted underwater to the length of time

Opposite: Nautical perfection: sun, sea and sails.

you can hold your breath. For many this becomes more than a little frustrating.

For those who feel the urge to explore further, scuba diving is the only way to really enjoy the undersea world.

Diving has come a long way in the last three decades: modern equipment is lighter and easier to use and professional dive instructors make learning remarkably easy. So if you have longed to follow in Cousteau's footsteps (or bubbles) there is no better place to start than in Maldives.

One traditional, diesel-driven *dhoani*, the *Magic of Maldives*, has been adapted as a 12-bed floating centre for minimum charters of six days.

Many dive centres in the islands have staff and instructors with international qualifications — your guarantee of a safe and enjoyable diving experience. Almost all resorts have dive centres, but the bulk of them are in **North** and **South Malé atolls**.

Once you feel at ease and your instructor considers you safe, it is time to test your new-found skills with your instructor to guide you around and introduce you to some of the multitude of marine creatures.

Once qualified, you can continue your diving education, either in the form of advanced courses or in special interest areas such as night diving or wreck diving.

Underwater photography, another popular course, takes you from holiday snap-shots in the deep right up to learning the advanced techniques needed to produce an underwater video programme.

If this all sounds too extreme, hire a "photo buddy" to photograph or video film your underwater exploits for you to show your friends back home.

Diving excursions are available daily from most centres and boats take you to the best diving spots in the vicinity. Instructors or dive masters should give you a thorough briefing on each dive site you visit.

The following points are also worth noting: remember that your legs will be much longer than normal, due to your fins, so take care not to kick the corals as you

Opposite: A high-flier, at one with wind and wave, skimming across the warm waters of a lagoon.

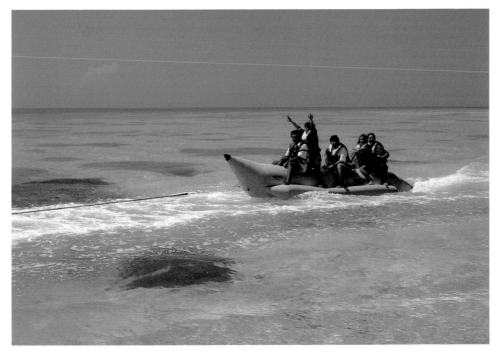

Above: The water sausage proves a popular diversion for many adventurous holiday-makers.

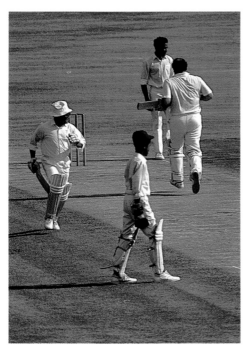

Above: Cricket is a popular sport on Malé, where the President often plays.

swim past. It only takes a few seconds to destroy decades of coral growth.

Never touch or handle coral structures. Their surfaces are covered by a thin, delicate skin and if they feel slimy it means you may have ruptured this protective membrane.

Never touch or handle marine life. Not all are as harmless as at first they might seem. Long-spined sea urchins are particularly unforgiving.

Never remove corals or shells, for even dead coral is important to the development of the reef — and "empty" shells are home to many different creatures.

Move slowly around the reef. Swimming fast allows you to see more coral, but fish sense you long before you approach and many go into hiding. By swimming fast over a coral reef, only the surface will be seen. Gentle swimmers inevitably see more fish as they do not pose a potential threat or disturbance.

You should also take time to look for smaller reef fish and other creatures as it will make your dive much more rewarding.

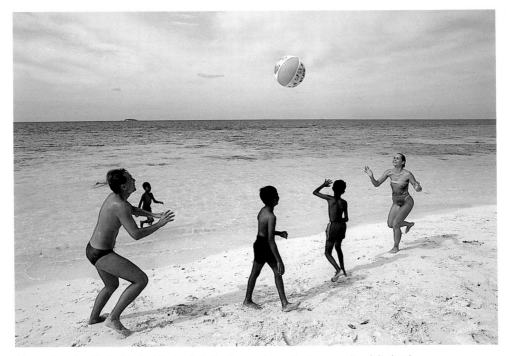

Above: Beach volleyball is the ideal activity for those who prefer the security of dry land.

Board games

Maldivians work hard to survive in their difficult marine environment but they enjoy their leisure. Although the vision of Maldives as a nation of "lotus eaters" waiting for coconuts to fall from the sky or fishes to hook themselves is a complete myth, there is time for games and dancing.

Older men on the islands often play cards in the shade of breadfruit trees in the village or under *cadjan* roofs by the seashore. Chess, a favourite game, is played very fast and with great gusto. The pieces are banged down hard.

Another favourite pastime is simply to sit under a tree in a kind of deck chair made from coir net, or on a flat wooden swing in the house.

Many children learn arithmetic playing a board game called *ovvalhu* in which cowrie shells are placed in sixteen different bowls carved in a wooden block. It probably originated in Africa.

Children also play an Arabic board game known as *carrom* in which they shove flat discs with their forefingers and try to knock others into the four corner pockets.

Athletics

More energetic sports include *bashi*, a girls' game. It is a mixture of cricket and tennis in which one girl knocks a ball over her shoulder with a racket while trying to keep the opposing team from catching it.

Cricket is played in Malé, but the sport that has really caught on is **football**, especially since a former president insisted every island should have a football pitch.

The inter-atoll championship is a big affair: the entire island turns out for the cup final — men, women and children — which takes place on the dusty pitch in the late afternoon. Presided over by chiefs and dignitaries, the game is followed by a big feast which sprawls into the streets. Later in the night the drums are brought out as winner and loser release their tensions in swirling, gyrating dances.

Arts and Crafts: Wood, Reeds and Lacquerware

Maldivians display extremely high standards of craftsmanship, especially in boat building. Although the art form has tragically been lost this century, their stone carving was also justly famous throughout the region.

Nevertheless, a wide variety of arts and crafts, many catering to the tourist trade, is still practised. In some cases this has brought about lower quality, but it is still possible to find fine examples of workmanship.

An exhibition of local works is held in the capital each year during November, when sales are at fixed prices. But in the tourist shops and inhabited islands near the resorts bargaining is an essential part of the ritual.

Wooden lacquered boxes

These hand-carved lacquered boxes — *liye laajehun* — are produced on Baa Atoll, especially on Thulhaadhoo Island (See "Baa Atoll: Land of Exiles", Part Two). Made from local *funa* (Alexandrian laurel), they come in various sizes and shapes; from small pillboxes to large round plates with oval lids (*maaloodh foshi*), used for family feasts on religious festivals.

Elegant vases, lacquered in strands of red, black and yellow resin delicately carved with flowing patterns, are also becoming popular.

Mats

Throughout the archipelago women weave beautiful and detailed reed mats. Perhaps the most impressive is the *thundu kunaa*, which ranges in size from a place mat to a mattress.

Locally grown reeds are dried in the sun and stained with natural dyes which vary from fawn to black. Woven on a hand loom, their intricate, abstract designs vary according to the talent and imagination of the weaver.

Musical instruments

The most common is the *bodu beru* drum, made from a hollowed coconut trunk and covered at each end with the skin of a manta ray or the stomach of a shark.

Jewellery

Maldivians have long been fine jewellers. Some craftsmen in the central atolls, especially on the so-called "Jewellers' Islands" in Dhaalu Atoll, still specialize in gold and silver, making delicate chains, earrings and bracelets (See "Dhaalu Atoll: The Jewellers' Islands", Part Two).

Yet most are unable to reach the high standards achieved by their forefathers, seen in the intricately carved heavy silver bracelets and armlets, long thin belts that wrap several times around the waist, silver charm boxes and gold necklaces that Maldivian women wear for special occasions.

Materials

Most men wear the *mundu* (sarong) and shirt while women wear the *libaas*, a long-sleeved, brightly coloured dress with an embroidered collar made from silver and gold thread.

It's worn tight across the arms and chest and loose around the hips over a black underskirt called a *kandiki*. Some of the older women still wear the traditional *feyli*, a heavy, white cotton sarong woven with brown and black strands.

Only a few people still know how to weave it, however. Most live on Eydhafushi Island in Baa Atoll, which was once the main centre of *feyli* production (See "Baa Atoll: Land of Exiles", Part Two). More recently Maldivians have taken to brightly coloured, polyester prints which are cheaper and easier to wash but less healthy in the tropical climate.

Island tailors make clothes for the local market, while tailors along every street of the capital are eager to create your own personal design. Since tourism has invaded the islands, cheap cotton T-shirts can be emblazoned with a personal motif as well as a typical Maldivian scene.

Above: Lacquering a vase carved from local Alexandrian laurel on Thulhaadhoo Island.

Marine products

Apart from these local crafts several marine products are available. But in some cases, the demand has led to a serious decline of species and visitors should consider the long-term effect of their purchase on the environment.

Black coral

Harvested by local divers at a depth of thirty metres (98 feet), demand for the beautiful brittle branches has virtually destroyed the coral in North Malé Atoll. The branches are cut, polished, and set into rings, earrings, pendants, bangles and jewellery boxes.

Tortoiseshell

Turtle's shells are made into tortoiseshell jewellery and all manner of decorative items. As a result Maldivian turtles are threatened. The government now prohibits the capture of smaller turtles. Although stuffed mature turtles are on sale in Malé, they cannot be taken out of the country. It is also illegal to import tortoiseshell into most countries.

Seashells

Thousands of shells lie along the island shores. Cowries and nautilus are abundant; conch, pearl and trident are rare. Although the government has banned the taking of shells — some diving sites have been seriously denuded — all can be bought in the tourist shops, either in their raw state or polished.

Ambergris

For centuries Maldives has been famous for its ambergris from the gut of the sperm whale. Extremely rare, it is an important ingredient in the manufacture of expensive cosmetics and perfumes. One kilo fetches around US$1,000 on the local market and ten times that overseas. The government imposes a fifty per cent tax on exports.

Above: Hand-carved lacquered boxes and vases, *liye laajehun*, Maldives' most distinctive craft.

Left: In the cool shade of their house compound, father and son work at embroidery, usually considered women's work.

Islam: Island Faith

Islam, central to the life of Maldivians, not only ordains the cultural background and life style, but lays down the smallest details of everyday behaviour.

Until recently, pre-Islamic history was ignored. But while the contribution of pre-Islamic culture is now appreciated, a non-believer still cannot become a citizen of the country.

The president is the religious as well as political leader. The law is based on the Muslim code of *shari'a*, which applies the principles of the Qur'an to society as interpreted by a *gazi* (judge). Indeed, like all Muslims, Maldivians do not distinguish between law and religion; *shari'a*, the nearest word for law, means the way, the true path of enlightenment.

The main events and festivals in Maldivian life follow the Muslim calendar. From the age of three children are taught the Arabic alphabet, memorize extracts from the Qur'an and learn the basic principles and history of Islam.

As they grow older they will be expected to say prayers with the family. On Fridays the boys go with their father in their best clothes to the local mosque; girls go with their mother to a mosque for women, if there is one, or stay at home.

When they grow up, the ambition of all pious Maldivians is to make the pilgrimage to Mecca.

Islamic beliefs

Belonging to the Sunnis, the largest and most traditional Islamic sect, Maldivians believe that "There is no God but Allah", confident that He is one, supreme and all powerful.

They also believe that Muhammad is the messenger of Allah. In a long line of prophets which includes Adam, Noah, Abraham, Moses, David, Solomon and Jesus, Muhammad is considered the last and greatest.

He is not divine — the archangel Gabriel brought him the message of Allah — but he is man at his best. It's the aim of all Muslims to practice Islam, which means literally "surrender to God".

At the same time, Maldivians follow the liberal Shafi'ite school, founded by Al-Shafi'i, an Arab-born Persian descended from the Qurayishi tribe. He usually gave equal weight to the Qur'an and to the words and deeds of the Prophet Muhammad as written down in the *Hadith*.

In some cases he preferred to rely on the latter in interpreting the principles of Islam for society. Maldivians, therefore, share similar beliefs to the Muslims of the East Indies, East Africa, lower Egypt and southern Arabia.

All Maldivians believe in an afterlife and a final judgement that decides whether they go to hell or heaven. Only right conduct can assure the latter, which entails keeping to the five pillars of the religion: to repeat the creed "There is no God but Allah, and Muhammad is the prophet of Allah" (*La ilaha illa Allah, Muhammad rasul Allah*); to say prayers five times a day (at dawn, midday, mid-afternoon, sunset and after darkness); to give alms to the poor; to make a pilgrimage to Mecca if possible at least once in a lifetime; and to fast during the month of Ramadan.

Islamic justice

In applying *shari'a*, or *sariyathu* as it is locally known, Maldives is fairly lenient compared with other Muslim states. The women do not generally observe *purdah* or cover themselves. Neither is punishment for breaking Qur'anic law too severe.

When Ibn Battuta became the *gazi* (chief minister of justice) and ordered the traditional Islamic punishment of cutting the hand off a thief, several Maldivians in his presence fainted at the thought of it (See "History: The Legend and the Mystery", Part One). Only once, during the reign of Amin Didi in this century, have thieves had their hands cut off.

Maldivians are peace-loving. Violent crime, like murder or rape, is extremely rare. In the old days a murderer would be flogged through the streets before banishment for life to a remote island.

Prisons for serious criminals and political detainees have been established

بسم الله الرحمن الرحيم

الحمد لله رب العالمين الرحمن الرحيم
مالك يوم الدين إياك نعبد وإياك نستعين اهدنا الصراط
المستقيم صراط الذين أنعمت عليهم غير المغضوب عليهم ولا الضالين

إن الصلاة كانت على المؤمنين كتاباً موقوتا

الله لا إله إلا هو الحي القيوم لا تأخذه سنة ولا نوم
له ما في السموات وما في الأرض من ذا الذي
يشفع عنده إلا بإذنه يعلم ما بين أيديهم وما خلفهم
ولا يحيطون بشيء من علمه إلا بما شاء وسع كرسيه
السموات والأرض ولا يؤوده حفظهما وهو العلي العظيم

Above: Young girls in a school yard on Dhiggaru Island in Meemu Atoll. All islanders attend primary school where they learn how to read and write and the rudiments of the Qur'an.

Opposite: The words of the Qur'an inscribed in the new Islamic Centre in Malé.

Right: A fisherman's daughter reads verses from the Holy Qur'an.

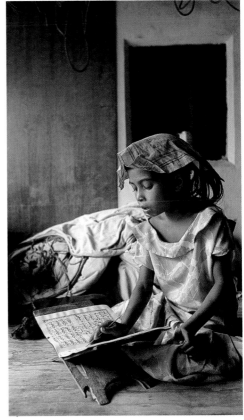

only recently. People are still flogged with a *dhurraa*, a taut leather strap with flat copper studs down the sides. Anyone caught committing adultery undergoes flogging on the thighs.

The most common and traditional punishment is house arrest or banishment to another island, far away from family and friends. Anyone caught drinking alcohol is usually banished for a year. Fines are imposed for petty crime.

If a banished person works hard they can become a respected member of the local community. With a new sense of self-esteem, it is extremely rare that they commit a crime again.

Dance and Drama

Suppressed Maldivian emotions find expression in popular music and dance. The most common is **bodu beru**. To begin, several men gather on a mat with a variety of drums while others clap to the beat and sing around them. The drums are made from hollowed coconut trunks, traditionally covered in manta ray skins or the lining of shark stomachs.

A lead singer chants the Arabic or Dhivehi lyrics while the chorus claps. Eventually, the strong slow rhythm builds to a frenzied crescendo.

Individuals, swaying as if in a trance, leap and jerk as the rhythm increases. If the lyrics are Arabic, the rhythm is undoubtedly African, a reminder of the influences that make up the complex culture of Maldives.

The dance is not only for the young. Old men, bent and desiccated by years of fishing under the merciless sun, suddenly catch a stray rhythm and throw themselves into the arena. To wild applause from the onlookers, they float, gyrate and grimace in their dance, passing on secret affinities from their ancestors.

Earlier this century spear dancing was often performed before the sultan on special occasions. Bell, for one, was not impressed by the "series of stereotyped braggart posturings in front of one another, representative of single combat, which soon pall to the uninitiated Western spectator".

But he enjoyed the "stick dancing", *dhandi jehun,* in which groups of men tap out the rhythm with tiny sticks, which was "at least quaint, if not unpleasing".

A dance rarely seen these days, the *thaara* was probably introduced from the Middle East in the seventeenth century. A line of men sit on the ground and beat hand drums while others dance between them, singing in Arabic.

In the *thaara's* wildest form, the dancer reaches such a climax that he stabs himself in the back of his neck with an iron spike. Such practices are common among Hindus in Sri Lanka, but the government has banned it in Maldives although some say it still continues in the northern atolls.

Another dying practice is the *raivaru*, a kind of poetic song, sometimes accompanied by a slow dance. It is a distinctive part of Maldivian culture and follows a strict metre.

Old fishermen sometimes croon them at the helm on moonlit nights and, after the day's work is done, you might hear the poignant lament of a *raivaru* singer on an anchored *dhoani*. Women also sing them as lullabies or love songs.

Above: Women *bodu beru* drummers on Huvarafushi Island, Haa Alifu Atoll in the north, accompany a dancer. Traditionally men drum and dance, but women are beginning to follow suit.

Top: Ecstatic *bodu beru* drummers singing songs of love and lament with an enthusiastic chorus.

Above: Dancing to rhythms of the *bodu beru* drums in Baa Atoll. Individual dancers, young and old, spontaneously take to the floor and work themselves into a frenzy, applauded and cheered by the audience.

Boat Building

Boats are central to Maldivian life, essential for earning a living, collecting wood and coconuts from other islands and for travel. Almost every family has a small boat, and richer families have several.

The caravel-styled boats known as *dhoanis* used by the Maldivians resemble sleek Arab dhows. Made from coconut and local hardwood, the boats are long and slender, with elegant curving prows.

At one time their planks were held together by coir to make them more flexible when passing over coral reefs.

In the late thirteenth century, the traveller John of Montecorvino noted:

"Their ships in these parts are mighty frail and uncouth, with no iron in them and no caulking. They are sewn like clothes with twine. And so if the twine breaks anywhere, there is a break indeed.

"Once every year therefore there is a mending of this, more or less, if they propose to go to sea.

"And they have a frail and flimsy rudder, like the top of a table, a cubit in width, in the middles of the stern; and when they have to tack, it is done with a vast deal of trouble; and if it is blowing in any way hard, they cannot tack at all.

"They have but one sail and one mast, and the sails are either of matting or some miserable cloth. The ropes are of husk."

By the sixteenth century sewn boats had given way to caravel-built boats, built with ribs using wooden pegs. Although iron nails were available along the Indian Ocean at the time, it was said the Maldivians preferred to used wooden pegs because they feared the magnetic island mentioned in *The Arabian Nights*, which would draw all iron nails out of passing ships.

But Maldivians were — and still are — expert and courageous mariners. In lieu of compass points, using simple nautical instruments, they sailed by different stars as far away as Sumatra, Penang, Calcutta and Aden, braving the storms in their small boats.

A favourite Maldivian poem entitled *Dioage Raivaru* goes:

Lo! our barque's upon the wave,
Dangers of the deep to brave,
Path 'mid ocean-wilds to pave —
To Aden.

Guiding stars with kindly ray
Will direct us on our way
Through the darkness, day by day —
To Aden.

Seas of strife as wide as deep,
Restless waves that never sleep,
Currents of terrific sweep —
To Aden.

Slender barque of bosom's sail,
Breasting bold the sternest gale
Till near haven's light she hail —
To Aden.

Until recently the southern atolls traded directly with Sri Lanka, using large *dhoanis* called *odis*, with three masts, four square sails and one triangular sail.

The boats, about fifteen metres (49 feet) long, five metres (16 feet) wide and three metres (10 feet) high, normally sailed at between two and three knots an hour, but in a good wind could reach up to five or six knots.

The crew usually consisted of the captain, bosun and cook. The passengers, between twenty-five and thirty-five of them, slept on deck and were expected to lend a hand if needed.

The *odi* sailed to Sri Lanka on the south-west monsoon carrying dried tuna fish, *hiki mas*, coconuts and syrup from the sap of coconuts palms, *diyaa hakuru*.

The passage took about six days, but the return voyage could not be made for about a month and a half — when the monsoon winds reversed. Carried along this time by the north-east winds, the *odi* sailed from Sri Lanka carrying rice, sugar, flour, cotton and clothes.

The last voyage of one of these beautiful and ancient vessels took place in 1978 from Fua Mulaku. Since then the diesel engine has replaced sail on long voyages and the only trace of the once proud and graceful *odis* is on Maldivian currency.

Within the archipelago smaller *baththelis*, about twenty metres (66 feet) long with two masts, a deckhouse and inboard engine, are used for long-distance travel.

Cargo-*dhoanis*, which are cumbersome looking vessels with top-heavy super-structures added to a traditional *dhoani* hull, are common. They carry up to 200 passengers, who usually sleep on the deck among their belongings. Not surprisingly, cargo-*dhoanis* roll in the slightest swell.

Whatever their appearance, these over-laden boats serve an important purpose and their arrival at any island is greeted with enthusiasm and interest. Some travel as far as Sri Lanka and India, but, unlike their graceful ancestors, without the worry of the monsoon winds.

Dhoanis are made by the local carpenter, *maavadin*, a highly respected member of the community. It takes a team of four or five carpenters about forty days to build the standard family *dhoani*, measuring ten metres (33 feet) long.

Most boats are made with simple tools. All depends on the eye and experience of the chief carpenter who does not need a written plan. The basic design and con-struction of the *dhoani* have changed little through the centuries.

The caravel-built hull is made from the trunk of a coconut tree and the yard pile that carries the lateen sail from the banyan tree. Nails have replaced the coir that was once used to sew the planking together, but the hull is still preserved with shark oil.

Originally the sail, which was made from coconut fronds, was square. This century Maldivians have recognized the advantage of the triangular lateen sail and now buy cotton strips from India to make them.

Major changes have taken place in ship building methods. Traditionally the hull was built first and then the frame added. At Alifushi Boat Yard in Raa Atoll (See "Raa Atoll: The Land of Kings", Part Two) the keel is laid first, frame and stern added and then planking.

Imported hardwoods from Malaysia result in a stronger, more seaworthy boat.

Copper rivets are used to nail the planks to the frame, and red oxide and cotton caulking is squeezed between them to make the hull watertight.

In the tropical climate and reef-strewn seas of Maldives, the boats should last at least twenty years. But however precise the planking and caulking, the boats take enough water to demand regular pumping of the bilges.

The future owner of a fishing *dhoani* normally pays the carpenters to build it for him. It often takes as long as two years to complete, for if the owner stops payment the carpenters drop tools.

In the new boat yard, however, the carpenters are paid by the twelve-hour day and owners have to guarantee payment. In this way their boat can be ready in as little as three months.

Extremely conservative, Maldivian fisher-men have not changed the basic design of their craft for centuries. If something works well, they see no need to change. Only in the last fifteen years have they recognized the advantage of engine over sail.

They invariably stick to the engine they know well; they see no reason to switch to a later or more powerful model. Such a view has its advantages, for the island black-smiths, using primitive techniques, have learned how to fashion spare parts for such engines.

The *dhoanis* usually carry a lateen sail in case the engine breaks down or the wind is particularly good and they can save fuel.

Overleaf: Cargo ships anchored in the roadstead off Malé, the nation's vital link with the outside world.

Sailing: The Freedom of the Waves

To become captain, *keyolhu*, of a *dhoani*, a man must be intimate with the reefs and entrances of the atolls. Although some *dhoanis* now carry compasses, most Maldivian mariners navigate by dead reckoning, the distribution and shape of the islands on the horizon, and distant clouds that sometimes reflect the green of an unseen island.

The skipper also takes into account currents and distances measuring their speed by throwing a piece of coir into the sea.

The helmsman — usually the captain — steers with a long tiller held between his legs. In rough weather he has to hang on with all his might to the crutch that holds the yard when the sail is not in use; it is like riding a bucking bronco. On approaching an island a member of the crew goes forward as a lookout to direct him through the narrow channels of the reef. One small mistake can ground the vessel.

Even when there's a bunk below, the crew prefer to sleep on deck under the stars. Comfort is less important than a sense of freedom and it's safer on deck when a sudden squall blows up or the anchor slips.

When the wind blows from the right direction even *dhoanis* with engines set the sail they always carry. The captain calls all hands on deck, including the cook, to hoist the long yard pole which carries the lateen sail. "Aa-haa-a, a-haa-ai", goes the cry as they heave on the rough rope.

As the yard reaches the top of the mast the sail billows out in the breeze — like the white wing of a magnificent bird. Now the *dhoani* leans over and cuts merrily through the waves as the sheet is pulled in and made fast astern.

All is transformed. The dull thud and shudder of the engine give way to the creak of rigging and the ripple of water rushing past the sleek hull. Nothing compares with the beauty and efficiency of the sail: canvas and wood are in harmony with wind and water, leaving no waste or pollution.

Visibly affected by the change from engine to sail, the crew gather peacefully on the cool foredeck in the shade of the billowing cloth — just as their forefathers before them.

But the euphoric mood can change suddenly. Squalls appear from nowhere and the sky grows dark as the stiffening wind whips up the white-flecked waves. Suddenly, the *dhoani* lunges, its rigging and sail straining taut.

In the galley, pots and pans go crashing to the deck. Whipped off the line, drying clothes disappear in the wake, and spray crashing over the prow of the ship is carried into the face of the anxious helmsman. Slacking sail, he turns his vessel bow on into the mounting sea.

Some captains make for the middle of the squall. If lucky, by some strange climatic quirk of this area of the Indian Ocean, it will divide into two separate storms. Sailing past the brooding, distended clouds on either side, the *dhoani* once again reaches calm sea, clear skies and blazing sun.

Sometimes there is no escape and they must weather the storm, leaving all in the hands of Allah who decides everything. As an added precaution, Maldivians may try to appease the spirits of the deep with rites and offerings. In the final outcome they depend on the tried and tested design of their boat. After all, the men who built it are their friends and neighbours.

Sailing in Maldives is ever dangerous. Foreign mariners who enter the atolls without a local pilot do so at their peril. The most modern charts, issued by the British Admiralty, carry the warning:

"The depiction of the reefs and dangers is based almost entirely on a lead-line survey of 1835. It is known that many uncharted dangers exist and that the positions and the shapes of many of the reefs are different from that shown. Mariners should navigate with extreme caution."

When approaching an island you sometimes see a rusty metal pole or tree branch, whitened by sun and sea, marking the channel through the shallows of the lagoon. Islanders navigate with great care; a

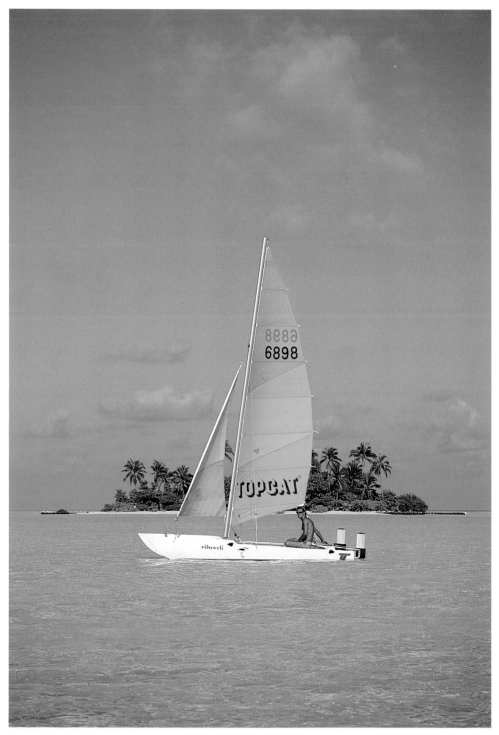

Above: Visitors to Rihiveli can discover the joy of sailing in translucent waters beneath an azure sky.

Overleaf: Like jewels across the equator, there are close to 1,200 islands in the Maldivian archipelago.

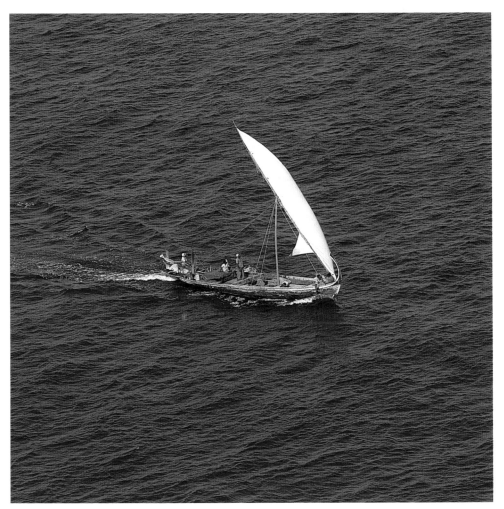

Above: A *dhoani* with its fine curving bow merrily sails across the Indian Ocean. Cousin to the Arab dhow, its superb design has not changed for thousands of years.

lookout in the bow strains to discern the slightest change in the colour of the sea bottom and gestures to the helmsman what direction to take to avoid submerged coral outcrops.

Even the most careful captain has heard the dreaded sound of his wooden-hulled *dhoani* grinding across the rugged coral. If lucky, the vessel breaks free; if not, the crew must wait for the tide or help. Boats under repair on the beaches of the islands reveal the scars of their unavoidable fate.

Currents between atolls run as fast as five knots an hour and boats are soon swept off course. In recent years a *dhoani* drifted thousands of kilometres to the East African coast.

Nevertheless, despite the dangers and difficulties, Maldivians are completely in their element at sea, moving about their tossing decks with great dexterity and balance — and no wonder: many spend more time upright in a boat than on land.

Opposite: The traditional lateen-sailed *dhoani* serves as a welcome 'water taxi' for locals and tourists alike.

The Stamps of Maldives:
A window on history

Since almost the beginning of the twentieth century, Maldives has reached out to the world through its postage stamps, delighting collectors with bold and colourful designs and offering fascinating historical, geographical and cultural information about the archipelago.

When postal services were first introduced in 1906, Maldives had no stamps of its own and for three years the overprinted stamps of Ceylon (now Sri Lanka) were used, where a postal system had been in operation since 1872. It was not until 1909 that an issue exclusive to Maldives was printed.

For those initial years, when Maldives and Ceylon were both countries of the British Empire and when cents and rupees were the national currency in Maldives, the six overprinted Ceylon stamps depicted the profiled head of King Edward VII and were the two-cent brown; the three-cent green; the four-cent orange and blue; the five-cent purple; the fifteen-cent blue and the twenty-five-cent brown. From a collector's point of view, they are considered a valuable acquisition now.

The early years

By 1909, the Crown Agents in Britain had produced stamps more representative of Maldives in a set of twelve from two cents to one rupee in value. Small, neat, slightly deeper in height than square, the stamp — with its central engraved illustration of the Juma Mosque, Malé — left no doubt of the Islamic faith of Maldives. All to the same design, the values differed from each other only in colour. A complete, well-franked set of these has commanded a good price amongst collectors for many years.

In 1933, the same stamp was redrawn and reduced in size by the well-known London printers Harrison & Sons and a set of ten stamps was issued in values of two cents up to one rupee. The colours of the new set, in order of value, were grey, red-

brown, claret, mauve, scarlet, green, black, brown, purple and — for the one rupee stamp — deep blue. All values had both vertical and horizontal watermarks, a factor of no small collector interest.

The 1933 issue remained in circulation until 24 December 1950, by which time the national currency had changed from 100 cents to the rupee to 100 larees. Recess printed by another reputable firm in the United Kingdom — Bradbury, Wilkinson & Co. — the stamp heralded the wonderfully evocative postage stamps which have continued to be issued until the present day. Its design of a palm tree on the shore, leaning towards a *dhoani* sailing landwards, appealed particularly to young collectors abroad before the Second World War, conjuring up exotic coral islands in a sunlit sea. Each stamp's value was printed in the top right-hand corner in English, and in the top left-hand in Arabic. "Maldive Islands" was clearly printed at the foot. The colours of the nine values from two larees to one rupee were olive-green, blue, emerald-green, red-brown, scarlet, orange, purple, violet and — for the one rupee — chocolate.

Two new stamps supplemented this issue in 1952: a blue horizontal three-laree stamp with a design of four swimming fishes, and an emerald five-laree stamp depicting locally made artefacts. Both were of interest to thematic collectors, as have been many of the Maldives postage stamps issued since.

A set of up to fifty larees in value issued in 1956 featured a Malé harbour scene and was emblazoned in the top right-hand corner by the crescent and star. The colours were purple, slate, red-brown, blackish-violet, emerald, chocolate, rose-red and orange. A different design figuring a fort and a palace in Malé illustrated the three higher value stamps of the same set.

1960-1992

From the 1960s onwards a great cascade of stamps has flowed from Maldives, indicative of a nation taking its place in the very competitive world of philately. The number of new stamps printed regularly has meant that, although they

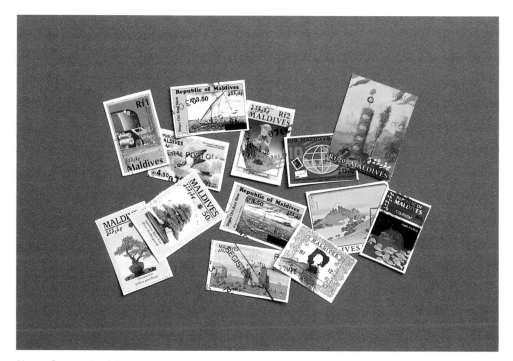

Above: Some colourful examples of Maldivian stamps with international themes.

are not so valuable to professional collectors as the earlier ones, they have nevertheless opened a window on the geography, flora, fauna and marine life of the islands and give an insight into the history, politics, religion, architecture, occupations and customs of the Maldivian people.

The year 1960 set the pattern for subsequent years. A new set of eleven stamps was issued on 15 October showing a Sultan's Tomb, the Customs House, Cowrie Shells, the Old Royal Palace, two more designs showing old tombs, the road to the Juma Mosque, the Council House, the New Government Secretariat, the Prime Minister's Office and Malé port. International notes were also struck on 20 August with a set of eight values to commemorate the 1960 Olympic games, followed by a further set of eight to celebrate World Refugee Year.

Special interest issues

A fine set of three stamps was issued in September 1961 for the 55th Anniversary of the First Stamps of Maldives. Each carries with its anniversary message a replica of the 1906 King Edward VII stamp. Designed by M. Shamir and photoprinted by Harrison & Sons, its recognition of the past has made it highly attractive to collectors. A special souvenir sheet of four imperforated one-rupee values was also issued in this series.

In May 1974 there were stamps to commemorate the Centenary of the Universal Postal Union; in September 1981 the 75th Anniversary of the Postal Service; in June 1984 the 19th Universal Postal Union Congress (held in Hamburg) and, on 21 September of the same year, the "Ausipex" International Stamp Exhibition, Melbourne. In 1986 (2 May), the "Ameripex" International Stamp Exhibition, Chicago, was commemorated and on 17 November 1989 two values were released for "World Stamp Expo 89" International Stamp Exhibition, Washington, one showing Walt Disney cartoon characters with Japanese cars. In 1990 (3 May) Maldives stamps to commemorate "Stamp World London 90" International Stamp Exhibition showed Walt Disney characters playing British sports. Three days later, on 6 May, an issue celebrated the 150th Anniversary of the Penny Black.

International themes

Stamps of Maldives have taken up international themes, celebrating anniversaries in the arts, sciences, sporting events, special campaigns and international organizations. In October 1963 a set commemorated the Red Cross Centenary; in 1964, the World Scout Jamboree; and in 1972, National Costumes of the World.

The United Nations has been featured regularly: in 1966, UNESCO'S 20th Anniversary was commemorated and its 40th in 1986. UNESCO's "Human Rights" campaign was commemorated in 1969 and, in 1978, the 30th Anniversary of Human Rights. The 25th Anniversary of United Nations did not pass unnoticed in 1970, nor, on 15 November 1972, the U.N. Environmental Conservation Conference in Stockholm.

There have been Maldives stamps to commemorate: 1971, Racial Equality Year; 1979, International Year of the Child and in 1985, International Youth Year. Highlighted events of 1988 included commemorating the 40th Anniversary of the World Health Organization on 7 April; World Environment Day on 9 May and on 1 December, World Aids Day.

In sport, Maldives' stamps commemorated the Olympic Games in Tokyo in 1964; Mexico in 1968; Munich in 1972; Montreal in 1976; Moscow in 1980; Los Angeles in 1984 and Seoul in 1988. For a country which takes its football seriously, it is not surprising to find that special issues appeared in 1967 to celebrate England's victory in World Cup Football and in 1974 and 1986 the World Cup Football Championships.

Transport themes have included 75 Years of the Automobile in 1970, Classic Motor Cars in 1983 and, in the same year, the Bicentenary of Manned Flight. The opportunity was not missed in Maldives in 1989 — a country with few roads and no railway — of celebrating on stamps the world's "Railway Pioneers".

Arts and sciences have also commanded their measure of representation: the 150th Anniversary of the Death of Ludwig van Beethoven in 1977; the 250th Anniversary of the Death of Albrecht Durer — the artist — in 1978 and in 1985 the Birth Bicentenaries of the Grimm Brothers. The first series of the Birth Centenary of the ornithologist John J. Audubon, on 9 March 1985, was followed by a second series on 9 October 1986. Great Scientific Discoveries — those of Euclid, Mendel and Galileo — were celebrated in 1988. An Eastern counterbalance to Western cultural emphasis was a set issued in September-October 1989 illustrated with Japanese Art Paintings by Hokusai.

In 1990 (11 December) International Literacy Year saw a cultural cocktail on stamps of Walt Disney cartoon characters illustrating fables by Aesop.

Western tilt

Although Maldives left the British Commonwealth at the instigation of Sultan Mohamed Farid Idi and became independent on 26 July 1965, it rejoined seventeen years later on 9 July 1982. Throughout, close cultural and emotional ties with Britain were retained. This is not only reflected in the stamps issued on 30 November 1974 to commemorate the Birth Centenary of Sir Winston Churchill, but a wealth of issues centered on events surrounding the British Royal Family.

These "Royals" include: 1972 (13 March) — the Visit of Queen Elizabeth II and Prince Philip; 1977 (6 February) — the Silver Jubilee of Queen Elizabeth II; 1980 (29 September) — the Queen Mother's 80th Birthday; 1981 (22 June) — the Royal Wedding of Prince Charles and Lady Diana Spencer; 1982 (1 July) — the 21st Birthday of the Princess of Wales; 1982 (18 October) — the Birth of Prince William of Wales; 1985 (20 August) — the Life and Times of Queen Elizabeth the Queen Mother; 1986 (29 May) — the 60th Birthday of Queen Elizabeth II; 1986 (1 July) — the Royal Wedding of Prince Andrew and Sarah Ferguson; 1988 (7 July) — the Ruby Wedding (40th Anniversary) of Queen Elizabeth II and the Duke of Edinburgh; and 1990 (6 July) — the 90th Birthday of Queen Elizabeth, the Queen Mother.

Of special interest to collectors of

"Royals" are the Maldives' 1982 Princess of Wales stamps surcharged in black and gold for an issue released on 20 August 1984.

The Maldives' tilt towards the West, noticeably the United States, is reflected in the stamps issued in 1976 (15 February) to commemorate the Bicentary of the American Revolution; in 1984, the 50th Anniversary of Donald Duck; in 1985, the 150th Birth Anniversary of Mark Twain; in 1986, the Statue of Liberty Centenary; in 1987, America's Cup Yachting Championship and, on 13 February 1989, the 25th Anniversary of the Death of John F. Kennedy.

Local themes

For many collectors, the most interesting stamps of Maldives will be those with Maldivian themes. They are not only beautiful in themselves but reveal much about the places, events and people of the islands.

The first directly political reference on stamps came in 1962 (29 November) when a series was issued to commemorate the Ninth Anniversary of the Enthronement of the Sultan. On 26 July 1965 Maldives became independent and in the following year, on 26 July, the First Anniversary of Independence was celebrated with stamps bearing the Maldivian Flag. Another set was issued on 26 July 1975 to celebrate the 10th Anniversary of Independence. In the same year (22 February) a series on the Historical Relics and Monuments of Maldives was released and in 1981 (27 June) the 50th Anniversary of the Citizens' Majlis was commemorated, the Maldivian equivalent of a parliament which listens to the grievances of the people.

On 11 November 1968, the country became a republic and the name changed from "Maldive Islands" to "Republic of Maldives". A special stamp issue was released that day. The Tenth Anniversary of the Republic was commemorated in stamps on 11 November 1978.

From 1980 onwards, stamps were used increasingly to forge national unity. In 1980 (19 January) an issue for National Day featured post-Ramadan dancing, the Sultan's ceremonial band, and musicians and dancers at an Eduu Festival and at a Circumcision Festival. In the same year in July, another series was devoted to the Seals of the Sultans. Special sets in the next five years appeared on 7 January 1981 (National Day); 15 November 1982 (National Education); 10 December 1983 (National Development Programme) and 6 June 1985 (National Security Service).

Religious themes are not absent in this strict Muslim country. On 10 August 1964 a "Maldives Embrace Islam" set appeared. Next, on 9 November 1980, the 1400th Anniversary of Hegira was commemorated in a set depicting the Munnaru mosque, the Hukuru Miskiiy mosque, and the shrine of the Maldivian saint Medhuziyaaraiy. In 1984 (11 November) the Opening of the Islamic Centre on Malé was recorded. In 1990, for Islamic Heritage Year, Thakurufaan's Palace and Malé's Friday Mosque were the subjects for stamps released on 26 July.

Maldives' economic interests are also depicted on stamps. On 1 December 1967 International Tourist Year was commemorated, suggesting a new interest in tourism, which was to become the country's principal source of foreign exchange. The same year (26 July) saw the Inauguration of Hulule Airport, an important event in Maldivian modern history since it linked the islands to the outside world. Malé International Airport, as it was renamed, was celebrated again on stamps on 11 November 1981.

The growing importance of tourism to the national economy was reflected in the series issued in 1975 (25 December), which featured a motor launch and small craft, sailing boats, underwater fishing, Hulule airport and motor cruisers. The tourism theme was taken up again in 1984 (12 September) and in 1985 (10 October) with the Anniversary of the World Tourism Organization.

Other political and economic interests of Maldives are reflected in sets issued in 1970 (26 July) for the 10th Anniversary of the Inter-governmental Maritime Consultative Organization and in 1990 (November) for the 5th South Asian Association for Regional Co-operation Summit.

The only sets showing support for radical causes in the Third World came in 1983 (29 November) with a show of "Solidarity with the Palestinians" and in 1984 (26 August) with a stamp depicting black hands breaking their manacles on Namibia Day.

Flora, fauna and marine life

Maldives' beautiful flora, fauna and marine life have been amply treated in a stream of special issues. Fauna was illustrated in 1973 (October), followed up on 16 December 1987. Birds were the selected subject in 1977 (26 July), 1980 (10 July) and 1990 (9 August). Butterflies were the topic for 7 September 1975.

Flowers of Maldives featured in December 1973 and again in 1979 (29 October) and 1987 (29 January). In 1976 (26 July) it was Vegetables; in 1975 (March) Fruits; in 1983 (31 December) Fungi and in 1987 (22 August) Trees and Plants.

With some of the most varied and spectacular marine life in the world, it was no surprise that a set of eight multi-coloured triangulars was issued on 2 February 1963 of colourful fish found in the waters around Maldives. Further Tropical Fish issues were released in 1967 (May), in 1970 (January), and in 1989 (October). The Fishes theme was taken up again in 1973 (August), followed by Marine Life in 1975 (6 June) and in 1980 (29 December). Marine Mammals featured in 1983 (6 September) and Marine Wildlife in 1986 (22 September). In 1975 (25 January) Seashells and Cowries were the subject; Crustaceans on 30 August 1978 and more Shells in January 1979. An issue in support of the Turtle Conservation Campaign was released on 17 February 1980 — although their shells are still used for jewellery throughout the archipelago.

Occupations

Since the country's principal livelihood comes from the sea, the various series printed showing ships on stamps are of special interest. In 1975 (August) the Ganges patela, the Indian palla, the odi (dhow), a Maldivian schooner and a Maldivian baggala were illustrated. In 1978

(7 April) the traditional Mas odi, bettela, baaduodi, Mas dhoani and baggala were featured. In 1985 (23 September) Maldives' ships and boats were again depicted, this time the battela, Addu odi, Mas dhoani and Baththeli dhoani.

Recognizing the importance of the fishing industry to Maldives, Fisherman's Day was commemorated on 10 December 1981 and in 1985, the latter depicting different species of tuna, the main commercial catch.

The different occupations of the islanders featured in a special issue in 1977 (11 November), including boat building. fishing, cadjan weaving, mat weaving and lace making. In 1975 (December) Maldivian lacquerware was represented, an art form also present in a series in 1979 (11 November) on a Handicraft Exhibition which included tortoiseshell jewellery and carved woodwork.

Maldivian women were the subject in 1979 (22 August) for a series on national costumes. In the special issue in 1981 (25 November) to mark the Decade for Women, they were depicted preparing fish; in 16th-century dress; farming and coir rope making. World Food Day in 1981 (30 December) illustrated the staple diet of Maldivians: bread fruit, chickens, maize, skipjack tuna, pumpkin and coconuts.

The rising generation has not been forgotten. In 1968 (1 January) Maldives followed up its celebration of the international Scouting movement with a special issue on Maldivian Scouts and Cubs. In 1985 (20 November) International Youth Year was commemorated with stamps showing young Maldivians playing drums, letting off steam in a tug-of-war and doing community service.

Since 1985 the Republic of Maldives has released an average of ten special issues a year.

NOTE: Spelling of names and places in this feature follows those which appear on the stamps. Current preferred spellings have been adopted in the body of the book.

Opposite: Tourists take time to relax in the welcoming shade of a tropical palm.

Tastes of Maldives

The basic diet of the islanders is **rice** and **fish broth**, *garudiya*, usually made from tuna. It is sometimes enlivened by a dash of salty **fish paste**, *rihaakuru*, or a spicy side dish of **onion and lime**, *asaara*. For breakfast, **unleavened bread**, *roshi,* and fish paste are served. Traditionally, Maldivians do not eat reef fish.

Another popular snack is unleavened bread and a salad mixture of grated coconut, dried fish, lime and spices, *mas huni*. There is also a wide range of mild, creamy **curries** made from home-ground curry pastes, fish and locally grown vegetables such as **breadfruit**, **pumpkin**, **sweet potato** and **eggplant**.

Short-eats

The most tasty culinary treats in Maldives are the savoury and sweet short-eats, *hedhi-kaa*, available in tea-shops and restaurants. The savouries, *kuli eche,* are usually based on a mixture of dried smoked tuna fish, grated coconut, lime juice, onion and chilli. The sweets, *foni eche,* are mixtures of flour, sugar and eggs and are best washed down with the national drink, hot **sweet tea**, *sai*.

Common savouries are:

Fihunu mas: fish brushed with curry paste and cooked slowly over hot coals; *gulha*: fish wrapped in a pastry ball and deep fried; *kavaabu*: deep-fried fish rissole; *keemia*: deep-fried fish roll; *kulhi bis*: fish mixture wrapped in oval-shaped pastry, steamed, turned in a thick, creamy curry paste and eaten with a spoon; *kulhi boakibaa*: mildly spiced fish cake; *samosa*: fish mixture wrapped in triangular shaped pastry, deep-fried, with a slightly sweet aftertaste; *theluli bambukeo*: breadfruit chips; *theluli kavaabu*: fish rissole dipped in yellow batter and deep fried.

Popular sweets are:

Banas: small bread rolls usually served with jam; *bondi*: white, finger-long coconut stick, sometimes wrapped in leaves; *bondi-baiy*: rice custard; *foni boakibaa*: gelatin-like cake; *foni folhi*: thick pikelets; *keyku*: fluffy, plain cake; *kastad*: custard served on a saucer, very sweet; *ussakuru gulha*: sugary rice balls; *rorst paan*: slices of bread dipped in egg and sugar then fried; *sooji*: cereal drink made with semolina, coconut milk and a few sultanas; *kanamadhu*: nuts, sugar and a dash of cinnamon and cardamon; *telali bambukeo*: strips of bread-fruit, deep fried until golden brown on the outside and mushy in the middle.

Chewing and smoking

After meals it's usual to pass round a tray with the ingredients to make a *dhufaaechchehi* — thin, crispy slices of areca nut, cloves, tobacco and lime wrapped in chewed betel leaf.

The habit dates back centuries. In the fourteenth century Ibn Battuta notes that betel was considered more precious than gold or silver. He wrote that taken with areca-nuts: "they sweeten the breath and aid digestion, prevent the disagreeable effects of drinking water on an empty stomach, and stimulate the faculties."

Although the areca nut is grown throughout Maldives, the Indian variety is preferred. From about the age of fourteen men and women chew it all day long and their teeth become stained from its red juice. In a world without alcohol, it's a mild stimulant.

Bidi, a local cigarette made from dark brown imported tobacco rolled very thin and tight in newspaper, is a great favourite with islanders.

Women prefer to smoke a water-cooled **hookah**, or hubble-bubble, in which the tobacco is flavoured with palm syrup and coconut.

Opposite top: A fine offering of wafer-thin crisps to grace a fish curry.

Opposite: Delicious "short-eats", Maldivian style. The cakes are both savoury and sweet and usually washed down with piping-hot tea. The thin slices of areca nut on the betel leaf are often chewed together afterwards.

Overleaf: Well-earned rest after a hard day's fishing under the equatorial sun.

265

PART FIVE: BUSINESS MALDIVES

The Economy

The Republic of Maldives, a chain of approximately 1,190 coral islands, spans an area of 90,000 square kilometres (34,749 miles) in the Indian Ocean. The islands occur in twenty-six natural atolls, but for administration purposes the country has been divided into twenty units: nineteen atolls and Malé.

Population

The population is growing at the rate of 3.2 per cent. The 1992 estimate puts the nation's population at over 230,000. There are 200 inhabited islands, of which twenty-five have more than 1,000 inhabitants. The most populous island is the capital Malé, whose population is growing at a faster rate than the rest of the country and stands at 70,000 (1992 estimate).

Labour force

The country's labour force (between fifteen and fifty-nine years of age) was estimated at 108,900 in 1988 — more than eighty per cent of the working age population. This reflects the large participation rate of women in the labour force.

Gross Domestic Product

From 1985 to 1990, the Gross Domestic Product (GDP) has grown between 8.6 and 13.8 per cent each year. The 1992 GDP was 1,121 million Rufiyaa (Rf) (US$157.9 million). GDP per capita for 1992 was Rf 4,857 (US$684).

The sectors of the economy that have contributed most significantly to the country's GDP are fisheries, tourism, shipping, agriculture and industries.

Policies for economic development

In light of the nation's development requirements, the government has outlined three principal objectives for the country's social and economic development.

- To improve the living standard of the people.
- To balance the population density and the economic and social progress between Malé and the atolls.
- To attain greater self-reliance for future growth.

Among the strategies for improving living standards are better health services, higher education and an increased national and per capita income.

The government hopes to attain greater economic independence by diversifying the productive base of the country and designing further cost-effective methods for increasing the strength and volume of local human and natural resources.

The government's development plan outlines the strategies to attain these objectives by rationalizing and diversifying the country's export products and markets, and by mobilizing internal financial resources for accelerated economic and social progress.

The plan also highlights priorities for development aimed at increasing the GDP and foreign exchange earnings; reducing infant, child and maternal mortality; achieving uniformity of integrated atoll development; and balancing the economic and social progress between Malé and the atolls. The plan also aims to relieve the population pressures in Malé and to protect the environment.

Maldives has maintained liberal, flexible and pragmatic economic policies and encouraged growth in sectors such as fisheries and tourism. Strategies are worked out to spread the benefits of such growth to the outer atolls by providing an essential social infrastructure.

The government's fiscal and monetary policy, while ensuring attractive investment opportunities for domestic and foreign investors, focuses on a phased programme of domestic resource mobilization.

The value of the national currency, the Rufiyaa, is not pegged to any basket of currencies, so foreign currency rates fluctuate according to market demand.

Fisheries

Fishing is the traditional occupation of the people and the principal means of livelihood. To realize its potential, the government is implementing a number of development projects to increase fish production and export.

Measures are being taken to tap the vast marine resources of the country and to this effect the government has established a 330-kilometre (200-mile) Exclusive Economic Zone. A Fisherman's Day is also being celebrated on the 10th of December every year to highlight the importance of fishing and the role of fishermen in the economic life of the country.

The predominant methods of fishing are pole and line for skipjack and trolling for surface fish such as little tuna, frigate, mackerel and wahoo. The traditional fishing vessel is the sailing *dhoani*, but the government has launched a programme to modernize the fishing fleet through mechanization.

In the past, Maldives exported fish to Sri Lanka, primarily *Hiki mas*, better known as "Maldive fish". Made by smoking fillets of tuna and then drying them in the sun, it has been the backbone of the economy for centuries. At present it cannot be exported to Sri Lanka in great quantities because of foreign exchange restrictions, but merchants in Colombo markets are known to pay up to four times the cost price for a kilo. Considered very nutritious and something of a delicacy, tourists are permitted to export up to four kilos when they leave.

As a result of Sri Lanka's attempt to curb its hard currency expenditure on "Maldive fish", there was a strong need for market diversification and adoption of alternative methods of fish processing. Today, Maldives exports canned, frozen and salted fish to the Far Eastern and European markets.

The fisheries sector, which in 1992 accounted for 13.63% of the GDP and engaged 22.4% of the labour force, is a vital source of foreign exchange, coming second only to tourism.

Tourism

Tourism has been the most dynamic sector of the economy during the last ten years. The country's natural assets — white coral beaches, the variety of marine life and the scenic beauty of the islands — are proven attractions.

Since the establishment of the first resort in 1972, nearly seventy resort islands have been developed. Of the registered resorts, less than half are leased by the government, and the rest to local and foreign operators.

Although most tourists are from Western Europe, especially Germany, Italy and France, new markets are now being tapped in East Asia and Australia. As a result the industry is less seasonal. Tourist arrivals in 1992 numbered more than 235,000.

In 1990, the tourism sector contributed 17.77% to the GDP and remains the number one foreign exchange earner, occupying an ever-increasing percentage of the country's labour force.

The cultural impact of tourism has been diminished by keeping the tourists isolated. No Maldivians live permanently on the resort islands and there is little contact betweem tourists and locals except in the tea and tourist shops of Malé.

The positive impact has been in employment, development and welfare services. The cash helps to pay for schools and health clinics in the outlying atolls. It also stimulates handicrafts such as mat weaving, lacquer work and jewellery. Traditional dances have also been resuscitated in order to show tourists something of Maldivian culture.

At the same time, the new tourist industry undoubtedly has an enormous influence on island life, even in the most remote atolls. Many men, particularly from the south, who learned English at the former British airbase on Gan, are separated from their families for most of the year while working in the resort satellites around Malé.

They learn skills and languages, but are also exposed to a new and strange way of life. When they return home sporting new-found wealth they are conspicuous in their western clothes.

Above: The luxurious Laguna Beach Resort is one of the seventy resort islands in Maldives

Shipping

The national shipping line, which is operated by Maldives National Ship Management Limited, handles ninety-five per cent of the country's imports. Since the mid-1960s the industry's surpluses have been an important source of foreign exchange.

This sector, however, has been adversely affected since 1982 by a number of external factors, including the stagnation in world trade, the Iran-Iraq war and the Gulf war. To minimize losses, the shipping line is being consolidated and operations streamlined.

Agriculture

Despite physical limitations such as lack of cultivable land, unfavourable climatic conditions and poor soil, several varieties of food and cash crops are grown. Coconut, breadfruit, mango, papaya, lime, banana, pumpkin, watermelon, taro and chilli all have considerable economic value.

Agriculture is usually a supplementary source of income, but given the growing demand for produce, there is a need to increase production and organize agriculture on a commercial scale.

The main market for agricultural produce is Malé and the tourist resorts. Large quantities of vegetables, fruits, meat and poultry products are imported, draining valuable foreign exchange. The government is taking measures to encourage and improve agriculture in the country. These include coconut rehabilitation, pest control, the provision of extension services and the maximum utilization of uninhabited islands.

Industry

Industry in Maldives consists of a traditional and a modern sector. The traditional industries include boat building, weaving, rope making, blacksmithing, handicraft production and other cottage industries.

This sector employs a considerable number of women as well as men and accounts for about a quarter of the work force. Its link with other parts of the economy, such as tourism, transport and construction, has also strengthened this sector. But as traditional livelihoods continue to flourish, new industries also emerge.

The main activities in the modern sector include fish canning, the manufacture of garments, the production of plastic pipes and washing powder and the bottling of aerated water.

Other enterprises such as boat yards, transport services, electrical and mechanical workshops, carpentry and brick making are also significant. The industrial sector accounts for 13.3 per cent of the GDP.

The size of the domestic market, shortage of skilled and semi-skilled labour, non-availability of raw materials, and difficulties of transportation characterize the constraints of industrial development.

It is recognized that the development of the industrial sector is important to meet the growing demands of the economy. Foreign investment, therefore, is encouraged by the government for initiating mutually beneficial investment projects.

It is expected that with the development of transport, communication and other infrastructure facilities, the economic base of the country will be broadened.

Monetary system

The value of the Maldivian Rufiyaa (Rf) is determined by the daily demand and supply at the Post Office Exchange Counter established by the Maldives Monetary Authority on March 1, 1987. Exchange rate (May, 1993): US$1.00 = Rf 10.45.

Economic Development

The Gross Domestic Product

Traditionally the economy of Maldives was based on the exploitation of fisheries and other marine resources. A second substantial sector was agriculture, followed by local industries including various crafts and carpentry. This structural pattern continued without change until the 1970s — a turning point in the economic history of Maldives.

The first attempt to assess the country's economic performance by estimating the Gross Domestic Product was made in 1979 with the help of the World Bank.

According to estimates of the Ministry of Planning and Development, the GDP in 1978 was attributed to twenty-two per cent fisheries and fourteen per cent agriculture. The services sector accounted for seventeen per cent government services and nine per cent tourism. Secondary sectors were responsible for only fourteen per cent.

In 1987 the picture was quite different, with a significant increase resulting from the growth of tourism in the services sector.

The secondary sector stayed unchanged at fourteen per cent while the primary sector's share decreased, indicating a movement away from primary production.

Nevertheless, the country increased exploitation of marine resources to an unprecedented level in the 1980s.

According to updated estimates, in the five years between 1985 and 1990 the gross domestic product (GDP) grew at the rate of 9.2%. The GDP was estimated at Rf 1,121 million in 1992 (at 1985 constant prices), which amounted to a per capita GDP of Rf 4,857.

The 1992 contribution to GDP by sectors was:

	Million USD	% of GDP
Tourism	27.9	17.77
Distribution	28.6	18.22
Fisheries	21.4	13.63
Construction	14.3	09.11
Agriculture	13.2	08.41
Government administration	14.1	08.98
Transport	10.1	06.43
Manufacturing	9.4	05.99
Services	9.5	06.05
Real Estate	6.6	04.20
Coral and sand mining	2.9	01.85

Increase of production

The growth of the country's GDP during the recent years has been dramatic and unusual. Estimates indicate that from 1978 to 1988 the GDP grew at an average rate of ten per cent a year in real terms.

The growth faltered only in 1982 due to the effect of collapsing markets for shipping, fisheries products and tourism. It was clearly the result of international economic stagnation, particularly in Europe, after the oil crises of the late 1970s.

The rapid economic growth attained in these ten years of development helped to raise the income level by offsetting the high population growth rate of 3.2 per cent per year between 1977-85. The per capita GDP increased from Rf 1,927 in 1977 to Rf 3,637 in 1987 and to Rf 4,857 (US$684) by 1992.

To be able to appreciate fully the achievements of the economy, one must judge its growth in the light of the country's special structural features and the problems they pose. These include the small size of the population, the dispersal of the population throughout 200 scattered islands separated by wide expanses of sea and the limited size and nature of land available on the islands. These physical limitations impose a heavy burden on the development processes.

Despite the handicaps, the Maldivian economy performed remarkably well. Fisheries and tourism in particular stimulated growth, with sound economic management, a mixture of pragmatic and flexible policies and a free economic environment all playing their part.

Emphasis on infrastructure development

Also contributing to the rapid growth was the emphasis on the development of infrastructure. A clear example of this was the effort made to complete the international airport followed by the incentive-oriented invitations to various international airline operators.

Other infrastructural achievements include upgrading the Felivaru Tuna Fish Cannery, the establishment of domestic regional airports, recommissioning Gan airport and the development of the garment export industry.

Institutions, money and banking

At the beginning of the 1980s, the basic economic institutions which are normally taken for granted in most countries were nonexistent in Maldives. This was particularly apparent in the case of the institutions and procedures essential for a sound and stable financial system.

The monetary system in Maldives has had a long and colourful history. The Maldivian cowrie shell, *Cyprea moneta*, was the medium of exchange in this region during the time of Arab and Portuguese trade (See "History: The Legend and the Mystery", Part One). Cowries were followed by or simultaneously used with the coinage of the country that dates back to the sixteenth century. Since then, successive governments have utilized different forms of money in the country.

By the end of the 1940s Maldives had an established system of notes and coinage, but there were major flaws in the system. For various reasons, reliable records documenting the issue of notes and coins had not been maintained; at best, only rough estimates were available detailing the amount of money in circulation. This situation posed major difficulties when the new administration took over in 1978.

The problems of monetary supply were further compounded by the existence of two commercial banks. Although both were providing useful services to the business life of the country, there were no regulatory mechanisms to oversee their performance and protect the customers, or the economy, from any possible harmful occurrences that might have arisen.

The new government formed in 1979 acted quickly to bring this situation under control. On 6 July 1981, the Maldives Monetary Authority (MMA) was established and immediately began a programme of monetary reform. At the outset it was decided to issue a new currency in order to bring the money supply under control. On 7 October 1983, the new currency was introduced, eliminating the confusion that had prevailed for years.

Since then the MMA has remained involved in the monetary policy of the government, and has done much to promote a healthy banking environment. The success of the government's monetary policies can be seen through the measures aimed at maintaining and promoting an open exchange system, with no restrictions.

On 26 February 1987, the country adopted a floating exchange rate system completely eliminating any parallel rates (under the earlier system of dual exchange rates the market rate was almost twice as high as the official accounting rate).

Maldives now enjoys the most liberal and market-oriented exchange rate system in the region, one comparable to any in the world.

The banking system has also been brought under the regulatory authority of the MMA. Between 1978 and 1987 three more commercial banks were opened to make a total of five.

In an effort to establish development banking within the country, as well as to establish local ownership in the banking sector, the Bank of Maldives Limited was incorporated in 1982.

This bank, with commercial and development banking functions, began as a joint venture between the government and a foreign concern.

Trade and industries

Traditionally Maldives has been involved in many forms of regional trade. In the past, exports included cowrie shells, coir rope, copra and dried and processed fish. These helped to pay for imports of grains, clothing, medicines and other commodities.

By the mid-1970s the major export was canned and fresh frozen tuna fish. But because processing was in the hands of foreign investors, much revenue was lost.

Traditional forms of handicraft and cottage industry also suffered from the increased impact of cheap imports, which threatened the survival of skills passed down through generations.

In the last decade major steps have been taken to improve the situation. Central to the strategies implemented was the role of the government. The Ministry of Trade and Industries was created in November 1982 to regulate and promote trade, to facilitate industrial development and to assist local and foreign investors.

A second major development was the positive role adopted by the State Trading Organization (STO) during this period. The traditional role of this government organization was to manage all state trade, including the export and import of essential commodities.

In the last decade, however, the STO has become an exemplary producer-exporter, a model emulated by many private commercial agencies. Its investment projects in fisheries and garments have been noteworthy successes.

In addition, the STO began to assist private local businesses in various forms, providing business information, for example, through a Trade Information Unit established in 1982. The unit became a very useful centre for new enterprises and small businesses.

The various institutions established and strengthened in recent years have provided an environment for sustained economic growth. The rapid growth in national income has been the most obvious indication of the success of these strategies.

Social Development

Along with economic growth, Maldives has made remarkable progress in social development. When the 1985-87 National Development Plan was devised, principal objectives were to improve living standards, to balance the population density and the economic and social progress between Malé and the atolls and to attain greater self-reliance for future growth.

To achieve these objectives the government has undertaken unprecedented development programmes, attaching high priorities to such services as health, education and social welfare.

Health

The Ministry of Health and Welfare is responsible for planning health services. Besides the Central Hospital in Malé, regional hospitals and health centres in the atolls, the Ministry also provides family care and health education. The ultimate goal is to provide adequate, essential services to all citizens by the year 2000.

The government spends a large proportion of the budget on health services and facilities.

Despite these efforts, however, a major constraint facing the health sector is a shortage of labour and facilities. The population per doctor is about 6,595; per nurse, 1,519; per health worker, 833; and

Just another day in Maldives.

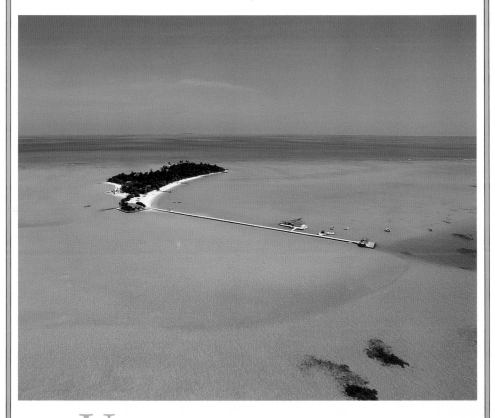

U pon your arrival, you will be overwhelmed by the beauty of the sight before you: a picturesque village of 35 private bungalows surrounded by a gigantic lagoon of crystal clear water. From Rihiveli Island you can wade to Rising Sun Island, Island of Birds, and the Sandbank of the Solitary.

French owner Pitt Pietersoone is determined that his guests experience their holiday to the fullest. Choose laying on the beach as a priority or enjoy a wealth of outdoor activities. The cuisine is unforgettable, as is a drink at the resort bar, presided over by Babar the barman and his parrot!

RIHIVELI

L'Atoll de Corail

For more information: Rihiveli Beach Resort, Ocean Store, Chandhani Magu, Malé
Telephone: 323767/323441/344775 Resort telephone: 443731/444775, Telex: 66072/66038

per midwife, 184. The population per hospital bed is 1,327.

The government is taking measures to remedy the situation by making primary health care available throughout the country. A greater part of this task involves the training of doctors, nurses, health workers, midwives and other health personnel. A large number of professionals are being trained and educated in the country and abroad.

Hospitals

Malé Central Hospital provides medical care at secondary and tertiary levels. During the past twenty-five years its services have expanded and improved to include natal care, maternal and child health services (including immunization, growth monitoring and birth control), surgery, gynaecology, pediatrics, ophthalmic and dental services, a diagnostic laboratory, radiological facilities and emergency services.

At present there are four regional hospitals: at Kulhudhuffushi, Haa Dhaalu Atoll; at Ugoofaaru, Raa Atoll; at Hithadhoo, Seenu Atoll; and at Muli, Meemu Atoll. These provide only primary and secondary level medical care for the regional population.

Atoll health centres

There are twenty-two atoll health centres in the country, each run by one or two community health workers and a supervisor trained at the Institute of Health Sciences.

These community health workers provide primary health care services to atoll populations, under the guidance and supervision of the Department of Public Health and the Ministry of Health and Welfare.

Family health workers

There are family health workers on all inhabited islands, usually one per 1,000 population. Their responsibility is to provide basic preventive and curative care for common ailments.

Education

The traditional system of education prevailing in Malé and in the atolls is comprised of three types of institutions: *kiyavaage, makthab* and *madhurasaa*.

The *kiyavaage* is a private home where the children learn to read the Qur'an, read and write in Dhivehi and to master basic arithmetic. The *makthab* provides further instruction in the same subjects as well as Islam, and classes are usually held in a separate building.

In the *madhurasa* the curriculum is expanded to include additional subjects. The range and level of subjects in *kiyavaages, makthabs* and *madhurasaas* vary across the country according to the abilities of the instructors.

Although the education attainment of the traditional system is low, it has contributed to a relatively high rate of literacy (ninety-three per cent) and the preservation of national culture and tradition.

English-medium education was introduced in the 1960s. There are seven government schools in Malé as well as many private schools supported by the government. A large number of students are enrolled in this stream of formal education and today students from all over the country attend these schools in Malé.

The education policy of the present government is to incorporate the two systems into one, so that the virtues of the traditional and the merits of the modern systems of education can be combined.

At present nineteen atoll primary schools in each of the nineteen administrative atolls have been built. Similarly there are nineteen Atoll Education Centres (AEC) funded by the government. These serve as "model" schools where the newly introduced curriculum is being taught by trained teachers using modern methods.

A Science Education Centre has been established allowing students who complete their secondary education to continue pre-university education. At present, Maldivian students must go abroad for university studies. The objective of the government is to make maximum possible use of overseas facilities and training programmes for an equal number of men and women.

The Institute for Islamic Studies also plays a very important role in education, providing Islamic religious instruction combined with general studies.

Human resource development

The education sector, which aims to provide universal primary education, is also responsible for training the labour necessary for national development.

The demand for skilled labour has been partly met through the training programmes conducted at the Vocational Training Centre (VTC). Courses are offered in engine repair, machinery, welding, sheet metal, air conditioning, refrigeration and electronics.

In addition, the School of Hotel and Catering Services, the Institute of Teacher Education, the Institute of Health Sciences and the Maldives Centre for Management and Administration all offer training courses in their various fields.

The focus in the Rural Youth Vocational Training (RYVT) programme is on basic skills such as engine maintenance/repair, carpentry, tailoring, sewing, handicrafts and boat building. The RYVT programme is supplemented and supported by the other sectors of the economy. It is a programme aimed at making the rural communities more self-sufficient and accelerating development in the atolls. There is also the Children's Reformatory (Is'Iaah'iyyaa) at Maafushi Island. Those who graduate from these institutions are readily absorbed into the dynamic sector of the economy.

Social welfare

The government accords high priority to social welfare and this is reflected in programmes designed to improve the living conditions of the people. Efforts are being made to provide physical rehabilitation and specialized vocational guidance for the disabled.

A National Committee for the Welfare of the Disabled was formed and in 1981, the International Year of the Disabled, a survey was conducted by the committee which revealed that nine people out of every thousand are physically and or mentally handicapped.

The National Committee for the Welfare of the Disabled undertakes to provide opportunities for the disabled to participate in the social and economic development of the country. Mass media campaigns also disseminate information about the need for prevention, detection and early cure.

A home for the aged and the disabled has been established on the island of Guraadhoo. The government also offers medical care for the handicapped due to paralysis, polio or leprosy; helps obtain expert treatment for the mentally retarded; and provides disabled persons with basic amenities required for their rehabilitation.

The government, in addition to providing free medical care for the poor at Malé Central Hospital, assists patients in obtaining special treatment in Sri Lanka and India.

Women's affairs

Throughout its history, women have participated in the affairs of Maldives. Some very noteworthy women sat on the Maldivian throne and ruled the country wisely and justly for many years (See "History: The Legend and the Mystery", Part One). Today women continue to play an important role in the socio-economic life of the country. One-quarter of government workers are women.

There is a male to female ratio of 100 to 107. Social indicators relating to women, such as the maternal mortality rate, have improved significantly during the last few years. The number of girls enrolled in public and private schools also remains proportionate to the population.

Traditionally women were found in professions such as fish processing, mat weaving, coir production, tailoring and other cottage industries. The garment manufacturing industry also employs a large number of women.

The process of development brought with it many strains, resulting in the loss of traditional employment opportunities for women. This prompted the women to reorganize in order to participate fully in the development process, and in 1979 the National Women's Committee (NWC) was established by the government to mark the International Decade for Women.

The Department of Women's Affairs was

established in 1986. The National Women's Committee and the Island Women's Committees have initiated and implemented various projects to generate income, supply information about nutrition and provide for the welfare of women in general.

Planning

The first development plan, issued in 1950 (covering the three years from 1950 to 1952), was more of a policy statement than an integrated plan for socio-economic development, due to the lack of established planning institutions.

In the subsequent period up to 1978, planning did not figure as a realistic strategy for development. The lack of an integrated and established policy for development meant that economic advance often took place at high social costs, and income and regional disparities became increasingly pronounced.

The National Planning Agency was established in 1978 to improve this situation and achieve balanced social and economic growth. In 1982 the agency was upgraded and renamed the Ministry of Planning and Development. Thus in 1985 the first technically consistent plan for socio-economic development in Maldives was formally issued by the government, along with proposed strategies for attaining its objectives. These were retained and implemented in the second development plan for 1988-1990.

Priorities

At the same time the following priority areas were drawn up, bearing in mind the resources available:
• To increase the Gross Domestic Product as well as national products.
• To increase foreign exchange earning.
• To increase the level of incomes, especially in the atolls.
• To provide better and balanced health and educational facilities throughout the country.
• To emphasize human resource development as the basis for all development activities.
• To give more emphasis to atoll development.
• To accelerate the decentralization process.

• To relieve Malé of its congestion.
• To accelerate the process of import substitution, especially in food and agricultural products.
• To preserve and manage properly the environment.

Strategies and policies

To achieve these short- and long-term objectives, the following strategies and policies have been adopted:

Production and export

Prospects in the fisheries sector are favourable. Fish prices, according to current world forecasts, are likely to increase tremendously in the future. The production and export of marine products are thus likely to increase considerably in the coming years.

Various measures are being undertaken to develop fisheries. These include the use of under-exploited and nonconventional resources to improve fisheries management. Future strategies also include the exploitation of fish species other than tuna, especially valuable reef fish.

In the agricultural sector, the coconut and forest rehabilitation activities and pest and disease control programmes are likely to result in increased agricultural production — especially poultry, fruits and vegetables. This will provide a wider base for import substitution.

Industrial growth will be boosted by measures taken to develop industrial and export processing zones. Such zones will provide the infrastructure required for the growth of manufacturing activities.

The good performance in the tourist sector is likely to be maintained, if not improved, due to the expected rise in the tourist arrivals and the development of a new tourism zone. Training activities in the field of hotel management and catering will result in a higher standard of resort services and further replacement of foreign labour by nationals.

In the field of health and education, the government is determined to improve the standard of services being delivered to the population.

The plan includes the provision of health facilities needed to lower the incidence of communicable diseases, to decrease infant and maternal mortality, and to improve nutritional standards. Of special significance is the intention to declare Maldives a malaria-free zone.

Activities in the education sector will encompass the objectives of universal primary education as well as the creation of an environmentally relevant education system that creates the human resources required for future development.

Atoll development

The government is determined to accelerate development in the atolls through the provision of a basic infrastructure as well as through the coordination of sectoral development programmes.

The strategy for the development of the atolls will also include the implementation of fisheries and agricultural development programmes.

Furthermore, it covers the accelerated provision of health, education and social services as well as training activities. The strategy of community-based integrated atoll development projects will also be continued.

A major impact on atoll development will be felt through the decentralization strategy begun in 1987. Large islands in the atolls are being selected to cope with the expected immigration and demands of industrial development. They should become future growth centres in the atolls.

Improvement

Malé, the centre of economic activity and administration of the country, is faced with the growing inability to provide the basic services needed by its population.

This is especially felt in the field of housing. Intensive efforts are being made by the government to meet the demand for housing through the development of nearby islands. The government has also declared the two islands of Viligili and Meerufenfushi as extended residential and industrial areas for the population of Malé.

Other major development activities in Malé include the construction of a water supply and sewerage system, a garbage disposal unit and a sports stadium, as well as port and harbour development. These activities will enable Malé to cope with the increasing demand for services triggered by the rising population.

Preservation of the environment

The government is determined to preserve and protect the country's environment. Hence the National Council for Environmental Protection has been entrusted with the tasks of setting up environmental standards and coordinating the activities of different agencies. The plan includes projects that further assist in this strategy to establish more efficient environmental management.

Investment

Since the birth of the tourist industry in Maldives, many foreign investors have shown a keen interest in leasing an island, constructing a resort and reaping the benefits of tax-free profits and duty-free imports.

Of course there are certain guidelines to adhere to, and there are as many failures as there are success stories. Information can be sought from the Ministry of Trade and Industries in Malé.

The Ministry will also provide details of investment opportunities in other sectors of the economy, especially in fisheries and agriculture.

FACTS AT YOUR FINGERTIPS

Visa and immigration regulations

All visitors need a valid passport. Israeli citizens should check with the immigration office in advance; officially no Israelis are permitted entry into Maldives.

Indians, Pakistanis, Bangladeshis and Italians are given a ninety-day visa on arrival. All other tourists are given a thirty-day visa. This can be extended for a nominal fee at the immigration department.

Visitors entering Maldives must have a minimum of US$10 a day for their stay (this does not apply to those with a tourist agency or going to work).

Visitors need confirmed hotel reservations for immigration clearance. Any visitor without a hotel reservation should seek help at the airport tourist information desk.

Health requirements

An international certificate of inoculation against yellow fever and cholera is required by visitors arriving from infected countries. Vaccinations against tetanus and typhus are recommended. Avoid drinking water from island wells; either boil it or drink rainwater. Though malaria has been eradicated in most of Maldives, occasional cases are reported in the northern atolls, and malaria tablets are recommended for travellers to this area.

International flights

Maldives is served by major international airlines. Scheduled services are operated by Air Lanka, from Colombo; Bulgarian Airlines, from Sofia and Bangkok; Emirates Airways, from Dubai via Colombo; Indian Airlines, via Trivandrum, India; Pakistan International Airlines from Karachi via Colombo; and Singapore Airlines from Brussels, Paris, Singapore and Zurich.

There are direct charter flights by many operators from London, Milan, Rome, Vienna, Zurich, Frankfurt, Dusseldorf, Munich, Berlin, Vienna, Stockholm, Copenhagen and Helsinki.

On arrival

Almost all visitors arrive by air. Malé International Airport is situated on Hulhule Island, about four kilometres (two miles) or ten minutes by boat from the capital, Malé.

Customs and immigration formalities are completed with a minimum of delay. Currency can be exchanged at airport banks and a tourist information bureau offers help and advice. These are open during regular business hours. There is a small duty-free shop and non-alcoholic beverage bar in the departure hall.

Departure tax

The airport departure tax is seven dollars, payable only in US dollars.

Customs

Firearms, drugs, alcohol and pornography (including publications like *Playboy*) are banned. As Maldives is an Islamic country, dogs, pigs and pork products are also forbidden.

Liquor

Alcohol cannot be imported without an official licence. You can buy alcoholic drinks in all major hotels and island resorts.

Travel permits

To visit an island outside Malé you need a travel permit from the Ministry of Atolls Administration. These are issued on request to anyone on an organized tour. Independent visitors must produce a letter from a "sponsor" offering accommodation.

Domestic flights

Air Maldives operates domestic flights to outlying atolls; from Hulhule to Gan in Seenu Atoll, Kadhdhoo in Laamu Atoll, and Hanimaadhoo in Haa Dhaalu Atoll.

Hummingbird Helicopters is also available for charters to many resorts, via nine helipads located in North Malé, South Malé, Alifu and Lhaviyani atolls.

Boat services

Specially adapted yacht-*dhoanis* can be hired from Voyages Maldives, Ocean Enterprise and Treasure Island Holidays all in Malé.

Taxi services

There are two roads — one in Malé and one, the longest, which is in need of repair, in Seenu Atoll. Taxi services operate in Seenu Atoll and on Malé, where taxis can be hired by telephone around the clock. The main operators are: Comfort Taxi 325120, Express Taxi 323132, Fine Taxi 328998, Khaleej Taxi 325060, Kulee Dhuveli 322122 and New Taxi 325757.

Capital

Malé, the capital of Maldives, is about 18 square kilometres (7 square miles) and has a population of about 70,000. It is the main business, administrative and political centre of the country.

Business hours

Business hours are 06.00-13.00, Saturday-Thursday. Government offices are open from 07.30-13.30, Saturday-Thursday. Banks are open 09.00-13.00, Sunday-Thursday. The post office is open from 07.30-13.30 and 15.00-17.00 daily.

Friday is the day of worship and government offices and banks close all day. Restaurants and shops close between 11.00 and 14.00 for prayers. On other days businesses close for prayer four times a day for fifteen-minute intervals.

During Ramadan, the Islamic month of fasting, working hours are shortened and some offices close altogether.

Currency

The unit of Maldivian currency is the Rufiyaa (Rf), which is divided into 100 Laari (L). Coins in use are 1, 2, 5, 10, 25, 50 Laari, and one Rufiyaa. The notes are in denominations of 2, 5, 10, 20, 50, 100 and 500 Rufiyaa. The exchange rate in May 1993 was US $1.00 = Rf 10.45.

Currency regulations

Foreign currencies can be exchanged with authorized money changers at banks, leading shops and tourist resorts. There is no restriction on the amount of foreign currency a passenger may bring in or take out of the country. The American dollar is the most common foreign currency in use.

Banks

There are several international banks with branches in Malé, including the Bank of Ceylon, Habib Bank and the State Bank of India. The Bank of Maldives is also located in the capital.

Payments

Hotel payments can be made with foreign currency, travellers' cheques or credit cards.

Credit Cards

American Express has an office in Malé and their credit cards are widely accepted throughout the capital and on the resort islands. Other major credit cards accepted include Visa, Mastercard, Diners Club and Eurocard.

Duty-free shopping

Malé has a large duty-free shopping complex. High quality electrical goods, stereo equipment, watches, cosmetics and many other products are available at reasonable prices. There is also a small, well-stocked duty-free shop in the departure lounge of Malé International Airport.

Tipping

Officially tipping is prohibited. Unofficially, many guests give a small sum to their room-cleaner and waiter. In the local tea-shops and guesthouses, *shukriyyaa*, thank you, is enough.

Security

Maldives is a peaceful country where violent crime and robbery are rare. However, do not leave your belongings unattended and lock your valuables in the resort safe.

Medical services

The Malé Central Hospital, located on Sosun Magu (emergency tel: 322884, registration tel: 322401), is equipped for routine health treatment. For any serious illness you should consider flying home. There are also health clinics in each of the atoll capitals which can treat minor illnesses or accidents.

Time

Maldives is five hours ahead of Greenwich Mean Time (GMT) and half an hour behind Sri Lanka and India.

Energy

The electricity supply on Malé is 240 AC using round-pin plugs. There are frequent failures and blackouts. All resorts operate their own generators. An increasing number of islands in the outlying atolls also have their own generators.

Postal services

Air mail takes about ten days to and from most destinations. Surface-mail parcels take up to six months. Allow at least half a day in the post office if you are sending parcels overseas.

Local handicrafts of gold, silver and brass need customs clearance. There is a fifteen per cent tax on lacquered boxes or wooden products and twenty per cent on jewellery made of black coral or turtle shell.

Communications

The satellite earth station in Malé provides telephone, telex and facsimile services to any part of the world. Inter-atoll communication is mainly through HF transmitters. There are VHF and UHF telephones in several islands.

Media

International magazines like *Time* and *Newsweek* are available every week. The Department of Information also issues a bi-weekly English news bulletin. The local Dhivehi daily newspapers, *Aa Fathis* and *Haveeru*, contain a few paragraphs in English.

The government-controlled Voice of Maldives broadcasts from 05.30 to 22.45 daily, with an English news bulletin at 18.00. TV Maldives screens local plays, Hindi films, Qur'anic recitals and imported Western programmes.

There is one local cinema which specializes in romantic and adventure-packed Hindi films.

Photography

Photography of people in mosques is discouraged and it is forbidden to film Theemuge, the President's residence, and the National Security Service (NSS) Headquarters. Film is available on Malé and the resort islands at reasonable prices.

Anyone wishing to make documentary, publicity or feature films requires permission from the Department of Information and Broadcasting.

Climate

The climate, determined by the two monsoons, is warm and humid. The rainy south-west monsoon begins during April and continues until October, while the generally fine north-east monsoon prevails from December to March. The average annual rainfall is 197 centimetres (77 inches). The mean daily maximum temperature is 30°C (86°F) while the daily minimum is 26°C (79°F).

Dress

Light cotton clothes are recommended to ward off the heat and humidity. As an Islamic country, Maldives prohibits nudity.

Religion

Maldives is 100 per cent Sunni Muslim. Islam is the religion of the state and the backbone of society. Only Muslims are allowed to marry or become citizens.

Language

Dhivehi, spoken throughout Maldives, is a language belonging to the Indo-Iranian group. Its present script, introduced in the late sixteenth century, is written from right to left. English is the second language, although an increasing number of Maldivians speak Arabic. All three languages are taught in schools.

Government

Maldives has been an independent state throughout its known history, except for a brief fifteen-year period of Portuguese rule in the sixteenth century. It was a British

Protectorate from 1887 to 1965, when independence was proclaimed.

The president is the head of state and the chief executive and defender of the faith. He is nominated by the Citizens' Majlis (or parliament) and elected by a public referendum for a renewable term of five years. He is also the commander-in-chief of the armed forces and the supreme authority entrusted with the protection of the country's religion.

The cabinet consists of the president, vice presidents and ministers. The president appoints all the ministers, who may or may not be members of parliament.

The Citizens' Majlis is comprised of forty-eight members elected for five-year terms (two elected from each district), and eight nominated by the president.

International relations

Maldives is a member of the United Nations and most of its specialized agencies: the Commonwealth, OIC, the Non-Aligned Movement and SAARC. At present Maldives has diplomatic relations with more than 100 countries. The country is also a member of international financial institutions such as the World Bank and the International Monetary Fund.

English — Dhivehi

Pronunciation

a as in cut   **o** as in hot   **ai** as in eye
e as in red   **u** as in put   **oa** as in moan
i as in fit   **aa** as in father   **ee** as in tree

Greetings and civilities

Hello	Salaam alekum
How are you?	Haalu kihineh?
Not bad	Goaheh noon
Very well	Vara gada
Good	Rangalu
I'm going	Aharen dani
See you later	Fahung baadaluvang
Thank you	Shukriyyaa

Small talk

What's the matter?	Kihineh vee?
It doesn't matter	Kame nu
What did you say?	Keekey?
What's happening?	Kihine vani?
Where are you going?	Kon taaka dhanee?
Wait there	Etanga hure
Come here	Mitana ade
Where?	Koba?
Why?	Keeve?
Who?	Kaaku?
What?	Kon echcheh?
Understand	Engije
Don't know	Nenge
Yes	Aanh
No	Noon

Personal talk

Who is that?	E-i kaaku?
Those people	E meehun
Who is this?	Mee kaakuge?
I	Aharen
Me	Ma
You	Kaley
He	Eyna
She	Mina
Man	Firihene
Woman	Anhen meehaa
Father	Bappa
Mother	Mamma
Uncle	Bodu beybe
Aunt	Bodu daitha
Brother	Bebe
Sister	Datta
Son	Darifulu
Daughter	Darifulu
Friend	Ratehi
Close friend	Rahumaiy'theriyaa

Time

What time is it?	Gadin kihaavare?
Sunday	Aaditta
Monday	Hoama
Tuesday	Angaara
Wednesday	Budha
Thursday	Buraasfati
Friday	Hukuru
Saturday	Honihiru
Yesterday	Iyye

Today	Miadhu		
Tonight	Mire		
Tomorrow	Maadhan		
Dawn	Fathis		
Sunrise	Iru arani		
Morning	Hendunu		
Midday	Mendhuru		
Afternoon	Mendhuru fas		
Sunset	Iru osani		
Early evening	Iraakolhu		
Night	Reygandu		
Two o'clock	De jahairu		
Quarter past three	Thineh gadi fanara		
Half past nine	Nua gadi ba		
Before	Kuring		
Now	Mihaaru		
After	Fahung		
In a little while	Tankule fahung		
Hour	Gadi		
Day	Dhuvas		
Week	Hafthaa		
Month	Maheh		
Year	Ahareh		

Numbers

Zero	Sume
One	Eke
Two	Dheiy
Three	Thineh
Four	Hathareh
Five	Faheh
Six	Haeh
Seven	Hate
Eight	Asheh
Nine	Nuvae
Ten	Dihae
Eleven	Egaara
Twelve	Baara
Thirteen	Theyra
Fourteen	Saadha
Fifteen	Fanara
Sixteen	Soalha
Seventeen	Sataara
Eighteen	Ashaara
Nineteen	Navaara
Twenty	Vihi
Thirty	Thirees
Forty	Saalhees
Fifty	Fansaas
Sixty	Fasdolas
Seventy	Haiydhiha
Eighty	Addiha
Ninety	Nuvadhiha
One hundred	Satheyka
Two hundred	Duisata
Three hundred	Thin satheyka
Four hundred	Atharu satheyka
Five hundred	Fas satheyka
One thousand	En haas
Ten thousand	Dhiha haas
One hundred thousand	Elaka

At the market

How much is this?	Mi kihavaraka?
What is that?	E korche?
Expensive	Agu bodu
Cheap	Agu heo
Fruit	Meyvaa
Vegetable	Tharukaaree
Fish	Mas
Banana	Dhon keyo
Mango	Anbu
Papaya	Falhoa
Breadfruit	Bambukeo
Pumpkin	Barabor
Cabbage	Bondi kopee
Chilli	Mirus
Lentils	Mugu
Rice (raw)	Handu
Coconut (aged)	Kaashi
Onions	Fiyaa
Garlic	Lonumedu

In the restaurant

What is there to eat?	Kong kaa-etche huri?
Rice (cooked)	Bai
Unleavened bread	Roshi
Curry	Riha
Tea (black)	Kalu sai
Tea (white)	Kiru sai
Tea (no sugar)	Hakuru naala
Water	Fen
Sugar	Hakuru
Milk	Kiru
Short-eats	Hedi-kaa
Knife	Valhi
Spoon	Samusaa
Fork	Uu
That's enough	Denheo
A little bit more	Adi kuda eti kole
Not too chilli hot	Kuli madu
Tasty	Raha meeru
Bad taste	Raha nubai
Dhal curry	Mugu riha
Vegetable curry	Tarukari riha
Cold drink	Fini bor eche
Drinking water	Bor feng
Much too sweet	Maa foni gada
I'm hungry	Aharen bandufai vejje
I'm thirsty	Aharen feng borvaiganejje
I'm full	Aharen bandu furifai
It's here!	Mihuvee mita!
A good restaurant	Rangalu horta

Travelling

When do you leave?	Dhanee kon irakun?
How long does it take?	Devenee kita duvahung?
Will you take me?	Aharen gendhaanan tha?
Good wind	Vai rangalu
A bad current	Oia nuba
I'm seasick	Aharen kandu bali
What's that island?	E otihee kon rasheh?
How much is the fare?	Fee kihaa vareh?
Is it time to go?	Furang vejje ta?
Bon voyage	Hing heo kurati
Hoist the sail!	Ria naga!

UNIVERSAL
GROUP OF RESORTS

PARADISE IN MALDIVES . . . Kurumba Village, Laguna Beach Resort, Nakatchafushi, Baros, Kuramathi, Maafushivaru, Blue Lagoon, and Fesdu.

Situated in Malé and Ari Atoll, Universal Resorts has untold delights waiting for you. Whether you are a beachcomber or an active water-sports enthusiast, Universal Resorts offer authentic and modern accommodation, first-class cuisine, evening discos and entertainment and, most of all, soft, seductive sands, swaying palms and boundless turquoise seas.

All Universal Resorts have international diving schools and windsurfing facilities. Various excursions are also available. Telephone, telex and fax facilities are available.

Universal Enterprises Ltd., 38, Orchid Magu, Malé 20-02, PO Box 2015, Republic of Maldives

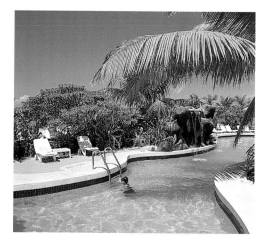

In Brief

Physical Geography

Every atoll is enclosed by a coral reef with several deep, natural channels as entry points. A protective coral reef and a shallow lagoon surround each island.

The islands are small and low-lying; most are no more than two metres above sea level. Common features are tall coconut palms, white sandy beaches, turquoise lagoons and crystal-clear waters.

There are no hills or rivers in Maldives. It is the flattest country on earth.

Area

The total area including land and sea is about 90,000 square kilometres (34,749 square miles). The archipelago is 823 kilometres (510 miles) long and 130 kilometres (81 miles) wide.

Marine life, fauna and flora

The protective coral reef surrounding every island creates a magnificent underwater garden, home to hundreds of multi-coloured fish species as well as a wide range of corals and shells.

There is no room on the islands for thick jungle. Plants of food value include breadfruit, banana, mango, papaya, screwpine, cassava, sweet potato and millet. The coconut palm is the most common tree.

The fauna and flora of Maldives are very similar to those found in other tropical island ecosystems. Very few terrestrial fauna are represented.

Below: Coconut palms, white sandy beaches, turquoise lagoons and crystal-clear waters are common features of the Maldivian landscape.

Wildlife

This is not a definitive list, but a profile of the wildlife you are most likely to see. Dhivehi names are in parenthesis.

Mammal Profile

Black rat (*Meedha*): Widely distributed. Introduced to the islands by arriving ships. Responsible for much crop destruction.

House mouse (*Meedha*): Widely distributed. Introduced to the islands by arriving ships.

Indian house shrew (*Hikandhi*): Widely distributed. Introduced species. Controls insects and other small creatures by feeding on them.

Bat, *Pteropus giganteus ariel*: Widely distributed on the larger islands. Fruit trees are the main source of food. **Flying fox**, *Pteropus hypomelanus maris*: Very rare, seen in the southern atoll of Seenu.

Bottlenose dolphin, *Tursiops truncatus*: Common. May be spotted swimming and playing at the edge of reefs. They are quite friendly with swimmers and divers.

Bird Profile

Herons

Grey heron, *Ardea cinerea rectirostris* (*Raabondhi*): Most common of Maldives' thirteen heron species. Found on all the islands. Feeds off small reef fish.

Maldivian little heron, *Butorides striatus didii* (*Raabondhi*): Extremely rare. Thought by some to be unique to Maldives.

Maldivian pond heron, *Ardeola grayii phillipsi* (*Raabondhi*): Extremely rare. Thought by some to be unique to Maldives.

Southern (or darker) Maldivian little heron, *Butorides striatus albidulus* (*Raabondhi*): Extremely rare. Thought by some to be unique to Maldives.

Waterfowl

Water cock, *Gallicrex cinerea* (*Hulhikukulhu*): Rare. Resembles a large moorhen.

White-breasted water hen, *Amaurornis phoenicurus maldivus* (*Kambili*): Common. Inhabits inland areas of dense vegetation. Identified by its white breast.

Birds of prey

Buzzard, *Buteo*: Extremely rare. Seen only when blown off course to the islands.

Falcon: Rare. Seen only during migration or when the strong monsoons blow them off course to the islands.

Harrier: Rare. Seen only during migration or during the heavy monsoon seasons when they are blown off course to the islands.

Kestrel, *Falco tinnunculus* (*Surumuthi*): Rare. May be spotted year-round. Once a migrating visitor, this species now permanently inhabits the islands.

Land birds

Indian house crow, *Corvus splendens* (*Kaalhu*): Most common Maldivian bird. Found on all settled islands. In some areas populations have reached pest proportions. Introduced by trading ships and arrived with the islands' first settlers.

Common sparrow, *Passer domesticus*: Rare. Small populations are found only in the capital. Originally introduced ten years ago.

Koel, *Eudynamys scolopacea* (*Kaalhu koveli* [m] *Dindin koveli* [f]): Most common Maldivian bird along with the Indian house crow. Found on inhabited islands. The male is identified by a shimmering black coat and green bill. The female has dull, spotted plumage brown and black in colour. She lays eggs in nests of the Indian house crow.

Plover: Common. There are at least seven species on the islands. Often spotted during its winter migration when it stops to rest.

Rose-ringed parakeet, *Psittacula krameri*: Common. Found on Malé and the surrounding islands. Identified by its green plummage, red bill, and long tail feathers.

Migratory birds

Curlew: Rare. May be spotted as its winter migration takes it by Maldives.

Godwit: Rare. Seen only during their winter migrations as they pass Maldives.

Sandpiper: Rare. May be spotted as its winter migration takes it by Maldives.

Turnstone: Rare. Only seen during its winter migration as it passes Maldives.

Whimbrel: Rare. Only seen during its winter migration as it passes Maldives.

Seabirds

Audubon's shearwater, *Procellaria iherminierei baflloni* (*Hoagulhaa*): Rare. Seen only when it visits the islands along the eastern seaboard to breed.

Common noddy, *Anous stolidus pileatus* (*Maaranga*): Common. May be spotted up and down the islands' coasts.

Lesser noddy, *Anous tenuirostris* (*Maaranga*): Common. Resides with the common noddy along Maldives' numerous coastlines.

Fairy tern, *Gygis alba* (*Kandhu-valla-dooni*): Found only on the atoll of Seenu. Considered by some to be the most beautiful of Maldives' birds. It is thought that they colonized the island from Seychelles, where they are quite common.

Greater frigatebird, *Fregata minor* (*Hoara*): Rare. Only small colonies exist. It is thought that these birds arrived from Seychelles, where there are larger populations.

Lesser frigatebird, *Fregata ariel* (*Hoara*): Rare. Only small colonies exist. It is thought that these birds arrived from Seychelles, where there are larger populations.

White-tailed tropicbird, *Phaethon lepturus lepturus* (*Dhandifuli-dooni*): Rare. This stunningly beautiful bird only visits the islands to nest. Their nests are usually built under the twisted roots of the screwpine tree.

Reptile Profile

Frog, *Rana breviceps* (*Boh*): Common. This short-headed species is the only variety found on the islands. It inhabits a wide range of areas.

Toad, *Bufo melanostictus* (*Boh*): Rare. Larger than most species. Inhabits a wide range of areas.

Geckos, *Hemidactylus brookii* (*Hoanu*) and *Hemidactylus frenatus*: Both species are widely distributed. Identified by their large unblinking eyes and ability to scale walls and hang from ceilings using the adhesive sucker-like tips of their toes.

Lizard, *Calotes versicolor* (*Bondu*): Widely distributed on most islands. Inhabits areas of dense vegetation. Males are identified by their reddish heads and yellow tails. Females are duller in colour.

Skink, *Riopa albopuctata* (*Garahita*): Rare. Most commonly seen when lying in the sun on a warm wall. It is quite fast-moving.

Snake, *Typhlops braminus* (*Harufa*): Common. Non-poisonous.

Wolf snake, *Lycodon aulicus capucinus* (*Nannugathi*): Common. Non-poisonous. Inhabits areas of dense vegetation and holes. Primary prey is the lizard.

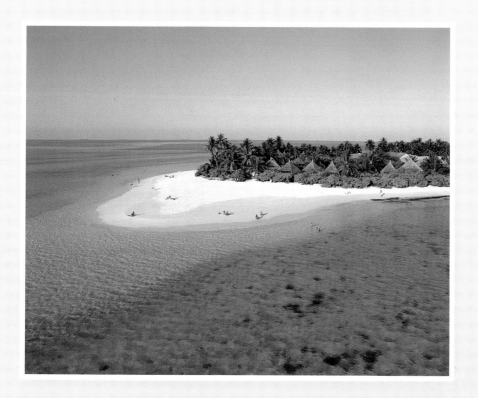

ANGAGA

Picture an endless stretch of white beach,
with 50 individual bungalows peeking out of the
luxuriant island vegetation.

Angaga offers a splendid combination of the full flavour
of Maldivian charm and modern facilities.
Private verandahs in each bungalow lead straight out to
your own section of secluded beach.

When you've had enough of privacy and peace, sip your
favourite cocktail in the Dolphin Bar and witness the
famous spectacle of a Maldivian sunset.
Or partake of the fabulous watersports on offer with
Angaga Pro Divers and Surfers.

There's something for everyone at Angaga. We take pride
in offering personalised service to all of our guests.
So, spoil yourself.
Come to Angaga — where all the little details count.

Angaga Island Resort, Ari Atoll, Republic of Maldives, Tel: 450520, Fax: 450520

Hawksbill turtle, *Eretmochelys imbricata* (*Velaa*): Common. Females come ashore to lay their eggs in the sand during the months of June through November. During the last ten years there has been a significant drop in the number of these Maldives residents.

Insect, Arachnid and Chelopod Profile

Armoured rhinoceros beetle: Common. These insects have been responsible for damage to coconut plantations by eating the roots and stems of these economically significant trees. The male is identified by the large rhinoceros-type horn protruding from the centre of its head.

Butterflies: Widely distributed. There are over sixty-seven identified species in Maldives.

Paper wasp: Common. Usually found constructing their nests under the eaves of buildings.

Scorpion: Widely distributed. The Maldivian species is quite small. Its sting is not fatal, but very painful.

Centipede: Common. Primarily found in damp areas such as under tree trunks and fallen leaves. Average size is ten centimetres (3.9 inches). Their venomous bite is quite painful though not fatal.

Seashell Profile

This is not a definitive list, but a profile of some of the more interesting and common shells you are likely to see.

Common bursa, *Tutufa bubo*: A large well camouflaged bursa found at depths of five to fifty metres (16 to 164 feet). It usually adheres to the underside of caves or at the rear of grottoes.

Geography cone, *Conus geographus*: A lightweight cone which is highly venomous and extremely dangerous to anyone handling it. All cones are highly specialized in their predatory nature; their radula are reduced and modified into a series of darts or harpoons which can be fired one at a time to inject venom from their poison gland. Although only a few have been shown to affect humans, all cones should be handled with great care (or not at all). The geography cone, together with the textile cone and a number of others with a distinctive "tented" marking on the shells, are fast-moving and actively aggressive with a highly potent toxin. Cones are normally nocturnal and have to be searched for by turning over dead coral and stones where they lie half-buried during the day. If rocks and coral are turned over, please remember to replace them as they were. Should this not be done, then hundreds of tiny creatures may die as a result.

Horned helmet, *Cassis cornuta*: A large heavy shell found in deep water, from a depth of twenty metres (65 feet), on sand and between coral banks.

Marlin spike, *Terebra maculata*: A heavy auger found in areas of clean sand.

Pink-lipped murex, *Murex virgineus*: A common largish murex found at depths of ten to fifty metres (32 to 164 feet), in the same locations as the common bursa, but with more regularity. This murex is a highly edible shell fish; the pure white body meat is chopped fine (after boiling) and used in salads and mixed seafood dishes.

Spider conch, *Lambri truncata*: A common species found in shallow water on reef flats, or areas of broken coral debris. It gets around by using its horny operculum as a hook and then moving forward with its muscular foot in a series of hops. It is this jerky movement which often gives its presence away on a broken coral sea bed, into which it can blend very well.

Tiger cowrie, *Cypraea tigris*: A large spotted cowrie found at depths of ten to fifty metres (32 to 164 feet), usually hidden in crevices and large niches under coral. Mainly nocturnal, it is best spotted during the night when its mantle is revealed and covers its shell.

Starfish Profile

Echinodermata are well represented in the waters of Maldives. The *crinoids* or **feather stars** can be found on almost any night dive and even on day dives if caves and grottoes are searched. They are multi-armed starfish which hold fast to the sea bed by a series of jointed legs known as cirri. Feather stars feed by catching plankton, using small sticky tube feet on their arms. This organic matter is transferred along ciliated grooves to the central mouth, utilizing the water vascular system.

Brittle starfish: Common in Maldivian waters. Being mainly nocturnal, they are rarely seen during the day, but on night dives many hundreds can be discovered.

Crown-of-thorns starfish, *Acanthaster planci*: A starfish with a bad reputation gained in Australian waters due to its voracious appetite for coral and the fact that they can multiply in large numbers and destroy the reef. They are covered by spines which, while looking innocuous, are in fact very sharp. The skin covering these spines has a venom which can be very painful. A starfish to leave strictly alone.

Cushion starfish, *Choriaster granulatus*: This common starfish has many colourful forms. The upper skin feels velvety to the touch with small gills which protrude through to give it a granular appearance; hence the Latin name. It feeds on coral polyps and other invertebrates.

Linkia starfish, *Linkia laevigata*: A long-armed starfish seen at most depths after five metres. It is self-coloured; sometimes blue, sometimes yellow.

Pin-cushion star, *Culcita novaeguineae*: A large puffy starfish, fairly common, which feeds off coral.

Spiny coral star, *Protoreaster lincki*: A shallow water species found commonly on sand with many colourful forms. It has a reticular skeleton with large thickened spines.

Many urchins, like the crown-of-thorns starfish, have mildly venomous spines. The long-spined black **sea urchin** (*Diadema savignyi*) causes the most problems for snorkelers and divers since the spines are sharp and brittle with pain-inducing venom.

In the event of being pierced by this urchin, do not attempt to remove the spines using a needle as with a splinter.

A much better method is to apply papaya to the skin. Papaya contains an enzyme which helps the body to dissolve these spines without the need to remove them. The pain caused by the penetration soon wears off, becoming a dull ache, and the spines dissolve within a week.

Above: Spiny coral stars are commonly seen in the shallow waters of Maldives.

Fish Checklist

Sharks
Black-tip Reef Shark
Grey Reef Shark
Hammerhead Shark
Mako
Nurse Shark
Sleeping Shark
Tiger Shark
Whale Shark
White-tip Reef Shark

Rays
Grey Sting Ray
Manta Ray
Round Ribbontail Ray
Spotted Eagle Ray

Morays
Black Cheek Moray
Dusky Moray
Geometric Moray
Leopard Moray
White Moray
Zebra Moray

Lizardfish
Variegated Lizardfish

Needlefish
Crocodile Needlefish

Flying Fish
Flying Gurnard
Glider Flying Fish
Tropical Two-Wing Flying Fish

Squirrelfish
Blotch-Eye Soldierfish
Shadowfin Soldierfish
Violet Soldierfish
Sabre Squirrelfish
Silverspot Squirrelfish
Spotfin Squirrelfish
Yellow-Tipped Squirrelfish

Trumpetfish and allies
Serrate Flutemouth
Razorfish
Trumpetfish
Yellow-Bellied Pipefish

Scorpionfish and allies
Frogfish
Bearded Scorpionfish
Paperfish
Stonefish
Long-Spined Firefish
Red Firefish (Lionfish)
Clearfin Lionfish
Ragged-Finned Lionfish

Goldie
Sea Goldie

Rock Cods and Groupers
Crescent Bass
Potato Bass
Yellowtail Fairy Basslet
Coral Rock Cod
Duskyfin Rock Cod
Lunar-Tailed Rock Cod
Peacock Rock Cod (Grouper)
Red-Edged Rock Cod
Sixspot Rock Cod
Slender Rock Cod
Vermilion Rock Cod
Black-tip Grouper
Comet Grouper
Four-Saddle Grouper
Honeycomb Grouper
Redmouth Grouper
Slender Grouper
Smalltooth Grouper
Spotted Grouper
White-Spotted Grouper
Orange Butterfly Perch
Black-Saddled Coral Trout

Bigeye
Crescent-Tail Bigeye

Sweetlips
Sailfin Rubberlip
Black-Spotted Sweetlips
Oriental Sweetlips

Opposite: Fierce moray eel in its coral hideaway threatens a passing bluefin jack.

Snappers
Green Jobfish
Small-Toothed Jobfish
Black-and-White Snapper
Blue-Banded Snapper
Bluestripe Snapper
Dory Snapper
One-Spot Snapper
Two-Spot Banded Snapper
Humpback Red Snapper
Red Snapper
Two-Spot Red Snapper

Fusiliers
Blue Fusilier
Blue and Gold Fusilier
Dark Banded Fusilier
Gold-Striped Fusilier
Rainbow Fusilier
Yellowfin Fusilier

Spinecheek
Yellowstripe Spinecheek

Batfish
Longfin Batfish
Orbicular Batfish

Moonie
Diamond Fish

Goatfish
Dashdot Goatfish
Doublebar Goatfish
Redspot Goatfish
Yellowstripe Goatfish

Angelfish
Blue Angelfish
Blue-Faced Angelfish
Emperor Angelfish
Empress Angelfish
Imperial Angelfish
Many-Spined Angelfish
Royal Angelfish
Three-Spot Angelfish
Yellow Angelfish
Dusky Cherub

Butterflyfish
Bannerfish
Indian Bannerfish
Schooling Bannerfish

Bennett's Butterflyfish
Black-Backed Butterflyfish
Black Pyramid Butterflyfish
Black Sickle Butterflyfish
Collared Butterflyfish
Double-Saddled Butterflyfish
Halfmoon Butterflyfish
Indian Butterflyfish
Klein's Butterflyfish
Long-Nosed Butterflyfish
Madagascar Butterflyfish
Meyer's Butterflyfish
One-Spot Butterflyfish
Orangebelly Butterflyfish
Purple Butterflyfish
Racoon Butterflyfish
Red-Fin Butterflyfish
Saddled Butterflyfish
Spotted Butterflyfish
Teardrop Butterflyfish
Threadfin Butterflyfish
Triangular Butterflyfish
Vagabond Butterflyfish
Yellowhead Butterflyfish
Zanzibar Butterflyfish
Gorgeous Gussy
Pennantfish
Schooling Coachman

Trevallies
Smallspotted Dart
Rainbow Runner
Bluefin Trevally
Golden Trevally
Bigeye Trevally

Pilotfish
Pilotfish

Dorado
Dorado

Sharksucker
Sharksucker

Hawkfish
Blackside Hawkfish
Freckled Hawkfish
Horseshoe Hawkfish
Spotted Hawkfish

Sweeper
Copper Sweeper
Slender Sweeper

Damsels
Blue-Green Chromis
Golden Chromis
Green Chromis
Chocolate Dip Damsel
Dicky Damsel
Dusky Damsel
Fusilier Damsel
Humbug Damsel
Jewel Damsel
Narrowbar Damsel
Sevenbar Damsel
Sulphur Damsel
Three-Spot Damsel
Whitebar Damsel
Domino
Threeband Humbug
Two-Bar Humbug
Zebra Humbug
Sergeant Major
Scissortail Sergeant
Sordid Sergeant
Blue Pete

Wrasses
Queen Coris
Turncoat Hogfish
Yellow-Tail Tamarin
Barred Thicklip
Banded Wrasse
Bird Wrasse
Bluestreak Cleaner Wrasse
Checkerboard Wrasse
Cleaner Wrasse
Crescent-Tail Wrasse
Floral Wrasse
Goldbar Wrasse
Humphead Wrasse
Moon Wrasse
Napoleon Wrasse
Queen Wrasse
Sixbar Wrasse
Slingjaw Wrasse
Tripletail Wrasse
Two Colour Cleaner Wrasse
Giant Maori Wrasse
Redbreasted Maori Wrasse

Opposite: A school of bluestripe snappers move gracefully together as if they were a single organism.

Parrotfish
Bicolour Parrotfish
Blue-Barred Parrotfish
Bullethead Parrotfish
Candelamoa Parrotfish
Daisy Parrotfish
Dusky Parrotfish
Heavybeak Parrotfish
Humphead Parrotfish
Singapore Parrotfish
Yellowscale Parrotfish

Mullet
Fringelip Mullet
Grey Mullet

Barracudas
Great Barracuda
Pickhandle Barracuda

Surgeons and Unicorns
Black Surgeon
Blacktail Surgeon
Blue Surgeon
Blue-Banded Surgeon
Chocolate Surgeon
Convict Surgeon
Dussumier's Surgeon
King Surgeon
Powder-Blue Surgeon
Yellowtail Surgeon
Unicorn Fish
Sailfin Tang
Two-Tone Tang
Bluespine Unicorn
Masked Unicorn
Orange-Spine Unicorn
Spotted Unicorn
Vlaming's Unicorn

Moorish Idol
Moorish Idol

Rabbitfish
Black-Eyed Rabbitfish
Fork-Tailed Rabbitfish
Orange Rabbitfish
Star-Spotted Rabbitfish

Kingfish
Kingfish (Wahoo)

Goby
Fire Goby
Sleeper Goby

Gamefish
Dolphin Fish
Indian Mackerel
King Mackerel
Black Marlin
Sailfish

Tuna
Big-Eye Tuna
Dogtooth Tuna
Eastern Little Tuna (Bonito)
Skipjack Tuna
Yellowfin Tuna

Triggerfish
Black Triggerfish
Boomerang Triggerfish
Chevron Triggerfish
Clown Triggerfish
Half-Moon Triggerfish
Ocean Triggerfish
Orange-Striped Triggerfish
Picasso Triggerfish
Red-Toothed Triggerfish
Titan Triggerfish
Wedgetailed Triggerfish
Yellowmargin Triggerfish

Filefish
Harlequin Filefish
Honeycomb Filefish

Boxfish
Blue-Spotted Boxfish
White-Spotted Boxfish

Toadfish
Starry Toadfish

Puffers
Blackdotted Puffer
Black-Spotted Puffer
Dog Puffer
Sharpnose Puffer
White-Spotted Puffer
False-Eye Toby
Honeycomb Toby
Model Toby

Porcupinefish
Porcupinefish

Coronetfish
Coronetfish

Jack
Bigeye Jack
Bluefin Jack

Goatfish
Doublebar Goatfish
Yellow Goatfish
Yellowsaddle Goatfish

Blenny
Striped Blenny

Monocle Bream
Two-Lined Monocle Bream

**Clown Fish
(Anemone Fish)**
Black-Footed Clown Fish
Maldive Clown Fish
Clark's Anemone Fish
Goldbelly Anemone Fish

Cardinalfish
Short-Toothed Cardinalfish
Wolf Cardinal

Sea Bream & Emperors
Gold Striped Bream
Large-Eyed Sea Bream
Blackspot Emperor
Orange-Spotted Emperor

Sandperch
Spotted Sandperch

Fun Island . . .

. . . ringed with soft, white, sandy beaches and a massive turquoise and aquamarine lagoon. Its secluded charm is enhanced by two virgin islets across the channel, which can be crossed on foot in low tide.

*A*ccommodation is in one of the 100 beautifully-appointed guest rooms overlooking immaculate beaches. The resort offers two tantalising restaurants and three well-stocked bars.

*T*here is a wide range of sports facilities to choose from: snorkelling, waterskiing, windsurfing, fishing or scuba diving. The giant house-reef, abounding with many-hued corals and tropical fish, is a diver's dream.

*W*hen the sun goes down, disco into the night or take time away on the picturesque open-air deck with stars above and islands beckoning across the sea.

*E*xcursions take you to a fishing village or our busy capital, Malé. Our popular island hopping tour and picnic on an uninhabited island is a memorable event.

Fun Island Resort (Bodufinolhu)
Villa Building, PO Box 2073, Malé 20-02
Tel: 444558/443957/441961/443959
Fax: 443958   Tlx: 77099 Funisle MF

Demographic Profile

The population of Maldives is growing at the rate of 3.2 per cent despite a high infant mortality rate of one in four. The 1992 estimate puts the nation's population at over 230,000. Since forty per cent of all Maldivians are under the age of fifteen, the population is expected to increase to about 300,000 by the end of the century. Maldives is the seventh most densely populated country on earth.

There are 200 inhabited islands, of which twenty-five have more than 1,000 residents.

The most populous of the inhabited islands is Malé, the capital and the centre of commerce. The population of Malé, which is growing at a faster rate than the rest of the country, stands at 70,000 (1992 estimate). Despite efforts to reclaim land, there is serious overcrowding.

The country's labour force totalled 108,900 in 1988 and consists of more than eighty per cent of the working-age (15-59 years) population. This reflects the wide availability of work and the high rate of participation by women.

Atoll Names

Location names in Maldives are often bewildering. Even official publications have different spellings. Often they are composite names — *Meerufenfushi*, for instance, means sweet-water island — or borrowed from other languages, like Sri Lanka's *Lankanfushi*.

In the 1940s, the traditional atolls were denoted by letters of the alphabet, and in some cases split into two parts for adminstrative purposes. As a result, the official maps carry the administrative title while most people still continue to refer to them by their traditional name.

Opposite: Sun, sea and sand — tourists enjoy the haven of a shady palm from the midday sun.

Administrative name	Common name
Addu	Seenu
Fua Mulaku	Gnaviyani
South Huvadhoo	Gaafu Dhaalu
North Huvadhoo	Gaafu Alifu
Hadhdhunmathee	Laamu
Kolhumadulu	Thaa
South Nilandhoo	Dhaalu
North Nilandhoo	Faafu
Mulaku	Meemu
Felidu	Vaavu
Ari	Alifu
North and South Malé	Malé (Kaafu)
Faadhippolhu	Lhaviyani
South Maalhosmadulu	Baa
North Maalhosmadulu	Raa
South Miladhummadulu	Noonu
North Miladhummadulu	Shaviyani
South Thiladhunmathee	Haa Dhaalu
North Thiladhunmathee	Haa Alifu

Gazetteer

(First line indicates kilometre distance from the capital, Malé.)

ATOLLS OF MALDIVES

Alifu (Ari)
64km
Capital: Mahibadhoo
Population: 7,800
18 inhabited islands, 61 uninhabited, 7 resorts

Baa (South Maalhosmadulu)
105km
Capital: Eydhafushi
Population: 7,000
14 inhabited islands, 67 uninhabited, 1 resort

Dhaalu (South Nilandhoo)
150km
Capital: Kudahuvadhoo
Population: 3,700
8 inhabited islands, 50 uninhabited

Faafu (North Nilandhoo)
120km
Capital: Magoodhoo
Population: 2,300
5 inhabited islands, 21 uninhabited

Gaafu Alifu (North Huvadhoo)
330km
Capital: Viligili
Population: 6,200
10 inhabited islands, 83 uninhabited

Gaafu Dhaalu (South Huvadhoo)
360km
Capital: Thinadhoo
Population: 9,000
10 inhabited islands, 150 uninhabited

Gnaviyani (Fua Mulaku)
430km
Capital: Mulah
Population: 7,000
1 inhabited island

Haa Alifu (North Thiladhunmathee)
280km
Capital: Dhidhdhoo
Population: 10,000
16 inhabited islands, 24 uninhabited

Haa Dhaalu (South Thiladhunmathee)
240km
Capital: Kulhudhuffushi
Population: 11,000
17 inhabited islands, 20 uninhabited

Kaafu (North Malé and South Malé)
Capital: Malé
Population: 88,700
10 inhabited islands, 105 uninhabited,
35 resorts

Laamu (Hadhdhunmathee)
224km
Capital: Hithadhoo
Population: 7,300
12 inhabited islands, 75 uninhabited

Lhaviyani (Faadhippolhu)
120km
Capital: Naifaru
Population: 7,000
4 inhabited islands, 55 uninhabited islands,
1 resort

Meemu (Mulaku)
120km
Capital: Muli
Population: 3,600
9 inhabited islands, 26 uninhabited

Noonu (South Miladhummadulu)
150km
Capital: Manadhoo
Population: 6,900
14 inhabited islands, 64 uninhabited

Raa (North Maalhosmadulu)
145km
Capital: Ugoofaaru
Population: 9,600
16 inhabited islands, 74 uninhabited

Seenu (Addu)
478km
Capital: Hithadhoo
Population: 15,000
7 inhabited islands, 26 uninhabited, 1 resort

Shaviyani (North Miladhummadulu)
192km
Capital: Funadhoo
Population: 7,800
15 inhabited islands, 39 uninhabited

Thaa (Kolhumadulu)
192km
Capital: Veymandhoo
Population: 7,200
13 inhabited islands, 54 uninhabited

Vaavu (Felidu)
67km
Capital: Felidhoo
Population: 1,500
5 inhabited islands, 19 uninhabited,
2 resorts

Museums & Historical Sites

Malé

National Museum
Medhuziyaaraiy Magu
Tel: 322254
Museum hours: 09.00–12.00 and 15.00–18.00 every day except public holidays.
Park hours: 09.00–18.00 Fridays only.

Set in part of the former Sultan's Palace, the National Museum contains archaeological finds, royal possessions, photographs, money and other curious artefacts.

Grand Mosque
Medhuziyaaraiy Magu
Hours: 09.00–17.00, closed for 15 minutes prior to prayer and for one hour following the commencement of prayer.

The mosque's *munnaaru*, or minaret, is the tallest structure in Maldives. Short trousers and short dresses are not allowed. Before entering you will be asked to remove your shoes and bathe your feet. A guide will take you through the main prayer hall, where there is beautifully carved woodwork to be admired.

Hukuru Miskiiy **(Friday Mosque)**
Medhuziyaaraiy Magu
Department of Religious Affairs tel: 322266

This is Maldives' oldest mosque, *miskiiy*, built in 1656. It is also recognized for its intricate carved interior, dating back to the thirteenth century. To visit this *miskiiy* you must first apply to the Department of Religious Affairs.

Other islands

Alifu Atoll
Thoddoo
Remains of Buddhist temple.

Dhaalu Atoll
Kudahuvadhoo
Ancient mosque built on the site of an earlier Buddhist temple.

Faafu Atoll
Nilandhoo
Aasaari Miskiiy, ancient mosque.

Faafu Atoll
Nilandhoo
Remains of Hindu Temple.

Gaafu Alifu Atoll
Dhevvadhoo
Hukuru Miskiiy.

Gaafu Alifu Atoll
Kon'dey
Four small *hawittas.*

Gaafu Dhaalu Atoll
Thinadhoo
Dhekunukolhu Miskiiy, Hukuru Miskiiy.

Gaafu Dhaalu Atoll
Vaadhoo
Malahandu Miskiiy, two *hawittas* known as Bodu and Vidamagh.

Gnaviyani Atoll
Fua Mulaku
Dhiguvaadu Miskiiy, ancient mosque.

Gnaviyani Atoll
Fua Mulaku
Kedeyre Miskiiy, ancient mosque.

Gnaviyani Atoll
Fua Mulaku
Redinge Funi, ancient monument.

Haa Alifu Atoll
Ihavandhoo
Ancient mosque.

Haa Alifu Atoll
Utheemu
Bodu Thakurufaanu Memorial Centre and the ruler's restored palace.

Haa Dhaalu Atoll
Kumundhoo
Unexplored ruins.

Haa Dhaalu Atoll
Vaikaradhoo
Hawitta known as *Jaadi Valhu Li Than.*

Laamu Atoll
Gan (Gamu)
Hawitta, also known as *Gamu Haiytheli*.

Laamu Atoll
Isdhoo
Ancient mosque.

Noonu Atoll
Lhohi
Hawitta known as *Haguraama Fas Gadu*.

Noonu Atoll
Landhoo
Hawitta known as *Maa Badhige*.

Seenu Atoll
Gan
Former British air base.

Seenu Atoll
Meedhoo
Koagannu cemetery.

Shaviyani Atoll
Kaditheemu
Ancient mosque.

Shaviyani Atoll
Lhaimagu
Hawitta known as *Fageeru Odi Baiy Than*.

Shaviyani Atoll
Nalandhoo
Hawittas known as *Us Fas Gadu* and *Happathi Gadu*.

Thaa Atoll
Buruni
Burunee Ziyaaraiy Miskiiy.

Thaa Atoll
Dhiyamigili
Ruins of Sultan Muhammad Imaaduddeen's residence.

Thaa Atoll
Kibidhoo
Hawitta.

Festivals and Holidays

Ramadan

The key events of the year are all Muslim religious feasts and festivals based on lunar movements. During *Roadha Mas* or Ramadan, everyone except those too young or sick (as well as pregnant and menstruating women) abstain from all food, water, cigarettes and sex from sunrise to sunset for a lunar month. As the sun sets, a horn shell is sounded to declare the day's fast is over; all the islanders then rush to drink coconut milk or tea and to enjoy "short-eats" while waiting for the piles of specially prepared rice and curried fish to be served. The next morning, they wake up before dawn to eat their customary rice and fish sauce, *rihaakuru*. It will be the last bite until evening: a long, dry and hungry day stretches out before them.

Kuda Id

At the end of Ramadan, there is a great feast called *Kuda Id*, held when the new moon rises in the sky. Every family usually sacrifices a precious chicken and a merry celebration takes place.

Bodu Id

Another important feast day is *Bodu Id*, two lunar months and ten days later, when those who can afford it set off on a pilgrimage to Mecca while those who can't remain at home and feast.

The Prophet's Birthday

As with all Muslims, Maldivians celebrate with great gusto the Prophet's Birthday or *Maulid*. For three days families invite one another to share their food in villages throughout the islands.

Huravee Day

This annual holiday commemorates the overthrow of the Malabars of India by Sultan Hassan Izzuddeen after their brief occupation in 1752.

Opposite: One of the countless tropical islands waiting to be discovered in Maldives.

Martyr's Day

Celebrated to honour the death of Sultan Ali VI by the Portuguese invaders in 1558.

Naming Day

When a child is seven days old close friends join the family for a naming ceremony with prayers, an Islamic recital called *Thaalud*, and a meal.

Circumcision

For boys this is the main celebration of their lifetime and takes the place of a wedding as an occasion for a big family party. Usually several six- or seven-year-old boys undergo the ceremony at the same time. After the operation, the boys lie side by side on a wooden platform in the main room of the house, with a sheet suspended in the middle by a piece of string over the lower part of their bodies. They lie on their backs for three days and the decorations, music, bright lights, food and general merriment are intended to take their minds off their recent ordeal.

Deaths

The deceased are buried in the local cemetery near the mosque as soon as possible, a necessary precaution in the tropics. During the next week prayers will be said at the burial-ground and at home. On the fortieth day a *faathihaiy* (memorial service) is held, featuring a long recital of Islamic texts (*maaloodhu*) and a feast. In memory of their loved ones, families will hold a *faathihaiy* on this same day every year. For important members of the family, this tradition may continue for several generations.

Weddings

Traditionally, weddings are not a grand affair, though some newly married couples arrange a *kaiveni sai*, a small reception with tea and snacks. The daughter of a wealthy family, though, may celebrate in style with up to 250 guests.

Public Holidays

January 1 .... New Year's Day

July 26 .... Independence Day

November 11 .... Republic Day

December 10 .... Fisheries Day

December 17 .... National Day

Also:

Huravee Day

Martyr's Day

Three holidays with religious significance are governed by the lunar calendar and their dates vary year by year. These are: *Kuda Id, Bodu Id* and *Maulid* (The Prophet Muhammed's Birthday)

LISTINGS

Airlines

Air Lanka
Ameer Ahmed Magu
Malé 20-05
Tel: 323459

Alitalia
C/O Maldives Air
Services Ltd
Marine Drive
Malé 20-02
Tel: 322436

Austrian Airlines
C/O Universal
Travel Department
18 Marine Drive
Malé 20-06
Tel: 323116

Balair/Air 2000/
Air Europe
C/O Voyages Maldives
2 Fareedhee Magu
Malé 20-02
Tel: 323617/323017
Fax: 325336
Telex: 66063

Balkan Airlines
C/O Maldives Air
Services Ltd
18 Marine Drive
Malé 20-06
Tel: 322436

Condor
C/O Universal
Travel Department
18 Marine Drive
Malé 20-06
Tel: 323116

Emirates Airways
Marine Drive
Malé 20-05
Tel: 325675

Eva Air
C/O Universal
Travel Department
18 Marine Drive
Malé 20-06
Tel: 323116

Indian Airlines
H Sifaa
Marine Drive
Malé 20-05
Tel: 323003

Transwede/Interflug
C/O Voyages Maldives
2 Fareedhee Magu
Malé
20-06
Tel: 323116

Lauda Air
C/O Fantasy Travel
Fareedhee Magu
Malé
Tel: 344668

LTU (Lufttransport-
Unternehmen)
C/O Faihu Agency
H Maleythila
Meheli Goalhi
Malé 20-05
Tel: 323202/327732
Fax: 327723
Telex: 66096

PIA (Pakistan)
H. Luxwood No. 4
Marine Drive
Malé 20-05
Tel: 323532

Singapore Airlines
2nd Floor
MHA Building,
Malé 20-03
Tel: 320777
Fax: 325699

Sterling Airways
C/O Voyages Maldives
2 Fareedhee Magu
Malé 20-02
Tel: 322019/325349
Fax: 325336
Telex: 66063

Air Charter Companies

Air Maldives
Fashanaa Building
Marine Drive
Malé 20-05
Reservations tel:
322437/322436
Fax: 325056
Telex: 77058

Hummingbird
Helicopters
P.O. Bag 6 GPO
MHA Building
Malé
Tel: 325708
Fax: 323161
Telex: 66185

Foreign Diplomatic Missions

BANGLADESH
Rukkara Magu
Malé
Tel: 323080
Fax: 322678
Telex: 66024

DENMARK
25 Marine Drive
Malé
Tel: 322451/325367
Fax: 323523
Telex: 66026

INDIA
Maafannuaage
Malé
Tel: 323176/324837
Fax: 324778
Telex: 66044

PAKISTAN
2 Moonimaage
Malé
Tel: 323005/322024
Fax: 321823
Telex: 66087

SRI LANKA
H. Sakeena Manzil,
Malé
Tel: 322845/323338
Fax: 321652
Telex: 66061

SWEDEN
25 Marine Drive
Malé
Tel: 322451/325367
Fax: 323523

UNITED STATES OF
AMERICA
Mandhuedhuruge
Violet Magu
Malé
Tel: 321981
Telex: 66028

Maldives Missions Abroad

AUSTRIA
21-250
A. 1190,
Weimarerstrasse 104
Tel: 345273/316340
Fax: 043222
Telex: 113248

BELGIUM
Rue de Vignes 16
1020 Brussels
Tel: (32) 2-478-1426
Fax: (32) 2-478-5682
Telex: 61323

EGYPT
16 Ahmed Omar Road
4th Floor
Flat 7,
El-Helmeya-El-Adida
Cairo
Tel: 391052
Fax: 342808
Telex: 94062

FRANCE
Zone Artisanale
5 Rue De Lafontaine,
21560 Arc Sur Tille
Tel: 80372660
Fax: 80372661

GERMANY
Immanuel-Kant
Strasse 16
D-6380 Bad
Homburg v.d.H.
Tel: (69) 6906789
Fax: (69) 692102
Telex: 415439

HONG KONG
201-5 Kowloon Centre,
29-39 Ashley Road,
Kowloon
Tel: (852) 376 2114
Fax: (852) 376 2366

ITALY
Via G. Caderini N-68
00196 - Rome
Tel: (396) 399660
Fax: (396) 3233181
Telex: 620377

JAPAN
Chiyoda Building 1-2
2 Chome Marunochi
Chiyodaku
Tokyo
Tel: 32 11 54 63
Fax: 32 11 69 21

MALAYSIA
15 Jalan Telawitiga
Bangsar Baru
59100 Kuala Lumpur
Tel: 03-2540941/
2547711
Fax: 03-2553780

PAKISTAN
PO Box 51
Campbell Street
Karachi
Tel: 737945/210125
Fax: 737817
Telex: 2692

SRI LANKA
25 Melbourne Avenue
Colombo 4
Tel: 580076/586762
Fax: 941-581200
Telex: 22469

SWITZERLAND
Gerechtigkeitsgasse 23
8002 Zurich
Tel: (01) 2028448
Fax: 2027505
Telex: 815562

UNITED NATIONS
Permanent Mission,
820 Second Avenue
Suite 800c
New York, NY 10017
Tel: (212) 599-6195
Fax: (212) 972-3970
Telex: (023) 096-0945

Maldives Trade Representatives

SINGAPORE
Maldives Government
Trade Centre
10 Anson Road
18-12 International
Plaza
Singapore 0207
Tel: (65) 2258955
Fax: (65) 2246050
Telex: 26007

UNITED KINGDOM
Unit 9
Printing House Yard
15A Hackney Road
London
E2 7PR
Tel: 071-729-5721/
071-729-5734
Fax: 071-729-1374
Telex: 295708

Maldives Tourist Offices Abroad

JAPAN
3-32-13 Horikiri
Katsushika-ku,
124 Japan
Tel: 03-692-4455
Fax: 03-692-3785

NORWAY
Stubbratan 20
1352 Kolsas
Tel: 02137221

UNITED KINGDOM
3 Esher House
11 Edith Terrace
London SW10 0TH
Tel: (071) 352 2246/351
0351
Fax: (071) 351 3382
Telex: 9413686

Resort Islands

Address shown is
the Malé booking office

ALIMATHA AQUATIC
RESORT
Safari Tours
SEK No. 1
Chandhani Magu
Malé
Office tel: 323524/
323760
Fax: 322516
Telex: 66030
Resort tel: 450575
Fax: 450544

ANGAGA ISLAND
RESORT
M. Thulagiri
Malé
Office tel: 313636/
326743
Fax: 323115
Resort tel: 450520/
450510
Fax: 450520
Telex: 66155

ANGELS BEACH
RESORT
(MACHAFUSHI)
G Greenlin
Neeloafaru Magu
Malé
Tel: 450616
Fax: 450615

ARI BEACH RESORT
(DIDHDHOOFINOLHU)
52 Marine Drive
Malé 20-01
Office tel: 327354/
321930/321931
Fax: 327355
Telex: 66177
Resort tel: 450513/
450607
Fax: 450512
Telex: 66178

ASDHOO SUN
ISLAND
C/O Shoanary
Henveiru
Marine Drive
Malé
Tel: 322149
Fax: 324300
Telex: 66091
Resort tel: 445051

ATHURUGAU
ISLAND RESORT
C/O Voyages
Maldives
2 Fareedhee Magu
Malé 20-02
Office tel: 324435
Fax: 324435
Telex: 77129
Resort tel: 450508
Fax: 450574

AVI ISLAND
RESORT
C/O Shoanary
Henveiru
Marine Drive
Malé
Tel: 322149
Fax: 324300
Telex: 66091
Resort tel: 450595
Fax: 450595

BANDOS
ISLAND RESORT
H. Jazeera
Marine Drive
Malé
Tel: 325529
Fax: 321026
Telex: 66050
Resort tel: 443310
Fax: 443877

BAROS
HOLIDAY RESORT
Universal
Enterprises
38 Orchid Magu
Malé
Office tel: 322971
Fax: 322678
Telex: 66024
Resort tel: 442672
Fax: 443497

BATHALA
ISLAND RESORT
Jetan Travel
Service
55 Marine Drive
Malé
Office tel: 323323
Fax: 324628
Telex: 66086
Resort tel: 450587
Fax: 450558

BIYADOO
ISLAND RESORT
Prabalaji Enterprises
(Pvt) Ltd
H. Maarandhooge
Malé
Office tel: 324699
Fax: 327014
Resort tel: 447171/
447070
Fax: 447272
Telex: 77003

BODUHITHI
CORAL ISLE
Safari Tours
SEK No. 1
Chandhani Magu
Malé
Office tel: 323524
Fax: 322516
Telex: 66030
Resort tel: 442637
Fax: 442634

BOLIFUSHI
ISLAND RESORT
Seesan Goalhi
Malé
Office tel: 320358
Fax: 320358
Resort tel: 443517
Fax: 445924
Telex: 66043

CLUB
MÉDITERRANÉE
(see "Farukolhufushi
Tourist Resort")

COCOA ISLAND
(MAKUNUFUSHI)
C/O M. Gulisthaanuge
Fiygathoshi Magu
Malé
Office tel: 322326
Fax: 322326
Resort tel: 443713
Fax: 441919
Telex: 77037

DHIGGIRI RESORT
Safari Tours
SEK No. 1
Chandhani Magu
Malé
Office tel: 323524
Fax: 322516
Telex: 66030
Resort tel: 450592
Fax: 450592

DHIGUFINOLHU
TOURIST RESORT
38 Orchid Higun
P.O. Box 2014
Malé
Office tel: 327058
Fax: 327058
Resort tel: 443599
Fax: 443886
Telex: 77006

ELLAIDHOO TOURIST
RESORT
Safari Tours
SEK No. 1
Chandhani Magu
Malé
Office tel: 323524
Fax: 322516
Telex: 66030
Resort tel: 450514
Fax: 450586

EMBOODHOO
FINOLHU ISLAND
RESORT
37 Chandani Magu
Malé
Office tel: 326483
Fax: 326482
Resort tel: 444451
Fax: 445925
Telex: 66081

EMBOODHOO
VILLAGE
Kaimoo Travels &
Hotel Services Ltd
Malé
Office tel: 322212
Telex: 66035
Resort tel: 442673
Fax: 442673
Telex: 66189

ERIADHOO
ISLAND RESORT
Ibrahim Hassan Didi
Magu
Malé
Office tel: 324933
Telex: 66031
Resort tel: 444487
Fax: 445926

FARUKOLHUFUSHI
TOURIST RESORT
(Club Méditerranée)
Ibrahim Hassan Didi
Magu
Majeedhee Bazaru
Malé
Office tel: 322976
Fax: 322850
Resort tel: 444552
Fax: 442415
Telex: 66057

FESDHOO FUN
ISLAND
Universal Enterprises
38 Orchid Magu
Malé
Office tel: 322971
Fax: 322678
Telex: 66024
Resort tel: 450541
Fax: 450547

FIHAALHOLHI
TOURIST RESORT
C/O Dhirham Travels
& Chandling
Athama Building
Faamudheyri Magu
Malé
Office tel: 323369
Fax: 324752
Telex: 66027
Resort tel: 442903
Fax: 443803
Telex: 66065

FULL MOON
Universal Enterprises
38 Orchid Magu
Malé
Office tel: 323080
Fax: 322678
Telex: 66024
Resort tel: 441976
Fax: 441979

FUN ISLAND RESORT
(BODUFINOLHU)
P.O. Box 2073
Villa Building
Ibrahim Hassan Didi
Magu
Malé
Office tel: 324478
Fax: 327845
Telex: 66090
Resort tel: 444558
Fax: 443958
Telex: 77099

GANGEHI ISLAND
RESORT
Holiday Club Maldives
H. Maizan dhoshuge
Sosun Magu
Malé 20-05
Office tel: 326687/
313937/313938
Fax: 313939
Telex: 66021
Resort tel: 450505
Fax: 450506

GASFINOLHU
ISLAND RESORT
C/O Imad's Agency
Chandhani Magu
Malé
Office tel: 324845
Fax: 322964
Telex: 66038
Resort tel: 442078
Fax: 445941
Telex: 77050

GIRAAVARU
TOURIST RESORT
C/O Phoenix Hotels &
Resorts
Marine Drive
PO Box 2089
Malé 20-05
Office tel: 323181/
323587
Fax: 325499
Telex: 66107
Resort tel: 440440
Fax: 444818
Telex: 66059

HALAVELI
TOURIST VILLAGE
Eastinvest (Pvt). Ltd.
Akiri
20-50 Marine Drive
Malé
Office tel: 322719
Fax: 323463
Telex: 77065
Resort tel: 450559
Fax: 450564

HELENGELI
TOURIST VILLAGE
Manta Office
Manta Reisen
Marine Drive
Malé
Office tel: 325587/
325625/323339
Fax: 325625
Resort tel: 444615
Fax: 444615

**HEMBADHOO
ISLAND RESORT**
Transit Inn
Maveyo Magu
61 Marine Drive
Malé
Office tel: 322016
Fax: 326606
Telex: 66084
Resort tel: 443884
Fax: 441948

**HOLIDAY ISLAND
(DHIFFUSHI)**
Villa Building,
Ibrahim Hassan Didi
Magu,
Malé 20-02
Office tel: 324195
Fax: 325177
Resort tel: 450011
Fax: 450022

**HUDHUVELI
BEACH RESORT**
H. Jazeera
Marine Drive
Malé
Office tel: 322844
Fax: 321026
Resort tel: 443396/
443982/443983
Fax: 443849
Telex: 77035

**IHURU
TOURIST RESORT**
Ihuru Investments Pvt.
Ltd
Ameeru Ahmed Magu
Malé 20-05
Office tel: 326720
Fax: 322700
Resort tel: 443502
Fax: 445933
Telex: 66099

**KANDOOMA
TOURIST RESORT**
Kandooma Malé
Office
0/46 Orchid Magu
Malé 20-02
Office tel: 323360
Fax: 326880
Resort tel: 444452
Fax: 445948
Telex: 77073

**KANIFINOLHU
TOURIST RESORT**
Cyprea Hotels
25 Marine Drive
Malé 20-05
Office tel: 322451/
325367
Fax: 323523
Telex: 66026
Resort tel: 445949/
443152/445566
Fax: 444859
Telex: 77096

**KUDA HITHI TOURIST
RESORT**
Safari Tours
SEK No. 1
Chandhani Magu
Malé
Office tel: 323524/
323760
Fax: 322516
Telex: 66030
Resort tel: 444613
Fax: 444613

**KUDA RAH ISLAND
RESORT**
2nd Floor
H. Merry Side
Marine Drive
Malé
Office tel: 322335
Fax: 322335
Telex: 66076
Resort tel: 450549
Fax: 450550

**KURAMATHI
TOURIST RESORT**
C/O Universal
Enterprises Ltd
38 Orchid Magu
Malé
Office tel: 323080/
322971
Fax: 322678
Telex: 66024
Resort tel: 450527
Fax: 450556

**KUREDHDHOO
ISLAND RESORT**
Champa Trade & Travel
KUM No 5
Malé
Office tel: 321751
Fax: 326544
Telex: 66140
Resort tel: 230337
Fax: 230332
Telex: 66201

**KURUMBA VILLAGE
(VIHAMANAA FUSHI)**
C/O Universal
Enterprises Ltd
38 Orchid Magu
Malé
Office tel: 323080/
322971/323512
Fax: 322678
Telex: 66024
Resort tel: 442324/
443081/443084
Fax: 443885
Telex: 77083

**LAGUNA BEACH
RESORT (VELASSARU)**
C/O Universal
Enterprises Ltd
38 Orchid Magu
Malé
Office tel: 322971/
323080
Fax: 322678
Telex: 66024
Resort tel: 443042
Fax: 443041

**LHOHIFUSHI
TOURIST RESORT**
Altaf Enterprises
8 Ibrahim Hassan Didi
Magu
PO Box 20109
Malé
Office tel: 323378
Fax: 324783
Telex: 66047
Resort tel: 441909
Fax: 441908

LITTLE HURAA CLUB
G. Bahaareege
Kalhu Huraa Magu
Malé 20-04
Office tel: 327387
Fax: 327387
Resort tel: 445934
Fax: 444231
Telex: 77032

**MAAYYAFUSHI
TOURIST RESORT**
Star Resort and Hotels
2/7 Ameeru Ahmed
Magu
Malé 20-04
Office tel: 320097
Fax: 326658
Resort tel: 450588
Fax: 450568
Telex: 77124

MADOOGALI RESORT
Hermosa Ltd. Inc.
H. Gaadhoo,
Malé
Office tel: 323223
Fax: 327442
Telex: 66196
Resort tel: 450581
Fax: 450554
Telex: 66196

**MAKUNUDHOO
CLUB**
Galena Maldives Pvt.
Ltd.
H. Buruneege
Malé 20-06
Office tel: 324742
Fax: 324465
Telex: 77068
Resort tel: 446464
Fax: 446565
Telex: 77059

**MEERUFENFUSHI
ISLAND RESORT**
Champa Trade &
Travels
5 Ahmadhee Bazaar
Malé
Office tel: 326545/
321751
Fax: 326544
Telex: 66140
Resort tel: 443157
Fax: 445946
Telex: 77002

**MIRIHI
MARINA**
M. Silver Star no: 3
Haveeree Higun
Malé
Office tel: 325448
Fax: 324711
Resort tel: 450500
Fax: 450501
Telex: 66131

**MOOFUSHI ISLAND
RESORT**
WDI Pvt. Ltd.
1/7 Marine Drive
Malé
Office tel: 326648
Fax: 326648
Resort tel: 450598
Fax: 450509
Telex: 66182

NAKATCHAFUSHI
TOURIST RESORT
C/O Universal
Enterprises Ltd
38 Orchid Magu
Malé
Office tel: 323512/
323080/322971
Fax: 322678
Telex: 66024
Resort tel: 443846/
443847
Fax: 442665

NIKA HOTEL
(KUDAFOLHUDHOO)
10 Fareedhee Magu
PO Box 2076
Malé 20-02
Office tel: 325087/
325091
Fax: 325097
Telex: 66124
Resort tel: 450516/
450565
Fax: 450577

OLHUVELI VIEW
HOTEL
Ma. Onyx
3/37 Chandhani Magu
Malé
Office tel: 313645/
313646
Fax: 313644
Telex: 66224
Resort tel: 441956/7/8/9
Fax: 445942

PALM TREE
ISLAND RESORT
(VELIGANDU
HURAA)
Orchid Higun
Malé
Office tel: 327058
Fax: 327058
Resort tel: 443882
Fax: 443886
Telex: 77006

PARADISE ISLAND
(LANKAN FINOLHU)
Villa Building,
Ibrahim Hassan Didi
Magu,
Malé 20-02
Tel: 324195
Fax: 325177
Resort tel: 440011
Fax: 440022

RANGALI FINOLHU
ISLAND RESORT
C/O Crown Company
Pvt Ltd.
1 Orchid Magu
Malé
Office tel: 322432
Fax: 324009
Telex: 66095
Resort tel: 450619
Fax: 450619

RANVELI BEACH
RESORT
(VILINGILIVARU)
2/44 Orchid Magu
Maafannu
Malé
Office tel: 322011
Resort tel: 450570/1/3
Fax: 450523
Telex: 66207

REETHI RAH RESORT
(MEDHUFINOLHU)
M. Shaazeevin
Fareedhee Magu
Malé
Office tel: 323758
Fax: 328842
Resort tel: 441905
Fax: 441906
Telex: 77121

RIHIVELI
BEACH RESORT
(MAHAANA ELHI
HURAA)
Chandhani Magu
Malé
Office tel: 323767
Fax: 322964
Resort tel: 443731
Fax: 443731
Telex: 66072

THUDUFUSHI
ISLAND RESORT
Voyages Maldives
20 Fareedhee Magu
Malé
Office tel: 324435
Fax: 324435
Resort tel: 450583
Fax: 450515
Telex: 77130

THULHAAGIRI
ISLAND RESORT
H. Jazeera
15 Marine Drive
Malé
Office tel: 325529
Fax: 321026
Resort tel: 445929
Fax: 445939
Telex: 77110

TWIN ISLAND
(MAAFUSHIVARU)
C/O Universal
Enterprises Ltd
38 Orchid Magu
Malé
Office tel: 322971/
323080
Fax: 322678
Telex: 66024
Resort tel: 450524
Fax: 450596

VAADHOO
DIVING PARADISE
H. Maarandhooge
Irumatheelai
Malé
Office tel: 325844
Resort tel: 443976/
443977
Fax: 443397
Telex: 77016

VABBINFARU
PARADISE ISLAND
Dhirham Travels &
Chandeling
Athama Building
Block A
Famudheyri Magu
Malé
Office tel: 323369/
323371
Fax: 324752
Resort tel: 443147
Fax: 443843
Telex: 77026

VELIGANDU ISLAND
Crown Company Pte
Ltd
1 Orchid Magu
PO Box 2034
Malé
Office tel: 322432/
324701
Fax: 324009
Telex: 66095
Resort tel: 450519/
450594
Fax: 450519

VILLIVARU
ISLAND RESORT
Prabalaji Enterprises
(Pvt) Ltd.
H. Maarandhooge,
Malé
Office tel: 324699
Fax: 327014
Resort tel: 447070/
447171
Fax: 447272
Telex: 77003

ZIYAARAIYFUSHI
TOURIST RESORT
Phoenix Hotels &
Resorts Pvt. Ltd.
H. Marine Drive
P.O. Box 2089
Malé
Office tel: 323181/
323587/322530/
325498
Fax: 325499
Telex: 66107
Resort tel: 443088
Fax: 441910
Telex: 66146

Hotels

HOTEL ALIA
Haveeree Higun
Malé 20-02
Tel: 322080
Fax: 322197

NASANDHURA
PALACE HOTEL
Marine Drive
Malé 20-06
Tel: 323380
Fax: 320822

OCEAN REEF
CLUB
C/O Phoenix Hotels
and Resorts
Marine Drive
Malé
Tel: 323181
Fax: 325499
Telex: 66107

Guesthouses and Lodges

Malé

AAZAADUGE
Tel: 322095

ALAFARU
Gololhu
(no phone)

ANDAAPOOLGE
GUESTHOUSE
Keneree Magu
Machchangolhi
Tel: 322173

ARAAROOTUGE
Machchangolhi
Tel: 322661

BORNEO
GUESTHOUSE
Handhuvaree Higun
Tel: 325324

BURUNEEGE
Hithaffinivaa
Henveiru
Tel: 322870

CAMELIA
Machchangolhi
Tel: 324642

CHAMPAA LODGE
NO. 1
Maafannu
Tel: 324733

CHAMPAA LODGE
NO. 2
Maafannu
Tel: 324733

DAWN SHINE
Machchangolhi
Tel: 322215

DHEREHA
Lainoofaru Magu
Maafannu
Tel: 323018

EVER PINK
Maafannu
Tel: 324751

FEGIVIDHUVARUGE
Fun Goalhi
Maafannu
Tel: 324470

GAADHO
GUESTHOUSE
Marine Drive
Henveiru
Tel: 323222

GINIRAAHI
GUESTHOUSE
Henveiru
Tel: 324893

GREEN LIN
Galolhu
Tel: 322279

HIAALEEGE
Maafannu
Tel: 322718/322795

KAIMOO
GUESTHOUSE
Marine Drive
Maafannu
Tel: 323241

KENEREE LODGE
No. 1/3 Majeedhee
Magu
Tel: 322468

KOSHEEGE
Kudhiraiymaa Goalhi
Machchangolhi
Tel: 323585

KURIBEE LODGE
Dhibahaaru Higun
Tel: 323078

LIFSHAM
GUESTHOUSE
Gulisthaanu Goalhi
Henveiru
Tel: 325386

MAAFARU
Champa Magu
Maafannu
Tel: 322220

MAAGIRI TOURIST
LODGE
Marine Drive
Henveiru
Tel: 322576

MALÉ TOUR INN
Maafannu
Tel: 326220

MAZAAGE
Nikagas Magu
Machchangolhi
Tel: 324669

MEEDHU
Henveiru
Tel: 322534

MERMAID INN
Maafannu
Tel: 323329

NIVIKOA
Chandhani Magu
Machchangolhi
Tel: 322942

OCEAN REED
Fareedhee Magu
Maafannu
Tel: 323311

REHENDHI
Galolhu
(no phone)

SAKEENA MANZIL
Medhuziyaaraiy Magu
Henveiru
Tel: 323281

SELVIO GUESTHOUSE
Kalhuthukkalaa Magu
Galolhu
Tel: 324671

SHABNAM LODGE
Orchid Goalhi
Tel: 322412

SONY GUESTHOUSE
Janavaree Magu
Henveiru
Tel: 325360

SUNNY LODGE
Shaheed Ali Higun
Tel: 325105

SUNSHINE
GUESTHOUSE
Maafannu
Tel: 322336

TETRA GUEST HOUSE
Hadheebi Magu
Galolhu
Tel: 322207

THAALIN
Machchangolhi
Tel: 324036

TWILIGHT INN
Sandhubaraka Goalhi
Tel: 323674

VELAGALI
GUESTHOUSE
Maafannu
Tel: 322267

Island Resort Operators

Dhirham Travel
Faamdheyri Magu
Malé
Tel: 323369
Bookings for:
Gasfinolhu, Fihaalhohi,
Vabbinfaru

Safari Tours
Chandhani Magu
Malé
Tel: 323524/323109/
322516
Bookings for: Dhiggiri,
Alimatha, Boduhithi,
Ellaidhoo, and
Kudahithi

Treasure Island
Marine Drive East
Malé
Tel: 322165/322537/
323745
Bookings for: Furana,
Bathala, Maayaafushi,
and Leisure Island

Universal Enterprises
Ltd
38 Orchid Magu
Malé
Tel: 322971/323512
Bookings for:
Baros, Fesdhoo,
Kuramathi, Kurumba,
Veligandu, Huraa and
Nakatchafushi resorts

Travel Agents and Tour Operators

Beach Travel & Tours
Pvt. Ltd
H. Green Avenue
Malé 20-05
Tel: 313628

Cosmos International
Pvt. Ltd
H. Labulaabuge
Ameeru Ahmed Magu
Malé
Tel: 313797

Cross World (Maldives)
Pvt. Ltd
H. Karanka Villa
(1st Floor)
PO Box 20172
Tel: 320912

Cyprea Hotels & Travel
(Pte) Ltd
25 Marine Drive
Malé 20-05
Tel: 322451/325367

Deens Orchid Agency
Marine Drive
Malé
Tel: 328437

Dhirham Travels
Fareedhee Magu
Malé
Tel: 323371

Galena Maldives Pvt.
Ltd.
Orchid Magu
Malé
Tel: 324743

Imad Agency
39/2 Chandhani Magu
Malé
Tel: 323441/324845

Land Mark Travel &
Trading Pte. Ltd.
52 Marine Drive
Malé
Tel: 324369

Phoenix Hotels and
Resorts Pvt. Ltd
Fasmeeru
Marine Drive
Malé 20-05
Tel: 323181/323587
Fax: 325499
Telex: 77080

Safari Tours
Chandhani Magu
Malé
Tel: 323524

Seasun Tours Pvt. Ltd
M. Sunny Coast
Malé
Tel: 325634

Sun Travel & Tours Pvt
Ltd
Ma Manaage
Malé
Tel: 325975/325977

Sunland Travel Pvt. Ltd
MTCC Building
Malé
Tel: 323467

The Travel Bureau
Maldives Air Services
Ltd.
Marine Drive
Tel: 322438

Universal Enterprises
Ltd
Orchid Magu
Malé
Tel: 323080

Voyages Maldives
Fareedhee Magu
Malé
Tel:322019/323017

Travel Agents and Tour Operators Abroad

Australia

Aquarius Travel
40-42 Taylor Street
Ashburton
Victoria
Tel: (03) 258863
Australian Himalayan
Expeditions
377 Sussex Street
Sydney
Tel: (02) 2643366

Club Méditerranée
500 George Street
Sydney
Tel: (02) 2648266

Detours
140 Pacific Highway
North Sydney
Tel: (02) 9570585

Dive Magic Tours
100 Clarence Street
Sydney
Tel: (02) 2676744

Island Affair Holidays
Singapore Airlines
House
17 Bridge Street
Sydney
Tel: (02) 2360101

Kuoni Travel
39 York Street
Sydney
Tel: (02) 2902577

New Horizons
95 St. George's Terrace
Perth
Tel: (09) 3217823

Penthouse Tours
109 Pitt Street
Sydney
Tel: (02) 2311455

Peregrine Expeditions
343 Little Collins Street
Melbourne
Tel: (03) 601121

Premier Travels
511 Willoughby Road
Willoughby NSW
Tel: (02) 9581622

Swingaway Holidays
33 Bligh Street
Sydney
Tel: (02) 2370300

Taprobane Tours
439 Albany Highway
Victoria Park WA
Tel: (09) 3625877

Vacations International
5 Hill Street
Perth
Tel: (09) 4264646

Europe

Hussain Afeef
Stubbratan 20,
1352 Kolsan
Norway
Tel: (021) 37221

Intravco
Via Albricci
20122 Milano
Italy
Tel: 573865

Lloyd Tours
Lilla Torg S-211
34 Malmo
Sweden
Tel: 104545

Manta Reisen
Meinrad Lienert-
Strasse 5
Zurich
Switzerland
Tel: 4615577

Neckermann
Postfach-119091
6000 Frankfurt 2
Germany
Tel: 26901

Nouvelles Frontieres
37 Rue Violet
Paris
France
Tel: 5786540

India

Taj Mahal Hotel
Apollo Bunder
Bombay
Tel: 243366

Japan

Ul Marine Pak
Nadaya Building
1-18-13 Shinbashi
Minato-ku
Tokyo 105
Tel: 5802804

Takekatzu Asakura
3-32-13 Horikiri
Katsushika-ku, 124
Japan
Tel: 03 692 4455

Singapore

American Express
96 Somerset Road
02-02 UOL Building
Tel: 2358133

Club Méditerranée
400 Orchard Road
14-06 Orchard Towers
Tel: 7377397

German Asian Travels
9 Battery Road
Straits Trading Building
Tel: 5335466

Maldive Island
Booking Service
96 Somerset Road
11-05 UOL Building
Tel: 7341041

Sri Lanka

Tradewinds
77 Robinson Road
01-00 SIA Building
Tel: 2254488
Sri Lanka

Aitken Spence
Sir Baron Jayatilaka
Mawatha
Colombo 1
Tel: 27861

Gemini Tours
40 Wijerama Mawatha
Colombo 7
Tel: 98446

Uniresort & Travel
77 Dharmapala
Mawatha
Colombo 3
Tel: 25032

Walkers Tours
130 Glennie Street
Colombo 2
Tel: 21101

United Kingdom

Indian Ocean
Hideaways
55a Rathbone Place
London W1
Tel: 071 631 4114

Maldive Travel
3 Esher House
11 Edith Terrace
London SW10 0TH
Tel: 071 352 2246

Speedbird Holidays
152 King Street
London RH10 1NP
Tel: 081 741 8041

Sea Freight Companies

India

Kumanar & Company
South Raja Street
Tuticorin
Tel: 21926

S. Albert & Company
South Raja Street
Tuticorin
Tel: 21276

V.V. Danushkodi Nadar
& Sons
South Raja Street
Tuticorin
Tel: 20038

Maldives

Huvadhoo Shipping
Maafannu
Malé
Tel: 322038

Marine Export Trading
Company
57 Marine Drive
Malé
Tel: 323121

Matrana Enterprises
Majeedhee Magu
Malé
Tel: 322151/322832

Omadhoo Shipping
Company
PO Box 20146
Malé
Tel: 324314

Sri Lanka

Pioneer Shipping
Agencies
676 Galle Road
Colombo 3
Tel: 87746

Taxi Hire

Express
Malé
Tel: 323132

Kulee Dhuveli Taxi
Service
Feeroaz Magu
Malé
Tel: 324996
and
Maafannu
Malé
Tel: 322122

Regular Taxis
Malé
Tel: 322454

Taxi Centre
Maafannu
Malé
Tel: 322560

Taxi Line
Maafannu
Malé
Tel: 323107

Taxi Zone
Henveiru
Malé
Tel: 322598

Wahoo Taxi Service
Marine Drive
Malé
Tel: 323574

Helicopter Hire

Hummingbird
Helicopters
P.O. Bag 6, GPO
MHA Building
Malé
Tel: 325708
Fax: 323161
Airport tel: 328857

Boat Hire

Altaf Enterprise
Majidi Bazaar
Malé
Tel: 323378

Nazaki Services
Marine Drive
Malé
Tel: 324314/324215

Rover Tours
10 Ever Glory
Malé
Tel: 323537

Sea Tracs Cruising
Marine Drive
Malé
Tel: 322597/324566

Treasure Island
Holidays
Marine Drive East
Malé
Tel: 322165

Voyage Maldives
2 Fareedhee Magu
Malé
Tel: 322019/323017

ZSS
Marine Drive
Malé
Tel: 322505

Medical Services

Central Hospital
Sosun Magu
Henveiru
Malé
Tel: 322400

Flying Swiss
Ambulance Clinic
Huvadhoo
Marine Drive
Malé
Office tel: 3234508/
324509
Telex: 77089
Emergency Number:
324500 (24 hours)

Banks

Bank of Ceylon
Ground Floor
Bodufaru
Orchid Magu
Malé
Tel: 323046

Bank of Maldives
Marine Drive
Malé
Tel: 323095/322948

Habib Bank Limited
Ship Plaza
Orchid Magu
Malé
Tel: 322051/322052

Maldives Monetary
Authority
(Central Bank)
Umar Shopping Arcade
Chandani Magu
Marine Drive
Malé
Tel: 322291/322292

State Bank of India
H. Zonaria
Marine Drive
Malé
Tel: 323053/323052

Cinema

Star Cinema
Majeedhee Magu
Malé
Tel: 323913/
322913

Bookshops

Asrafee Bookshop
Orchid Magu
Malé
Tel: 323464

Nishaan Book Shop
Sosun Magu
Malé
Tel: 322825

Novelty Bookshop
Faridi Magu
Malé
Tel: 322564

Papyrus Book Shop
Majeedhee Magu
Malé
Tel: 323293

Libraries, Museums and Cultural Centres

National Centre for
Linguistics and
Historical Research
Director
(Culture & History)
Malé
Tel: 323077
Director (Language)
Tel: 324396

National Museum
Sultan Park
Malé
Tel:322254

National Library
Majidi Magu
Malé
Tel: 323943

Media

Newspapers

Haveeru — daily
Husnuheenaa Magu
Malé
Tel: 325671/323685

Aafathis — daily
Haveeree Higun
Malé
Tel: 328730/328731

Government Offices

Atolls Administration
Fashanaa Building
Marine Drive
Malé 20-05
Tel: 322826/323070

Immigration &
Emigration
F/2 Huravee Building
Ameeru Ahmed Magu
Malé 20-05
Tel: 323913

Information &
Broadcasting
F/3 Huravee Building
Ameeru Ahmed Magu
Malé 20-05
Tel: 323837

Tourism
F/2 Ghazee Building
Ameeru Ahmed Magu
Malé 20-05
Tel: 323224/323228

Trade & Industries
F/1 Ghazee Building
Malé 20-05
Tel: 323668

Bibliography

General

Archives and Resources for Maldivian History, published by University of Khartoum, Sudan.

Constitution of the Maldive Islands (AH 1383), Malé.

Etudes interdisciplinaires sur le monde insulindien, "The Mosque in the Maldive Islands", Archipel 26, Paris.

Isdhoo Loamaafaanu (1986), by Hassan Ahmed Maniku and G. D. Wijayawardhana, published by the Royal Asiatic Society of Sri Lanka, Colombo.

The Islands of Maldives (1983), published by Novelty, Malé.

Journal of the Ceylon Branch of the Royal Asiatic Society, vol. XXVII (1986), "Maldivian Linguistic Studies", by Wilhelm Geiger, published by the Royal Asiatic Society, Malé.

Journal of the Royal Asiatic Society (vol. 78, 1925), "A Description of the Maldive Islands: c. 1683", published by the Royal Asiatic Society, Colombo.

Linguistic Strands in the Maldives (1978), published by the School of Oriental and Asian Studies, London.

The Maldive Islands (1974), by C. H. B. Reynolds, published by the Royal Central Asiatic Society, London.

The Maldive Islands: An Account of the Physical Features, Climate, History, Inhabitants, Production, and Trade (1883), by H. C. P. Bell, published by Government Printer, Colombo.

The Maldive Islands: Monograph on the History, Archaeology, and Epigraphy (1940), published by Ceylon Government Press, Colombo.

The Maldive Islands: Report on a Visit to Malé January 20 to February 21, 1920 (1921), published by Government Printers, Colombo.

Maldives (1984), by S.H. Mirza, published by the Centre for South Asian Studies, University of Punjab, Lahore.

The Maldives: An Introductory Economic Report, (1980) by K. Sarwar Lateef, published by World Bank, Washington DC.

The Maldives: A Profile (1977), by Hassan Maniku, published by the Department of Information, Malé.

The Maldives Mystery (1988), by Thor Heyerdahl, published by Unwin Hyman, London.

Maldives 25 Years of Independence (1990), published by Media Transasia, Bangkok.

Maldives: Winds of Change in an Atoll State (1985), by Urmila Phadnis and Ela Dutt Luithi, published by South Asian Publishers, New Delhi.

People of the Maldive Islands (1980), by Clarence Maloney, published by Orient Madras, Longman.

Report on the Maldive Islands (1883), published by the Ceylon Government, Colombo.

Report on the Survey of Island Women (1980), by Helen Seidler, published by the National Planning Agency, Malé.

Say it in Dhivehi (1990), by Hassan Ahmed Maniku, published by Lake House, Colombo.

Some Observations on the History of the Maldivian Language (1970), by M. W. S. De Silva, published by the Philological Society, Oxford.

Southern Arabia and the Islamication of the Central Indian Ocean Archipelago (1981), by Andrew Forbes, Archipel 21, Paris.

The Story of Mohamed Thakurufaanu (1986), by Hussain Salahuddeen, published by Novelty, Malé.

The Strode Venturer (1965), by Hammond Innes, published by Collins, London.

Ten Years of Development 1978-1988 (1988), published by the Ministry of Planning and Environment, Malé.

Vanavaru (1 October, 1988), "Dhevi", by Hassan Ahmed Meniku, published by Novelty Press, Malé.

Vanavaru (2 March, 1989), "Nakaiy", by Hassan Ahmed Meniku, published by Novelty Press, Malé.

Vanavaru (4 October, 1989), "Filaaveli", by Hassan Ahmed Meniku, published by Novelty Press, Malé.

Guides and Travel Books

A Visit to the Maldive Islands (1961), by C. Smallwood, published by the Royal Central Asian Society, London.

An Illustrated Account of some Maldivian Plants, by R. N. Fouseka and S. Balasubramanium.

The BMW Tropical Beach Handbook (1980), by Nick Hanna, published by Fourth Estate, London.

Catalogue of Fishes of the Maldives — 3 volumes, Malé.

Common Fishes of the Maldives (1987), by Charles Anderson and Ahamed Hafiz, published by Novelty, Malé.

Discover Maldives (1977), by Adam Maniku, published by Fotoart, Malé.

Diversions of a Diplomat in Ceylon (1957), by Philip K. Crowe, published by Van Nostrum, New York.

An English Lady's Visit to the Maldives (1920), by Lawson Robins, published by the Ceylon Observer Press, Colombo.

The Fascinating Maldives (1985), by Mohamed Farook, published by Novelty, Malé.

The Fauna and Geography of the Maldive Islands and Laccadive Archipelago (1901), by Stanley J. Gardiner, published in Cambridge.

A Field Guide to the Coral Reef Fish of the Indian and West Pacific Oceans (1977), by R.H. Carcasson, published by Collins, London.

Give Me a Ship to Sail (1958), by Alan Villiers, published by Hodder & Stoughton, London.

A Guide to the Common Reef Fish of the Western Indian Ocean (1987), by K.R. Bock, published by Macmillan, London.

Island World of Maldives (1988), published by Media Transasia, Bangkok.

Journey Through Maldives (1992), by Mohamed Amin, Peter Marshall and Duncan Willetts, published by Camerapix Publishers International, Nairobi.

Ladies and Gentlemen — The Maldive Islands (1949), by M. A. Didi, published by the Ministry of External Affairs, Malé.

Land of 1000 Atolls (1966), by Irenaeus Eible-Eibesfeldt, published by World Publishing, New York.

Maldives (1987), by Stuart Bevan, published by Other People, Australia.

The Maldives — Home of the Children of the Sea (1990), by Mustag Hussain and Rohan Gunaratna, published by Novelty, Malé.

Maldives: A Nation of Islands (1983), published by the Department of Tourism, Malé.

Maldives & Islands of the East Indian Ocean: A Travel Survival Kit (1990), by Robert Willox, published by Lonely Planet, Australia.

Maldives: le plus beau des livres (1984), by Christophe Valentin and Emmanuel Valentin, published by Richer-Hoa Qui, Paris.

Maldives: People and Environment (1988), by Paul A. Webb, published by Media Transasia, Bangkok.

Memoir on the Inhabitants of the Maldive Islands (1844), by I. A. Young and W. Christopher, published by the Bombay Geographical Society, Bombay.

Nautical Directions for the Maldive Islands (1840), by Robert Moresby, published by Allen & Company, London.

Papineau's Travel Guide to the Maldives (1987), published by MHP Publishing, Singapore.

Travels in Asia & Africa 1325-54 (1983), by Ibn Battuta, published by Routledge & Kegan Paul, London.

The Tropical Traveller (1982), by John Hatt, published by Pan, London.

The Two Thousand Islands: A Short Account of the People, History, and Customs of the Maldive Archipelago (1935), by T. W. Hockly, published by Witherby, London.

Underwater Maldives (1989), by Bob Friel, published by Novelty, Malé.

The Voyages of François Pyrard of Laval to the East Indies, the Maldives, the Moluccas, and Brazil — vol. I (1887), by François Pyrard de Laval, published by the Hakluyt Society, London.

INDEX

(Illustrations are indicated in bold.)

A

Aasaari Miskiiy 142, 301
Abdulla, Sultan Dharmas Mohamed Ibn 38, 142
Addu Atoll see Seenu Atoll
Addu Development Authority 179
Adiri Adiri, Captain 42
Agriculture 269
Air charter companies 305
Air Maldives 22, **23**, 279
Airlines, international 279, 305
Al-Adrisi 39
Al-Barbari, Abu al-Barakat Yusuf 38, 85, 173
Al-Biruni 211
Al-Mas'udi 35
Al-Thabreyzee, Abdul Rikaab Yusuf see Al-Barbari, Abu al-Barakat Yusuf
Ali Rajas, the 40, 42, 156
Ali Rasgefaanu Ziyaaraiy memorial 85
Ali VI, Sultan 42, 85, 168
Ali, Sultan Mohammed Ibn Al-Haj 160, 173
Alifu (Ari) Atoll **24, 27**, 130-136, 298; map of **131**; resorts in 130-136
Alifushi Boat Yard 162, 249
Alimatha 138
Alimatha Aquatic Resort 138
Ambergris 241
Andre, Captain Andreas 42
Angaga 130
Angelfish 206
Anthem, national 30
Arabs 38-39
Arachnid profile 290
Arachnids 197
Ari Atoll see Alifu Atoll
Ari Beach Resort (Diddu Finolhu) 130
Ariadhoo Channel 130
Arts 240-242, **241**, **242**
Aryans 17
Asdhoo 99, 118
Asdu Sun Island 118
Athurugau 130
Atoll Education Centres 274
Atolls, central 96-153; map of **97**
Atolls, development of 278
Atolls, formation of 52-53
Atolls, names of 298
Atolls, northern 156-169; map of **157**
Atolls, southern 171-187; map of **172**

B

Avi Island Resort (Velidhoo) 130-131

Baa (South Maalhosmadulu) Atoll 158-160, 298; map of **161**
Baarah 168
Banana Reef 221
Banana Split 221, 225
Bandaara Kulhi 177
Bandos 99, 106, 221, 230
Banks 280, 313
Bannerfish 206
Barbosa, Duarte 59
Baros 99, 106, 230
Barracuda 205, 208
Barracuda Giri 225
Bat 196, 287
Batfish 206
Bathalaa 130, 135
Battuta, Ibn 38, 40, 58, 59, 60, 100, 160, 176, 192, 211, 243
Beetle, rhinoceros 197, 290
Bell, H.C.P. 37, 57, 59, 76, 150, 152, 176, 177, 183
Bihuroazu Kamanaa Miskiiy 85
Bird profile 287-288
Bird, koel 198, 287
Birds 198-202, **198, 199, 200-201, 202**, 287-288
Birds of prey 287
Birds, land 287-288
Birds, migrant 198, 202, 288
Birds, wading 198
Biyadoo 99, 122
Blue Lagoon 225
Boat building 162, 248-249
Boat services 280, 312-313
Bodu Id 303
Bodu Thakurufaanu Memorial Centre 169, **170**, 301
Bodufinolhu 99, 123
Boduhithi 99, **101**, 109
Bolifushi 99, 118
Bomasdhoo 163
Bookshops 313
Bougainvillea **101, 191, 194-195**
British, the **42**, 44-45, 178-179, 183, 185
Buddhism 37, 38, **39**
Bursa, common 290
Buruni **110-111, 127**, 148, 303
Buruni Ziyaaraiy mosque 148
Business hours 280
Butterflies 197, 290
Butterflyfish **204**, 206, **215**
Buzzard 198, 287

C

Centipede 197, 290
Children's Reformatory 275
Christopher, Wilmott 59
Cinemas 313

Circumcision 304
Citizens' Majlis 19, 48
Climate 20, 53-56, 281
Clothing, traditional **46, 180**, 240
Clownfish 205
Club Méditerranée see Farukolhufushi
Club Vacanze 73
Cocoa Island (Makunufushi) **1**, 73, 99, **116-117**, 122
Coconut 190, 192-193
Cod, vermillion rock **189, 220**
Coir rope, making of 63, 171
Conch, spider 290
Coral Garden 225
Coral, black **144**, 146, 217, 241
Coral, fire **183**, 205
Coral, mining of 213
Corals 203, 205, **217**, 218, **227**
Cowrie, tiger 291
Cowries 38, 210-211, 213, **218**
Crab, ghost 213
Crab, hermit 213
Crab, land 213
Crab, porcelain 213
Crabs 213
Crafts 240-242, **241, 242**
Crow, Indian house 198, 287
Crown-of-thorns 214
Cultural centres 313
Curlew 198, 288
Currency 280
Currency regulations 280
Customs 279

D

Da Gama, Vasco 36, 41
Dance 169, 246, **246, 247**
Darwin, Charles 52
De Almeida, Dom Lourenço 36
De Barros, Joao 59, 211
Deaths 304
Demographic profile 298
Dhaalu (South Nilandhoo) Atoll 144-146, 298
Dhadi Magu 178
Dhadimage Kulhi 177
Dharaboodhoo 142
Dhekunukolhu Miskiiy 173, 301
Dhevi 59-60, 176
Dhevvadhoo 171, 173, 301
Dhidhdhoo 167
Dhiggaru 139, **245**
Dhigufinolhu 99, 122
Dhiguvaadu Mosque 178, 301
Dhiraagu Earth Station **25**
Dhivehi 17, 19, 37, **49**, 171, **186, 281**, 282-283
Dhives Akuru **186**, 187
Dhiyamigili 148, 303
Dhoani 20, 22, 66, **112, 120-**

121, 143, 162, 248-249, 252, **256, 257**, 257
Dhoonidhoo 100
Diddu Finolhu see Ari Beach Resort
Didi, Abdullah Afif 45
Didi, Muhammad Amin 45, 76
Didi, Muhammad Farid 45
Didi, Sultan Abdul Majeed 45
Diggiri 138-139
Diplomatic missions, foreign 305
Diving 219, 220-231, **226, 228-229, 231**, 235-238
Diving guide 225-230
Diving, night 221
Diving, wilderness 221
Divorce 64
Dolphin, bottle-nose **196**, 210, 287
Dolphins 196, 210
Drama 246
Dravidians 17, 37
Drums, bodu beru 246, **246, 247**
Drums, traditional **44**
Dugong 196
Dutch, the 43-44

E

Ecology 213-218
Economic development 267, 270-272, 277-278
Economy 267-270
Education 65, 79, 274
Eel, moray 208, **292**
Eels 205
Ellaidhoo 130, 135
Emblem, national 30, **30**
Emboodhoo Channel 225
Emboodhoo Express 225
Emboodhoo Finolhu 99, 118, 225
Emboodhoo Village 99, 118
Emboodhoo Wall 225
Equatorial Channel 175
Eriadhoo 99, 113
Eriadhoo Island Resort 113
Export 277
Eydhafushi 159, 160, **162, 166**

F

Faadhippolhu Atoll see Lhaviyani Atoll
Faafu (North Nilandhoo) Atoll 142-144, 300
Fahala 148
Falcon 198, 287
Family life 62-64, **67**
Fanditha 60, 176, 192
Faridhoo 167
Farukolhufunadhoo see Funadhoo
Farukolhufushi (Club Med) **72**, 73, 99, **99**, 106, 113-114, 225

Fauna 196-197
Fehendhoo 159
Felidhoo 138
Felidhoo Kandu Channel 136
Felivaru 158, **159**
Fesdhoo 130, 135
Festivals 303-304
Feydhoo 183
Fihaalhohi 99, 126
Fioari 174
Fish **188**, **189**, **204**, 205-209, **210**, **211**, **212**, **214**, **215**, **216**, **220**, **222-223**, **224**, **226**, **295**
Fish checklist 293-294, 296
Fish, pilot 205
Fish, reef 205-209
Fishing **12-13**, **50**, 50, **66**, 66, **71**, **78**, **88**, 89, **94-95**, 149, 158, **159**, **164**, **168**, **182**, 217, 268
Flag, national **5**, 30
Flights, domestic 279
Flights, international 279
Flora **30**, 30, **101**, **108**, **139**, **140-141**, 190-195, **191**, **192**, **193**, **194-195**; cultivated 191-193
Flower, national 30, **30**
Food 174, **178**, 264, **265**
Fox, flying 196
Frangipani **192**
Friday Mosque (Laamu Atoll) **149**, **150**
Friday Mosque (Malé Atoll) 85
Frigate bird, lesser 202, 288
Frigatebird, greater 202, 288
Frog 197, 288
Fua Mulaku 174, **175**, 175, 176, 177, 178, **182**, **184**, 192, 301
Fua Mulaku Atoll see Gnaviyani Atoll
Fulhadhoo 158, 159
Fun Island Resort 123
Funadhoo (Malé Atoll) 100
Funadhoo (Shaviyani Atoll) 163, 165
Furana 99, 106, 114, 225, 226, 230
Fusilier 206
Fusilier Reef 225

G
Gaadhoo 149
Gaafaru 103
Gaafu Alifu (North Huvadhoo) Atoll 171-173, 300
Gaafu Dhaalu (South Huvadhoo) Atoll 173-175, 300
Gaathafushi 135
Gadhdhoo 174
Gallandhoo Kadu 169
Gan (Gaafu Dhaalu Atoll) 174

Gan (Gamu) (Laamu Atoll) 149-150, 152, 303
Gan (Seenu Atoll) 178-179, 181, 183, 303
Gan Holiday Village 179, 181, 183
Gangehi Island **8-9**, **14-15**, **109**, 130, 135
Gasfinolhu 99, 118
Gayoom, President Maumoon 37, 46, 48
Gazetteer 298, 300
Gecko, house 197, 288
Geiger, Professor Wilhelm 20
Geography 52-56, 286
Geography cone 290
Giraavaru (island) 34, 99, 103
Giraavaru (people) 37, 58, 103
Girifushi 225, 230
Global warming 217-218
Gnaviyani (Fua Mulaku) Atoll) 175-178, 300
Godwit 198, 288
Goidhoo 159
Government 281-282
Government offices 313
Grand Mosque 301
Gross Domestic Product 267, 270
Groupers 205
Guesthouses, listing of 310
Guraadhoo 148

H
Haa Alifu (North Thiladhunmathee) Atoll 167-170, 300
Haa Dhaalu (South Thiladhunmathee) Atoll 166-167, 300
Hadhdhunmathee Atoll see Laamu Atoll
Hadhdoo Kadu 148
Hakeems 61
Halaveli 130, 135
Hanna's Reef 225
Harley, Richard 221
Harrier 198, 287
Hass, Hans 52
Hassan IX, Sultan 41
Hassan X, Sultan 185
Hawkfish 207
Health 20, 65, 272, 274
Health requirements 279
Health Sciences, Institute of 275
Helengeli 73, 99, 103
Helicopter hire 312
Helmet, horned 290
Hembadhoo 109, 113
Heron, grey 198, **199**, **202**, 287
Heron, Maldivian little 287
Heron, Maldivian pond 198, 287
Heron, Southern Maldivian little 287
Herons 198, 287

Heyerdahl, Thor 37, 142, 146, 173, 174, 177, 178
Hibiscus **193**
Himithi 142
Himmafushi 103, 230
Hinnavaru 158
Historical sites 301, 303
History 33-50
Hithadhoo (Laamu Atoll) 149
Hithadhoo (Seenu Atoll) 179, 183, 185, 274
Hiyala, Dhon 148
Hockly, T.W. 76
Holidays 303-304
Homes 62, 185
Hospitals 274
Hotel and Catering Services, School of 275
Hotels, listing of 309
Huadadhoo 177
Hudhuveli 114
Hukuru Miskiiy (Dhevvadhoo) 173, 301
Hukuru Miskiiy (Malé) 85, 301
Hukuru Miskiiy (Thinadhoo) 173, 301
Hulhudhoo 185
Hulhule Island 19, **21**, 70, 76, 79, **90-91**, 100
Human resource development 275
Hummingbird Helicopters 22, **28-29**, 279
Huraa 103
Huravee Day 303
Hussain, Khatib 42
Hussain, Sheikh 61
Huvadhoo Atoll 171, 202
Huvadhoo Kandu see One-and-a-Half-Degree Channel
Huvarafushi 169, **246**
Huvarafushi Youth Association 169

I
Ibrahim, Sultan 173
Ihavandhippolu Atoll 169
Ihavandhoo 169, 301
Ihuru **74-75**, 99, 109
Imaad-ud-deen VI, Sultan Muhammad **42**, 148, 185
Immigration regulations 279
Independence 46
Industry 269-270, 272
Insect profile 290
Insects 197
Investment 278
Isdhoo **149**, 149, **150**, 152, 303
Isdhoo loamaafaana 38, **47**
Iskandar I, Sultan Ibrahim 43, 85
Islam 36, 38, **83**, 83, 85, 243-245
Islamic Centre **48**, **83**, 83, **84**, **85**, **244**
Island Women's Committees 277

J
Jack, bluefin 208, **292**
Jacks **211**

K
Kaadedhdhoo 22, 279
Kaafu Atoll see Malé Atoll
Kaashidhoo 100
Kaashidhoo Kandu Channel 96, 156
Kabaafaanu, Mariam 43
Kaditheemu 165, 303
Kaduma 99, 123
Kalegefan, Abdul Naib 178
Kaliminja, King 38
Kaloa, Prince Koimala 34, 38, 60, 160
Kandu Giri 226
Kandu Oiy Giri 114, 225, 226
Kanifinolhu 99, 118
Kanu Huraa (Tari Village) 99, 118
Kedeyre Mosque **175**, 178, 301
Kelai 169
Kestrel 198, 287
Kibidhoo 148, 303
Kilege, Sultana Khadeeja Rehendhi Kabaidhi 39, 40
Kinolhas 160
Koel 198, 287
Kolamaafushi 173
Kolhufushi 139
Kolhumadulu Atoll see Thaa Atoll
Kon'dey 173, 301
Koravalu Mosque 185
Kuburudhoo 167
Kuda Bandos Island **54-55**, 100
Kuda Hithi 99, 109
Kuda Id 303
Kuda Malé 158
Kuda Rah 130
Kudafolhudhoo see Nika Hotel
Kudahuvadhoo 146, 147, 301
Kudahuvadhoo Kadu see Maa Kadu Channel
Kulhudhuffushi 167, 274
Kumundhoo 167, 301
Kunfunadhoo 73, 159, 160
Kuramathi Tourist Resort **68**, 73, **106**, **113**, 130, 136
Kuredhdhoo 156
Kuredhdhoo Island Resort 158
Kuredhivaru 163
Kurumba Village (Vihamanaafushi) 73, 99, **100**, 103, 106

L
Laamu (Hadhdhunmathee) Atoll 148-153, 300; people of 153
Labour force 267
Lacquerware, production

of 160, 240, **241**, **242**
Laguna Beach Resort
(Velassaru) 73, 99, 118,
269
Lakshadweep Islands 52,
156, 169
Landhoo 163, 165, 303
Language 281
Lankanfushi 99, 114, 226,
230
Lhaimagu 166, 303
Lhaviyani (Faadhippolhu)
Atoll 156-158, 300; map of
158; resorts in 156, 158
Lhohi 163, 303
Lhohifushi 99, 118
Libraries 313
Lion's Head 226
Lionfish 207, **214**, **216**
Little Huraa 99, 118
Lizard, garden 197, 288
Lizardfish 207
Lodges, listing of 310

M
Ma Huan 35, 211
Maa Kadu Channel 147
Maabaidhoo 149
Maadheli 146
Maafushi 100, 275
Maafushivaru *see* Twin
Island
Maagari 226
Maakadoodhoo 165
Maamakunudhoo 167
Maamendhoo 149
Maamutaa 173
Maavah 149
Maayyafushi 130, 136-137
Madoogali 130, 136
Magoodhoo 142, 144
Makunudhoo 99, 113
Makunudhoo Club 113
Makunufushi *see* Cocoa
Island
Malahandu Mosque 173,
181, 301
Maldive Fish 66, 268
Maldive Victory, wreck of
100, 114, 226
Maldives Centre for
Management and
Administration 275
Maldives missions abroad
305, 306
Maldives Monetary
Authority 271-272
Maldives' National Day
85
Maldives National Ship
Management Limited 19,
50, 96, 269
Maldives tourist offices
abroad 306
Maldives trade
representatives 306
Malé 19, **25**, **69**, 76-93, **77**,
78, **80-81**, **82**, **83**, **84**, **85**, **86**,
87, **88**, **89**, **92**, **93**, 301; map
of **79**
Malé Atoll 99-127, 300;
map of **98**; resorts in 99

Malé International Airport
19, **21**, 22, **90-91**, 100
Mammal profile 287
Manadhoo 163
Maniku, Hassan Ahmed
59-60, 148
Manta Point 114, 226
Maradhoo 183
Marine life 203-218
Marine products 241
Marriage 64-65, 304
Martyr's Day 42, 304
Medhu Ziyaaraiy
memorial 85, **86**
Medhufinolhu *see* Reethi
Rah
Media 281, 313
Medical services 280-281,
313
Medicine, traditional 60-
61, **177**, 192
Meedhoo 185, **186**, 303
Meemu (Mulaku) Atoll
139, 300
Meerufenfushi 99, 118
Migoodhoo 165
Minicoy 169
Mirihi 130, 137
Monetary system 270,
271
Moofushi 130, 137
Moresby, Captain 173
Mouse, house 196, 287
Mu'in-uddin II, Sultan
Muhammad 44
Muhameed, Sultan 60
Muhammad, Khatib 42
Muhammad, Sultan Kalhu
40, 41
Mulah 175
Mulaku 139
Mulaku Atoll *see* Meemu
Atoll
Muleeaage 86
Mulhadhoo 169
Muli 139, 274
Munnaaru Minaret 85
Murex, pink-lipped 290
Museums 301, 303, 313
Music **44**, **45**, 169
Musical instruments 240

N
Naga 37
Naifaru 156, 158
Naikay system 56, 59
Nakatchafushi 99, **108**,
109, **194-195**
Nalandhoo 166, 303
Naming Day 304
Nasir, Ibrahim 45-46
National Centre for
Linguistic and Historical
Research 187
National Committee for
the Welfare of the Disabled
275
National Council for
Environmental Protection
278
National Museum **33**, **36**,
39, 86, 301

National Planning Agency
277
National Women's
Committee 275
Nika Hotel
(Kudafolhudhoo) 130,
132-133, 136
Nilandhoo 142, **145**, 301
Noddy, common 288
Noddy, lesser 288
Nolhivaranfaru 166
Noonu (South
Miladhummadulu) Atoll
162-163, 300
Noonu 163
North Huvadhoo Atoll *see*
Gaafu Alifu Atoll
North Maalhosmadulu
Atoll *see* Raa Atoll
North Malé Atoll, resorts
in 99, 103-118
North Miladhummadulu
see Shaviyani Atoll
North Nilandhoo Atoll *see*
Faafu Atoll
North Thiladhunmathee
see Haa Alifu Atoll
Nuruddin II, Sultan
Hassan 45

O
Olhuveli 99, 123
One-and-a-Half Degree
Channel 96, 152, 171
Opera House, the 230

P
Palm Tree Island
(Veligandu Huraa) 99, 122
Pappus of Alexandria 35
Paradise Pass 230
Paradise Rock 230
Parakeet, rose-ringed 198,
288
Parmentier, Jean 36, 58,
176
Parmentier, Reoul 36, 58,
176
Parrotfish 206, **226**
People **18**, 57-66, **58**, **61**,
64, **65**, **66**, **151**, **187**, **245**
Perch, orange butterfly
222-223
Pink rose 30, **30**
Plover 198, 288
Plover, crab **199**
Political system 46, 48
Population 267
Porcupinefish 207
Portuguese rule 17, 41
Portuguese, the 41, 59
Postal services 281
Presidential Palace 86
Prophet's Birthday, the
303
Ptolemy 35
Puffer 207
Pyrard de Laval, François
43, 58, 60, 158

R
Raa (North

Maalhosmadulu) Atoll
160-162, 300; map of **161**
Rainbow Reef 230
Ramadan 303
Ranin, Buraki 60
Rannalhi 99, 126
Ranveli Beach Resort
(Vilingilivaru) **27**, 130, 136
Rasdhu 136
Rasgefaanu 175-176
Rat, black 196, 287
Ray, manta 207
Ray, spotted eagle 207
Ray, sting 208
Redin, the 37, 148, 149,
152, 159, 163, 173, 177, 178
Redinge Funi 301
Reethi Rah
(Medhufinolhu) 99, 113
Religion 36, 38, **83**, 83,
243-245, 281
Reptile profile 288, 290
Reptiles 197
Resort islands 70-73;
listing of 306-309
Resort operators, island
310
Ribudhoo 146
Rihiveli 70, 99, 123, **124-
125**, **253**
Robins, Lawson 76
Ruins, archaeological 34,
37, 130, 142, **145**, 146, 148,
149, 150, 152, 163, 165, 167,
173, 174, 177, 183, 185
Rural Youth Vocational
Training 275

S
Sailing 252-257, **253**, **256**,
257
Sandpiper 198, 288
Science Education Centre
274
Scorpion 197, 290
Scorpionfish 207
Sculptures, ancient **33**, **35**,
36, **39**, 86, 142, 173
Sea freight companies 312
Sea urchin 291
Seabirds 202, 288
Seagulls 202
Security 280
Seenu (Addu) Atoll 178-
187, 300; resorts on 179,
181
Shallow Point 230
Shamsuddeen, Mohamed
187
Shamsuddin III,
Muhammad 44, 86
Shari'a law 63, 243, 245
Shark, grey reef **206**, 209,
228-229
Shark, nurse 209
Shark, silver-tip 209
Shark, whale 207, 210, 230
Shark, white-tipped reef
209
Sharks 209-210
Sharks, feeding of 221,
224, 226

Shavi, Abdulla 176
Shaviyani (North
Miladhummadulu) Atoll
163-166, 300
Shearwater, Audubon's
202, 288
Shell profile 290-291
Shells 210-213, 241
Shells, common bursa 290
Shells, conch 210
Shells, cowrie 38, 210, 211,
213, **218**, 291
Shells, geography cone
290
Shells, giant triton 211
Shells, horned helmet 290
Shells, marlin spike 290
Shells, nautilus 210
Shells, pearl 210
Shells, pink-lipped murex
290
Shells, spider conch 290
Shells, trident 211
Shipping 269
Shopping, duty-free 280
Shrew, Indian house 196,
287
Sinhalese 37
Skink, rapid 197, 288
Snake 197, 288
Snake, wolf 288
Snappers, bluestripe **295**
Snipe 198
Snorkeling 220, 235
Social advisory 19-30
Social development 272
Society 57
Sodré, Vincent 41
Soldierfish, large-eyed 206
South Huvadhoo Atoll see
Gaafu Dhaalu Atoll
South Maalhosmadulu
Atoll see Baa Atoll
South Malé Atoll, resorts in
99, 118-126
South Miladhummadulu
Atoll see Noonu Atoll
South Nilandhoo Atoll see
Dhaalu Atoll
South Thiladhunmathee
Atoll see Haa Dhaalu Atoll
Sparrow, common house
198, 287
Spike, marlin 290
Spirits, belief in 59-60
Sports **63, 162**, 185, 235-
239, **238, 239**

Sports, water 70, **122, 123,
126**, 219-231, **226, 228-229,
231, 232-233, 234**, 235-238,
236-237, 238
Squirrelfish 206
Stamps 258-262, **259**
Star, feather 291
Star, pin-cushion 291
Star, spiny coral 291, **291**
Starfish profile 291
Starfish, brittle 291
Starfish, cushion 291
Starfish, linkia 291
State Trading
Organization 272
Stonefish 207
Sulaiman the Merchant
35, 39
Sultan's Palace 86
Sultan's Park 86
Superstitions 59-60
Surgeonfish 206, **210**
Surgeonfish, blue **210**
Surgeonfish, chocolate **224**
Sweetlips, oriental **212**

T
Tamil 37
Tari Village see Kanu
Huraa
Tax, departure 279
Taxi services 280, 312
Tea-shops **73**, 92, 139, 173,
185
Teacher Education,
Institute of 275
Tern, fairy **198**, 202, 288
Terns 202
Thaa (Kolhumadulu) Atoll
127, 147-148, 300
Thakandhoo 169
Thakurufaanu Mosque
185
Thakurufaanu, Ali 169;
tomb of 169
Thakurufaanu,
Muhammad 42-43, 83,
167, 168-169, 168;
birthplace of 168, **170**;
tomb of 85
Thakurufaanu, Yousuff
Naib Kalheihaara 185
Thimarafushi 148
Thinadhoo 173, 301
Thoddoo 130, 301
Thudufushi 130, 137
Thulhaadhoo 160, 240

Thulhaagiri 99, 106, 109,
107
Thulusdhoo 103
Tipping 280
Toad 197, 288
Toddy tapping 192-193
Tombstones, carved **47**,
85, 146, 165, 173, **186**, 187
Tortoiseshell 241
Tour operators 311
Tour operators abroad
311
Tourism 50, 268
Trade 272
Traditions 26
Travel agents 311
Travel agents, abroad 311
Travel brief 19-30
Travel permits 279
Tree, national 30
Triggerfish, clown **207**
Tropicbird, red-billed 202
Tropicbird, red-tailed 202
Tropicbird, white-tailed
202, 288
Tuna, skipjack **188**
Turnstone 198, 288
Turtle, green 197
Turtle, hawksbill 197, **197,
208**, 210, 290
Turtle, leatherback 197,
210
Turtle, loggerhead 197
Turtle, olive Ridley 197
Turtles, marine 197, 210
Twin Island
(Maafushivaru) 130, 137

U
Ugoofaaru 160, 162, 274
United Suvadive Islands
45
Usman, Sultan 148
Utheemu 168, **170**, 301
Utheemu brothers 166

V
Vaadhoo (Gaafu
Dhaalu Atoll) 173, **181**,
301
Vaadhoo (Malé Atoll) 99,
118, 225, 230
Vaadhoo Caves 230
Vaadhoo Coral Garden
230
Vaadhoo Kandu Channel
100, 103, 118, 226, 230

Vaavu (Felidu) Atoll 136-
138, 300; map of **136**;
resorts in 138
Vabbinfaru Paradise
Island **74-75**, 99, 106
Vaikaradhoo 167, 301
Vattaru Reef 138, 139,
230
Velassaru see Laguna
Beach Resort
Velidhoo see Avi Island
Resort
Veligandu 130, 137
Veligandu Huraa see Palm
Tree Island
Veymandhoo 147, 148
Vihamanaafushi see
Kurumba Village
Viligili (Gaafu Alifu Atoll)
171
Viligili (Malé Atoll) 118
Viligili (Seenu Atoll)
183
Viligilivaru (Vilivaru) 99,
123
Vilingilivaru see Ranveli
Beach Resort
Vilivaru see Viligilivaru
Visa requirements 20,
279
Vocational Training Centre
275
Voightmann, Herwath
221

W
Wasp, paper 197, 290
Water cock 198, 287
Water hen, white-breasted
198, 287
Waterfowl 287
Whale, sperm 210
Whales 196, 210
Whimbrel 198, 288
Wildlife 196-197, 287-
291
Women's Affairs,
Department of 275
Wrasse, cleaner 205
Y
Yakka 37
Young, Gavin 196
Young, I.A. 59

Z
Zaki, Ahmed 46
Ziyaaraiyfushi 99, 113